CONTENTS

How to Use This Guide

Every component of *Food & Wine Magazine's Official Wine Guide 1998* is designed to help you find wines that you will enjoy, no matter what your budget or level of wine knowledge.

The book is easy to use. Brief introductions to each country, region or important grape type answer essential questions for wine lovers: What do the wines taste like? How good a value do they represent? What recent vintages should you look for? What kinds of foods do the wines complement? The accompanying tasting notes present recommended wines arranged by price category, beginning with less expensive examples.

To make the guide even more useful, a series of indexes are provided to help you quickly locate the bottles you're after—by price, by food pairing and by grape variety. In addition, the book features a number of short essays on topics ranging from "Surviving the Restaurant Wine List" (page 207) to "Starting a Wine Cellar" (page 200).

FEATURED WINES: Best of all, unlike most wine books, *Food & Wine Magazine's Official Wine Guide 1998* focuses on specific producers and vintages. This means that, whenever possible, I've reviewed the vintage currently available on wine store shelves. For a handful of wine regions—Alsace, Burgundy, Barolo and Barbaresco, Germany—I've highlighted top producers and their best bottles rather than specific vintages of a particular wine. Producers in these areas tend to release numerous wines each year (sometimes as many as 30 or 40), mostly in extremely limited quantities. Your odds of locating *something* from one of these wineries are much higher than your chances of finding any particular bottling.

This book is not padded out with mediocre or overpriced wines. I taste upward of 10,000 wines each year, the majority of which I would not recommend. Every wine in this book is here because it offers high quality and unusually good value for its price. Wine areas that currently provide a wealth of very good wines at attractively low prices—such as southern France and Australia—are given more coverage. I strongly recommend that you experiment in these areas, rather than pay far too much for wines from regions where the prices are currently skyrocketing (such as California and Bordeaux).

THE ORGANIZATION OF THE GUIDE: *Food & Wine Magazine's Official Wine Guide 1998* is organized geographically. As a rule, information is presented by region for European countries (e.g., Bordeaux) and by grape variety for the New World (e.g., Cabernet Sauvignon) because that is how wine bottles are typically labeled, as well as how wines are organized on restaurant wine lists and store shelves.

ABOUT THE TASTING NOTES: My brief tasting notes for each wine are designed to answer the following questions: What are the wine's aromas and flavors? What does the wine feel like in the mouth? (Is it velvety and soft, or is it unforthcoming and austere? Is it moderately concentrated or extravagantly rich and deep?) Does the wine's fruit come across as ripe to the point of sweetness, or is it dry or even austere? (Many delicious wines give an impression of sweetness that comes from thoroughly ripe fruit, although they are technically dry.) How tannic is the wine? And how long is the finish? (The finish is the amount of time the flavor of the wine lingers in your nose and mouth after you have swallowed it—perhaps the single most revealing indicator of wine quality.)

Each wine reviewed in this guide has been rated with one to four stars, according to the following scale:

★ A soundly made, satisfying wine for everyday drinking

★★ A very good wine with noteworthy intensity of flavor

★★★ An excellent wine of concentration and character, true to its variety and region

★★★★ An outstanding, world-class wine worth a special search

A sample:

★★★ **PAULO SCAVINO 1996 DOLCETTO D'ALBA VIGNETO DĖL FIASC:** Deep red-ruby color. Dark berries and licorice on the nose. A vibrant floral component enlivens unusually concentrated, sappy black cherry flavor. Strong but harmonious acidity gives the wine a juiciness and a firm, bright finish. Long on the palate.

In most cases, tasting notes are based on my sampling of bottled wines. Occasionally, though, my wine descriptions are from samples tasted from barrel or tank shortly before bottling. However, in every instance in which I have published a note on an unbottled wine, it is from a producer with a proven track record for bottling wine without compromising its quality.

The wines and producers highlighted in this book are not meant to be comprehensive lists of the best in every category. Rather, they represent my own highest recommendations at a wide range of price points. In several sections of the guide, additional "Splurgeworthy" wines are listed. These are superb, pricier bottles for wine lovers willing to spend a little more for the very best.

VINTAGE CHARTS: Brief, highly specific vintage charts are liberally scattered through the book, focusing on current and recent vintages you're likely to come across on wine store shelves. Vintages are rated from A+ to F. If a vintage rates reasonably well—B- or higher—you can purchase the *next* vintage of any wine listed in the book (i.e., a bottle not yet reviewed) with a strong assurance of getting a good bottle.

AVAILABILITY OF WINES: Many of the wines recommended here should be available in most large metropolitan markets on the shelves of any retailer specializing in wine. (For a list of the best wine stores in the United States, please refer to "Where to Buy Wine" on page 204.) Wines with more limited availability may require a special search of the marketplace. But once you establish an ongoing relationship with a wine merchant, he or she will likely be willing to do the legwork on your behalf.

FRANCE

FRANCE IS THE UNDISPUTED GROUND ZERO OF WORLD wine culture. Second only to Italy as the largest producing nation, France provides the benchmark for virtually every wine type popular in the international marketplace: Cabernet Sauvignon and Merlot (at its finest in Bordeaux), Chardonnay and Pinot Noir (Burgundy), Sauvignon Blanc (the Loire Valley), Syrah (the Northern Rhône Valley), sparkling wine (Champagne) and sweet dessert wine (Sauternes).

For a country smaller than Texas, France covers a remarkable range of climates. In the cool northeastern region, spring frosts and harvest-time rains are a constant concern. On the sun-baked Mediterranean rim, the challenge is more often to get sufficient build-up of flavor in the grapes before they become overripe.

ON THE LABEL: Whereas New World wines are normally labeled according to grape variety, most of France's wines are named after places. Behind the use of these place names is the almost mystical French notion of *terroir*, which incorporates all the factors (soil, sun exposure and microclimate) that contribute to the distinctiveness of a particular vineyard site. To most French wineries, expressing the individual character of the wine's vineyard or region is, at least in theory, more important than showcasing the winemaker's own style.

GRAPES & STYLES: French wine features most of the world's highly valued grapes. Of course, cause and effect

English Channel

CHAMPAGNE
◆Rheims

Paris ◆

Strasbourg ◆

ALSACE

Colmar ◆

Orléans ◆ ◆ Auxerre

LOIRE   Angers   CHABLIS

Nantes ◆   CÔTE D'OR ◆Dijon

Saumur   Tours   BURGUNDY

CÔTE CHALONNAISE
MÂCONNAIS
BEAUJOLAIS

◆Geneva

Lyon ◆

Atlantic
Ocean

Bordeaux ◆   NORTHERN
RHONE
BORDEAUX
◆ Valence

0   100   SOUTHERN
miles   RHONE

Avignon ◆

Montpellier ◆   PROVENCE

Toulouse ◆ LANGUEDOC
Marseilles ◆

ROUSSILLON

Mediterranean Sea

Wine growing
regions

Loire

Rhône

can be hard to separate: These grapes are considered great because of the heights they reach in France. Note that many of France's best wines (Bordeaux and Champagne, to name just two) are blends of two or more varieties.

What are the chief stylistic differences between French wines and those of the New World? First and foremost, French wines are less obviously fruity. They tend to express the soil and climate that produced them rather than simply varietal character. The best French wines are more complex, as well as suaver of texture and less apparently alcoholic. Their lighter touch and harmony also make them more food-friendly.

Many of the best traditionally made wines are not intended to provide instant gratification, but are meant to be aged. The most prized wines have a track record of developing in complexity after extended cellaring.

THE BOTTOM LINE: The last two years have witnessed surging prices for the renowned wine names of France. Behind this rise is strong worldwide demand, especially from markets in the Far East. More than ever before, finding value in French wine requires looking beyond the chic neighborhoods and the most famous names. The good news is that France still offers such bargains in abundance.

FRANCE'S APPELLATION CONTRÔLÉE SYSTEM

Most of France's finest wines are entitled to the designation Appellation d'Origine Contrôlée (AOC), or "controlled name of origin." This widely copied approach to signifying wine quality was designed to protect producers in delimited areas from imitators elsewhere and to guarantee authenticity to consumers. Within each appellation, strict regulations control the land area included, the grape varieties that may be planted and a number of other variables, including maximum grape yields per hectare, allowable vinification techniques, the date each year's harvest may begin and minimum grape ripeness levels and/or alcoholic strength.

The superior appellations are usually the smaller ones—for example, the famous St-Julien appellation lies within the larger appellation Haut-Médoc, which in turn is part of Bordeaux. Any wine made within the broad boundaries of Bordeaux can call itself Bordeaux. Only wines made from vines within the St-Julien appellation can use that more restricted name. An AOC can be the name of a large region (such as Burgundy), a district within the region (Côte de Nuits), a village or *commune* (Vosne-Romanée), or a specific vineyard (Richebourg).

The next rank of French wine after AOC is VDQS (delimited wines of superior quality), followed by *Vins de Pays* (van duh pay-EE), or country wines. The phrase *Vin de Pays* is always followed by a place name, such as Côtes de Thongue (no pun intended). Finally, there is simple *vin de table* (van duh TAH-bluh), everyday drinking wine that carries no geographic indication other than the broadest of all: "France."

BORDEAUX

The port city of Bordeaux and its environs constitute the planet's largest and most famous source of fine wines. Bordeaux is the model for Cabernet Sauvignon- and Merlot-based wines produced from Bulgaria to Australia. Its top châteaux—the "classified growths" named back in 1855—are considered by many connoisseurs to produce the world's greatest red wines. Yet these most renowned wines constitute only a drop in the vast ocean of wine produced within the Bordeaux appellation, some of it distinguished, some of it basic plonk.

About three quarters of Bordeaux's wine is red (traditionally called claret by the English), but the region also makes excellent dry white wines and some of winedom's most prized sweet white wines (from Sauternes).

WINE GEOGRAPHY: The sprawling Bordeaux region covers both banks of the Gironde estuary in southwest France, as well as the Garonne and lower Dordogne rivers to the south and southeast. Bordeaux's highest-quality red wines generally come from seven major appellations: St-Estèphe, Pauillac, St-Julien and Margaux in the Médoc (meh-DOCK) region, Graves to the south of the city of Bordeaux, and Pomerol and St-Émilion to the east (areas commonly referred to as the "right bank," as it lies east of the Dordogne). The best dry whites come from Graves, while the finest sweet wines are made in Sauternes, an enclave within the southern reaches of the Graves appellation.

══════ RED WINES ══════

GRAPES & STYLES: In general, red wines from the left bank, particularly from the Médoc region, are based on Cabernet Sauvignon (with varying amounts of Merlot and Cabernet Franc—and often lesser portions of Petit Verdot and Malbec—included in the blends). These wines are dry and firm, with a solid tannic spine, and are often austere in their youth. They are among the longest-lived wines made anywhere. The wines of the Médoc display aromas and flavors of black currant, black cherry and herbs—plus cedar, cigar box, vanilla and spice notes from aging in small oak barrels. Red wines from the gravel and sand soils of Graves often show more texture earlier in their evolutions, as well as roasted aromas of smoke and tobacco.

Wines from Bordeaux's right bank *communes* of St-Émilion and Pomerol are usually blends based on the softer Merlot grape. They are generally fleshier and more pliant than wines from the Médoc and are accessible earlier even though the best are capable of improving in the bottle for decades.

AT THE TABLE: Red Bordeaux is most often served with beef and lamb; it can also accompany hard cheeses such as Cheddar. But note that maturing, aromatically complex and

THE BORDEAUX HIERARCHY

Any wine made within the borders of Bordeaux is entitled to the basic appellation "Bordeaux." "Bordeaux Supérior" is a modest step up. Bordeaux from districts singled out for their special quality (such as Pauillac) carry the name of their specific appellation on the label. While the "big seven" appellations are most familiar to wine lovers, lesser-known districts such as Moulis, Côtes de Bourg and Fronsac also produce excellent wines, generally at much lower prices.

All the best wines of Bordeaux also carry the name of the specific château, or vineyard. More than 200 of the finest châteaux of the Médoc, Graves and St-Émilion (and Sauternes as well) have been awarded *cru classé*, or classi-fied growth, status. The famous Médoc Classification of 1855 established four *premiers crus*, or first growths—Lafite-Rothschild, Latour, Margaux and Haut-Brion (in 1973, Mouton-Rothschild, too, was declared a first growth)—as well as a host of second through fifth growths. Three right-bank wines—Châteaux Pétrus, Cheval Blanc and Ausone—are now commonly considered to be equivalent to the official first growths. In addition, St-Émilion has its own classification system. There are also dozens of *crus bourgeois*, some of very good quality, as well as hundreds of lesser-known properties throughout the Bordeaux region commonly referred to as *petits châteaux*.

less tannic clarets should be paired with simpler, less aggressive meat dishes that don't overwhelm their delicate flavors.

THE BOTTOM LINE: Classified-growth red Bordeaux and their right-bank equivalents are the last place to look for wine value: Prices have skyrocketed in the past two years. Futures prices for 1996s (i.e., the prices that consumers are paying now for delivery of the wine in the fall of 1998 or the spring of 1999), especially for renowned first growths such as Lafite-Rothschild, Latour and Margaux, are now $2,000 per case and up, more than double the prices asked for 1994s two years ago.

A number of factors are behind the recent surge in prices, including the mostly very-good-to-excellent quality of the 1995s and 1996s following a string of less exciting years (1991–1994), strong demand from a number of new markets, and speculators banking on even higher prices ahead.

You will get better value from châteaux of lesser pedigree: *crus bourgeois, petits châteaux* and wines from outlying appellations that lack the cachet of the big names. Prices here have risen too, but these wines are generally not targets for speculators. From a value perspective, the good-to-very-good 1993 and 1994 vintages may be better bets for most wine drinkers than the excellent but far more expensive 1995s.

Vintage Rating

	1988	1989	1990	1991	1992	1993	1994	1995	1996
MÉDOC	B-	A-	A+	D+	C	B-	B	B+	A-
GRAVES	A-	A	A-	C-	C	B	B+	B	B
RIGHT BANK	B-	A	A	F	C	B-	B	A-	B-

CLASSIFIED GROWTHS AND RIGHT-BANK EQUIVALENTS

Tasting Notes

UNDER $30

★ ★ ★ **CHÂTEAU LAFON-ROCHET 1994 (ST-ESTÈPHE):** Deeply pitched, thoroughly ripe smoke and mineral aromas. Dense, sweet and smoky, with tobacco and black currant flavor. Has good fat and sweetness, but maintains a brightness thanks to solid acidity. Finishes strong.

★ ★ ★ **CHÂTEAU PONTET-CANET 1994 (PAUILLAC):** Black cherry on the nose, with notes of menthol and nutty, pungent oak. Minerally, rich and sweet, but with a firm, fresh Cabernet structure. Offers good density.

★ ★ **CHÂTEAU BEAUREGARD 1995 (POMEROL):** Aromas of currants, lead pencil and smoky oak. Sweet, fat and easygoing; in a gentle style but with good stuffing. Intriguing mineral nuance. Finishes with even tannins and sweet fruit.

★ ★ **CHÂTEAU CLERC-MILON 1994 (PAUILLAC):** Black currant and a hint of oak spice on the nose. Bright and nicely delineated, but could use a bit more personality. Finishes with notes of chocolate and smoke and some chewy tannins.

★ ★ **CHÂTEAU HAUT-BAGES-LIBERAL 1995 (PAUILLAC):** Toasty, cassis-scented nose, with a floral top note. Nice sweetness on entry, then firm and penetrating. Offers good intensity and freshness, but the acidity will need time to harmonize with the fruit. Not especially tannic.

★ ★ **CHÂTEAU LANGOA-BARTON 1995 (ST-JULIEN):** Exotic, rather open aromas of red currants and coconut. Lush and layered in the mouth; dominated by caramel and toffee oak notes. A bit loosely knit but has good length. Finishes with rather substantial tongue-dusting tannins.

★ ★ **CHÂTEAU LA TOUR-HAUT-BRION 1994 (GRAVES):** Deep ruby-red color. Pungent black cherry and spice nose, with a sappy mineral note. Sweet and firm in the mouth; a taste of roasted chestnuts suggests superripeness. Finish is velvety, with substantial but even tannins.

$30–$60

★ ★ ★ **CHÂTEAU CANON-LA-GAFFELIÈRE 1994 (ST-ÉMILION):** Minerals, black raspberry, oak spice and roasted coffee on the pristine nose. Dense, sweet, black cherry fruit offers excellent flavor intensity and texture. Finishes with substantial chewy tannins that require bottle aging. Notes of earth and smoke on the aftertaste. Large-scaled but bright.

★ ★ ★ **CHÂTEAU COS D'ESTOURNEL 1994 (ST-ESTÈPHE):** Gingery sweet oak, black raspberry, black cherry and spice on the nose. Dense and firm, with very good concentration. Expressive and enticing thanks to the very ripe Merlot component. Deep and long, with enough acidity to give the wine excellent balance.

★ ★ ★ **CHÂTEAU DUCRU-BEAUCAILLOU 1994 (ST-JULIEN):** Multidimensional nose of cassis, licorice, mint and ethereal spices. Rich and mouth-filling after a supple, sweet entry. Larger-scaled and solidly structured; finishes with substantial tannins.

★ ★ ★ **CHÂTEAU FIGEAC 1995 (ST-ÉMILION):** Perfumed, tangy black raspberry and smoky, spicy oak aromas. Succulent, silky and gently oaky in the mouth with expressive cassis, raspberry and mocha flavor. A wine of considerable richness and finesse.

★ ★ ★ **CHÂTEAU GAZIN 1995 (POMEROL):** Floral, high-toned aroma of crushed berries, licorice, smoke, chocolate and coffee. Smooth and flavorful in the mouth, with a lovely velvety texture and the density of the 1995 vintage. Finishes with a lingering fruit sweetness and fine tannins. A gently styled Pomerol, but with no shortage of structure.

★ ★ ★ **CHÂTEAU LÉOVILLE-BARTON 1994 (ST-JULIEN):** Pungent black currant and black cherry nose, with bright oak aromas. Tight and high-pitched in the mouth; dense and very concentrated. The pungent, smoky oak is balanced by deep fruit. Youthful and strong, with a firm tannic spine and a minerally austerity. Quintessential claret.

★ ★ ★ **CHÂTEAU MONTROSE 1994 (ST-ESTÈPHE):** Brooding, roasted nose is quite enticing; faint note of damp earth. Lush, sweet black fruit in the mouth; has a glycerine, mouth-filling texture. Lingering finish, with thoroughly ripe, even tannins. A lovely '94.

★ ★ ★ **CHÂTEAU RAUZAN-SÉGLA 1994 (MARGAUX):** Excellent deep red-ruby color. Explosive aromas of sappy black currants, minerals and smoky oak, with a floral top note and a hint of chocolate. Wonderful sweetness and inner-mouth flavor. Enticing cedary oak on the back end. Concentrated, solidly structured and persistent.

Splurgeworthy:

★ ★ ★ **CHÂTEAU L'ANGÉLUS 1994 (ST-ÉMILION):** Black ruby color. Sweet, expressive aromas of bitter cherry, cocoa powder, smoked meat and woodsmoke. Very dense and rich, yet fresh and pure. Substantial, even tannins coat the mouth, but are buried under an avalanche of fruit.

★ ★ ★ **CHÂTEAU LÉOVILLE-LAS CASES 1994 (ST-JULIEN):** Excellent deep, saturated ruby color; inviting aromas of black cherry, cassis and toasty, smoky oak; wonderful sweetness and texture, with terrific perfume; firm but impeccably integrated tannins.

★ ★ ★ **CHÂTEAU PICHON-LONGUEVILLE-COMTESSE DE LALANDE 1994 (PAUILLAC):** Pungent oak, talc and black raspberry on the nose, with a suggestion of superripeness; lush and sweet; not at all a blockbuster but quite suave; should give pleasure reasonably early.

═══ RED BORDEAUX OF LESSER PEDIGREE ═══

Tasting Notes

UNDER $15

★ **CHÂTEAU GREYSAC 1994 (MÉDOC):** Currants, bitter cherry, licorice and herbs on the nose. Firm, flavorful and rather elegantly styled, with a restrained sweetness. Not particularly fleshy but avoids dryness. Finishes with dusty, even tannins and notes of tobacco and spice.

★ **CHÂTEAU DE PEZ 1994 (ST-ESTÈPHE):** Brooding aromas of bitter cherry, leather and herbs. A supple midweight, with a chocolatey ripeness and good acidity. Finishes with slightly dry tannins and an earthy note.

★ **CHÂTEAU ROLLAND DE BY 1995 (MÉDOC):** Ripe black raspberry, chocolate and smoke aromas. Thick, concentrated and juicy; ripe, chocolatey black fruit is leavened by a menthol note. Has weight and breadth on the palate. Finishes with tongue-dusting tannins.

$15–$30

★ ★ **BAHANS-HAUT-BRION 1994 (GRAVES):** Black cherry nose. Sweet and velvety, with lovely roasted, meaty flavor in the mouth; also a faint menthol note. Finishes very long, with fine, even tannins. A harmonious, rich wine with beautifully integrated acidity. The second wine of the great first growth, Haut-Brion.

★ ★ **CHÂTEAU CHASSE-SPLEEN 1995 (MOULIS):** Highly aromatic nose of red and black currants and smoky, spicy oak. Supple and lush, with very good inner-mouth flavor and lovely balance. Hints of iron and game on the finish, which shows ripe, fine tannins.

★ ★ **CHÂTEAU MEYNEY 1994 (ST-ESTÈPHE):** Black currant, smoke and leather aromas. Supple, concentrated and layered; thick and substantial, with lovely sweet fruit. Classic claret smoothness. Finishes with tongue-dusting but ripe tannins.

★ ★ **CHÂTEAU POTENSAC 1995 (MÉDOC):** Warm aromas of black plums, currants, grilled nuts and licorice. Supple and plummy in the mouth. Finishes with chewy, slightly rustic tannins. Satisfying for the price.

★ ★ **CHÂTEAU POUJEAUX 1994 (MÉDOC):** Aromas of spicy berries and licorice, along with an exotic note of citric skin. Attractive floral, ripe fruit offers spicy berry flavor. Finishes with good grip and length and tannins under control.

★ ★ **CHÂTEAU SOCIANDO-MALLET 1994 (HAUT-MÉDOC):** Roasted, sweet raspberry nose, with a minerally quality that gives it lift. Supple and lush; ripe and rather gentle for this wine. Rather soft acids and chewy, ripe tannins will not prevent early drinking. Very tasty.

★ ★ **CHÂTEAU TAYAC PRESTIGE 1989 (CÔTES DE BOURG):** Extravagant maturing Merlot aromas of currant, blackberry, tobacco, cinnamon and roasted nuts. Soft, lush currant and tobacco flavors offer the compelling, almost roasted sweetness of the '89 vintage. Ready to drink, but capable of further bottle aging.

★ ★ **CLOS DU MARQUIS 1994 (ST-JULIEN):** Spicy cassis and currant aromas, and a suggestion of damp earth. Very expressive, perfumed bitter cherry flavor in the mouth. Firm acids carry the fruit to a penetrating, fresh finish. Quite serious and solidly built. The second wine of the outstanding second growth Léoville-Las Cases.

★ ★ **LA DAME DE MONTROSE 1994 (ST-ESTÈPHE):** Expressive nose combines smoked meat, earth, black cherry, roasted chestnut and grilled nuts. Not especially rich, but vinous and suave, with subtle flavor intensity and lovely shape. Finishes with substantial but fine-grained tannins and an iron nuance. The second wine of Château Montrose.

SAUTERNES

SAUTERNES (SAW-TAIRN), WHICH REPRESENTS BARELY 1% OF total Bordeaux production, is the name for sweet wines made in five *communes* southeast of the town of Bordeaux: Sauternes itself, Fargues, Preignac, Bommes and Barsac. At its most glorious, Sauternes is a remarkably complex, unctuous wine that can develop in bottle for 20 years or more. But making great Sauternes, as opposed to ordinary sweet wine, is a risky business: château proprietors must leave their grapes on the vines well into autumn in the hope that the beneficent fungus botrytis cinerea (bo-TRY-tiss sin-eh-RAY-ah), known as "noble rot," will develop. This occurs, on average, about three or four years a decade. In other years, the region is more likely to have no rot at all or to be afflicted with destructive gray rot, noble rot's evil twin. The 1996 vintage, for example, was the first with good levels of botrytis since the unprecedented 1988–1990 trio of superb vintages. The Sauternes Château d'Yquem (dee-KEM) is the world's most famous botrytis-affected wine.

GRAPES & STYLES: Sauternes is made of a blend of white varieties, typically about 80% Sémillon with most of the rest Sauvignon Blanc. It is usually quite sweet (5-8% residual sugar) and high in alcohol (14%+), unlike many other famous sweet wines (Germany's, for example) from cooler climates. Most of today's top Sauternes are at least partially aged in new oak barrels, which augments their fruit flavors with notes of spice, vanilla and crème brûlée.

AT THE TABLE: Sauternes with Roquefort is a classic, playing on the contrast between the sweetness of the wine and the salty, acidic blue cheese. Sauternes also works well with desserts such as fruit tarts, almond cookies and vanilla pudding.

THE BOTTOM LINE: Look for wines from 1990, 1989 and 1988. While replacement costs for these wines are currently extremely high, reflecting the general price inflation that has

THE NOBLE ROT

Botrytis cinerea, or noble rot, is a mold that develops under the right climatic conditions (alternating humidity and dry heat), turning grapeskins purplish gray and shrivelling them. While the chemical action of this fungus is imperfectly understood, botrytis has the beneficial effect of concentrating sugars and acids and increasing glycerine as the grape dehydrates. Certain grape varieties—notably Sémillon, Riesling and Chenin Blanc, and, to a lesser extent, Sauvignon Blanc—are especially prone to noble rot. Botrytis wines are generally very sweet and sumptuous in texture, with exotic aromas and flavors of apricot, marmalade, pineapple, honey and licorice and an uncanny persistence on the palate.

occurred in Bordeaux in the last two years, many retailers around the nation still hold stocks purchased at or close to original prices. Sharp-eyed shoppers may be able to find the following wines in the $30–$45 range.

Vintage Rating 1988/A 1989/A- 1990/A+ 1991/C- 1992/F 1993/F 1994/C+ 1995/B- 1996/B+

Tasting Notes

The Bordeaux region has suffered through several mediocre to poor years for sweet wine in the 1990s, and bottles from the promising 1996 vintage will not appear in the market until at least the fall of 1998. Few wines from the intervening years were blessed with noble rot, and many show aromas that are sure signs of destructive gray rot. Even the less expensive wines from satellite appellations like Loupiac and Cadillac offer little value at current prices. So, what's a Sauternes lover to do? Seek out wines from 1990, '89 and '88.

★ ★ ★ ★ **CHÂTEAU LAFAURIE-PEYRAGUEY 1990:** Fabulously complex aromas of smoke, truffle, licorice and tropical fruits. Layered and mouth-filling, but bracing acidity gives the wine uncanny freshness. Terrific balance of sugar and acidity. Powerful finishing fruit goes on and on.

★ ★ ★ **CHÂTEAU DOISY DAËNE 1990:** Tobacco and mint on the nose. Moderately viscous in the mouth, with terrific spicy, resiny flavor intensity. A rather powerful Sauternes with high alcohol and moderate residual sweetness; quite long and dusty on the aftertaste.

★ ★ ★ **CHÂTEAU DOISY VÉDRINES 1990:** Vibrant, complex aromas of honey and apple; unusually delicate for 1990. Lovely harmonious, youthful fruit is lively and delineated. Not especially weighty or alcoholic, despite possessing considerable power. Long, subtle, spicy finish.

★ ★ ★ **CHÂTEAU DOISY VÉDRINES 1989:** Copper-tinged golden-straw color. Exotic notes of chocolate, toffee and honey on the nose. Very sweet and fat, with a honeyed ripeness and noteworthy depth of flavor. Very long, ripe aftertaste shows a slight burnt sugar note.

★ ★ ★ **CHÂTEAU LAFAURIE-PEYRAGUEY 1988:** Honey, dried fruits, apple and fresh herbs on the nose, along with a faint flinty nuance. Rich and pliant in the mouth, with complex flavors of honey, damp earth, tobacco and oak spice. Spicy and very long in the aftertaste.

★ ★ ★ **CHÂTEAU DE RAYNE-VIGNEAU 1990:** Slightly high-toned aromas of lime and licorice. Harmonious and very intensely flavored; offers a silky texture. Gives an impression of strong extract. An understated, but very long wine with intriguing herbal nuances.

★ ★ **CHÂTEAU DE MALLE 1990:** Highly aromatic nose of dried fruits, pineapple, fresh apple, honey and grilled nuts; plenty of noble rot character. Thick, fairly viscous and mouth-filling, with excellent concentration and a hint of licorice. Long, honeyed aftertaste.

DRY WHITE WINES

MANY CHÂTEAUX IN THE GRAVES REGION MAKE A DRY WHITE WINE from the same blend of varieties used to make Sauternes: Sémillon for a subtly honeyed richness and Sauvignon Blanc for acidity and freshness. The quality of these wines has vastly improved in the past 15 years. Numerous wines previously made mostly from Sauvignon Blanc in stainless steel now feature a higher percentage of Sémillon, are vinified and aged in oak barrels and spend many months being enriched by contact with their spent yeasts.

AT THE TABLE: Leaner white Graves make excellent aperitifs and are also good with raw shellfish; pair them with delicately flavored dishes, as you would a Loire Valley Sauvignon Blanc. The much richer new-wave versions, with their layered textures and strong oak component, will take on richer, spicier fare: fish steaks, lobster, scallops with butter or preparations using curries, chilies or pungent herbs.

THE BOTTOM LINE: The "big three" white Graves (Château Laville Haut-Brion, Château Haut-Brion Blanc and Domaine de Chevalier) are scarce and exorbitantly priced, and even the midrange wines are now quite expensive ($30–$50). Some of the recently improved lesser names of the area offer interesting values in the $15 range. Dry white wines from the more generic Bordeaux or Entre-Deux-Mers appellations are generally even cheaper and can offer excellent value.

Vintage Rating 1993/B **1994**/A- **1995**/B+ **1996**/B

Tasting Notes

UNDER $15

★ ★ ★ **CHÂTEAU DE ROCHEMORIN 1994 (PESSAC-LÉOGNAN):** Subtle, leesy aroma of figs, smoke and citrus skin. Rich and layered on the palate; a seamless, mouth-filling wine with lovely sweetness of fruit. Long, ripe finish features a late kick of spicy oak. From the heart of the Graves appellation.

★ ★ **CHÂTEAU BONNET 1995 (ENTRE-DEUX-MERS):** Lively aromas of fresh herbs, minerals and orange peel. Clean, juicy and penetrating, yet quite supple, with ripe citrus notes of tangerine and orange peel. Has very good flavor intensity and length.

★ ★ **CHÂTEAU LA CAUSSADE 1996 (BORDEAUX):** Highly aromatic lemon, smoke and fig nose. Juicy, tangy and floral in the mouth, with strong but harmonious acidity giving the fruit splendid clarity. Bright and clean. The blend is 90% Sauvignon Blanc.

★★ **LES COMTES DE JONQUEYRES 1995 CUVÉE ALPHA (BORDEAUX):** Figs, resin, honey and orange peel on the nose. Spicy, textured and refreshing; has a softly citric character and fairly good flavor intensity. Ends with lemon and spice notes.

★★ **CHÂTEAU DE CRUZEAU 1994 (GRAVES):** Pungent, lively aromas of herbs, smoke and melon. Creamy and intensely flavored, with good ripeness, a gentle, dusty texture, and a firm shape. The overall impression is crisp and refreshing. Finishing notes of flowers, spice and smoke.

$15–$30

★★★ **CLOS FLORIDENE 1995 (GRAVES):** Lemon, earth and a butterscotch note. Rich and ripe on the palate, with the layered, suave texture of a more expensive white Graves. From very concentrated grapes—in this case, mostly Sémillon.

★★ **CHÂTEAU GUIRATON 1995 (GRAVES):** Deep lemon-lime nose. Fresh and delineated, but quite supple for the category; in fact, this shows a juicy richness and lovely inner-mouth perfume. Has real thrust and a lingering aftertaste.

★★ **CHÂTEAU LA LOUVIÈRE 1995 (PESSAC-LÉOGNAN):** Smoke, mint, oak spice and an undertone of mineral on the nose, with bright citrus and mineral flavors. Finishes with a kiss of oak spice. Would have merited three stars if it had a bit more flesh and concentration.

★★ **CHÂTEAU TALBOT 1994 CAILLOU BLANC (BORDEAUX):** Slightly high-toned aromas of lemon and oak spice. Vibrant, quite dry and citric, with very good flavor intensity and noteworthy texture. Has sufficient concentration of fruit to support the subtle oak treatment.

BURGUNDY

Burgundy, beloved by connoisseurs, produces arguably the planet's most aromatically complex and ethereally lovely dry red and white wines, as well as some of its most irritating rip-offs. The famous labels of Burgundy—it's *Bourgogne* (boor-GOHN-yuh) in French, by the way—are among the world's rarest and most expensive wines. You'll think you've died and gone to heaven when you get a great one, yet it is all too easy to spend $60 for a bottle of shockingly ordinary juice. With Burgundy, more than with any other wine, you must trust your wine merchant or do enough research on your own to know what you're getting.

GRAPES & STYLES: Pinot Noir, the most elegant, complex and sensuous of red wine grapes, reaches its apotheosis in the Côte d'Or, at the heart of Burgundy. The same area is the source of the world's finest Chardonnays, and the reason that enophiles can't get enough of this variety. Happily, less swanky Burgundy neighborhoods like Mâcon and the Côte Chalonnaise produce delicious and more easily affordable Pinot Noirs and Chardonnays. Burgundy is also home to Beaujolais, an easygoing, considerably cheaper wine made from the red Gamay grape.

AT THE TABLE: Thanks to its flavor intensity without excess weight, red Burgundy (Pinot Noir) makes a remarkably flex-

THE CLASSIFICATION OF BURGUNDY

The wines of the Côte d'Or are classified into five basic categories based upon the quality of the vineyard site. At the lowest level is generic Burgundy (the label simply reads Bourgogne), which may come from anywhere in Burgundy. Next is a special category of generic wines entitled to use a regional appellation (for example, Côte de Nuits-Villages) on the label. Third, the category of Burgundy popularly referred to as village wine comes from vineyards located entirely within the boundaries of a group of favored villages (the label normally lists only the name of the village—for example, Chambolle-Musigny).

First growths (*premiers crus*) are specially designated vineyards with particularly good soil and sun exposures. The name of the *premier cru* vineyard is added to the village name on the label (such as Vosne-Romanée Les Suchots). The label will always specify *premier cru*.

At the top of the Burgundy pyramid are the *grands crus* (e.g., Chambertin, La Tache), world-famous, ideally situated vineyards that over the centuries have consistently produced the region's greatest wines. Several villages long ago capitalized on the reputations of these famous vineyards by appending the name of the local *grand cru* to their own village name, which can cloud the important distinction between a vineyard (Musigny) and the village in which it is located (Chambolle-Musigny). The very fact that so many Burgundy fanatics are willing to wade through all this confusion is a testimony to the strong allure of the wines.

ible food wine, complementing everything from fish to pasta dishes to chicken and lamb. Regional favorites are boeuf bourguignon and game birds, but mature Burgundies also go well with lamb and full-flavored cheeses. White Burgundies, with their distinct soil and mineral tones and generally sound acidity, tend to be more versatile at the table than softer versions of Chardonnay from the New World.

THE BOTTOM LINE: The world's greatest and most maddening source of Pinot Noirs and Chardonnays, often at breathtaking prices. If you have to ask.... Anyway, there's always Beaujolais.

CÔTE D'OR

THE "GOLDEN SLOPE," A 30-MILE-LONG RIBBON OF VINEYARDS stretching from just south of Dijon to just south of Beaune, is the wine world's most expensive strip of real estate, yielding the finest examples of Pinot Noir and Chardonnay. Winemakers from Portland to Perth have tried to duplicate the perfumed fruit flavors of red Burgundy, as well as its silky texture and subtle hints of flowers, spices, minerals and earth. Meanwhile, the region's whites (plus those of Chablis to the north) are the reason Chardonnay is virtually synonymous with white wine, even if relatively few consumers can afford this mother of all

THE CONCEPT OF TERROIR

Terroir (tair-WAHR) is a semi-mystical notion, near and dear to the Burgundian heart, that incorporates everything unique about a particular vineyard site: its soil and subsoil, drainage, slope and elevation and microclimate (including temperature, rainfall and exposure to the sun). The concept of *terroir* is crucial to a variety like Pinot Noir, because the grape is hypersensitive to its environment, reflecting the slightest nuances of soil and climate in its tastes and textures. This concept is not just a marketing scheme: Burgundian vineyards literally 50 yards apart can yield very different styles of wine.

Outside of Burgundy, the concept of *terroir* is most important where wines are made from a single variety, grown in highly specific vineyard sites and in regions where vintages vary widely, like Riesling in Germany and Alsace, or the great Nebbiolo wines Barolo and Barbaresco in Italy's Piedmont region.

Chardonnays. The best wines of Burgundy are prized for the way they convey a strong, specific sense of place, a vinous expression of the very plot of soil and microclimate that produced them.

THE BOTTOM LINE: *Grand cru* Côte d'Or Burgundy, red and white, generally begins at about $60 per bottle and can easily climb to three digits, with *premiers crus* typically in the $35–$60 range. The least expensive "Bourgogne" appellation wines typically start at around $12. "Village" wines sell for $20 and up. Unfortunately, with the high prices Burgundy fetches these days, there is a financial disincentive for growers to limit production. The name of a conscientious producer on the label is thus often a more reliable indicator of Burgundy quality than the vintage or vineyard. The notes below focus on producers *whose wines can actually be found in the U.S. retail market*, singling out their most reliably interesting wines at various price levels. Look for wines from the '96 and '95 vintages.

Vintage Rating

CHARDONNAY	1994/B-	1995/A	1996/A	
PINOT NOIR	1993/B+	1994/C+	1995/A-	1996/B+

=========== CÔTE D'OR RED WINES ===========

Tasting Notes

Recommended Producers and Wines

★★★★**DOMAINE ROBERT CHEVILLON:** Benchmark examples of Nuits-St-Georges: aromatically complex, seamlessly textured, packed with fruit and solidly built, thanks to firm acidity and a substantial tannic spine. Particularly consistent across vintages. *Look for*: Nuits-St-Georges Cailles, Nuits-St-Georges Vaucrains, Nuits-St-Georges Les St-Georges, all from extremely old vines.

★★★★**DOMAINE DUJAC:** Flamboyantly aromatic, stylish, impeccably balanced wines that showcase pure Pinot red fruit and spice rather than power. Deceptively accessible in their youth due to their silky texture and enticing new oak component, the Dujac wines have a solid track record for ageability. These wines appeal to Burgundy neophytes and veterans alike. *Look for*: Morey-St-Denis, Charmes-Chambertin, Clos St-Denis, Clos de la Roche, Echezeaux and Bonnes-Mares.

★★★★**DOMAINE ROUMIER:** Classically structured, aromatically complex, slow-developing wines from very low-yielding vines. Their spicy red fruit character gives them an uncanny succulence. At once strong and refined: quintessential red Burgundy. *Look for*: Chambolle-Musigny, Morey-St-Denis Clos de la Bussières and Bonnes-Mares.

★ ★ ★ **DOMAINE MARQUIS D'ANGERVILLE:** The paradigm of the Côte de Beaune village of Volnay: ageworthy wines of finesse, with sweet cherry and raspberry fruit and graceful but substantial structure. An understated style that does not rely on the sweetening influence of new barrels. Very reasonably priced. *Look for*: Volnay Champans, Volnay Taillepieds and Volnay Clos des Ducs.

★ ★ ★ **DOMAINE BARTHOD-NOËLLAT:** The richer, more solid side of Chambolle-Musigny: densely fruity but detailed wines with dark berry and cherry flavors and the balance and backbone to age. A perfect *terroir* exercise for the Burgundy aficionado, as Barthod bottles several *premiers crus* from various vineyards within a very small area. *Look for:* Chambolle-Musigny Charmes, Chambolle-Musigny Cras and Chambolle-Musigny Beaux-Bruns.

WHY BURGUNDY IS SO DIFFICULT TO BUY

There are three reasons the amateur of Burgundy is widely viewed as the masochist of winedom: one historical, one climatological and one a function of market conditions. After the French Revolution, the best Burgundy vineyards, previously owned by the church and the aristocracy, were confiscated and auctioned off, many to wealthy speculators who in turn subdivided and resold them. The parceling of vineyards was accelerated by French inheritance laws established by the Napoleonic Code, which required property to be equally divided among all heirs. The upshot is that today's typical vineyard has been divvied up among a gaggle of owners. The most famous example, the 125-acre, walled Clos Vougeot, is carved up among more than 80 owners—all of whom have the right to produce a "Clos Vougeot." The problem is that wines from the same vineyard and vintage sell for roughly the same price but vary dramatically in quality, depending mostly on the standards of the individual grower.

In addition, the great wines of Burgundy are made from a single grape variety grown in a closely defined site, rather than a blend of grape varieties and vineyard sites. In this coolish, difficult climate, vintages vary markedly, with cold or rainy harvest-time weather always a possibility. Winemakers do not have the luxury, as in Bordeaux, of being able to increase the proportion of a particular grape that fared better or to favor a site that did relatively well.

And finally, supply and demand are seriously out of whack. When thirsty (and well-heeled) Burgundy aficionados around the world are all vying for the same fashionable grower's 900 bottles of Musigny, prices can quickly climb to absurd levels.

★ ★ ★ **DOMAINE GRIVOT:** Back on track after a rough spell in the 1980s; a venerable estate producing harmonious, intensely flavored wines. Tangy aromas and flavors of sweet black fruits, minerals and spices; firm acidity and substantial but pliant tannins. **Look for**: Vosne-Romanée Beaumonts, Nuits-St-Georges Boudots and Echezeaux.

★ ★ ★ **MAISON LOUIS JADOT:** Traditionally made, powerfully structured, slow-to-unfold Burgundies from an astounding array of sites spanning virtually the entire Côte d'Or. The rather uncompromising style here favors expression of *terroir* rather than simply fresh Pinot fruit. Jadot bottles wines both from its own vineyards and from purchased fruit and wine. **Look for**: Beaune Clos des Ursules, Corton Pougets, Clos Vougeot, Bonnes-Mares, Gevrey-Chambertin Lavaux St-Jacques, Gevrey-Chambertin Clos St-Jacques and Chambertin-Clos de Beze.

★ ★ ★ **DOMAINE ALBERT MOROT:** Deeply fruity, solid, consistent wines from several of Beaune's best *premiers crus*. Extensive use of new oak helps round out the tannins of the normally somewhat rustic Beaune style. These are bargains for their quality. **Look for**: Beaune Cent-Vignes, Beaune Grèves, Beaune Marconnets, and Beaune Teurons.

SOME OTHER RELATIVE VALUES TO SEEK OUT (ALL 1995s): Bertrand Ambroise Côtes de Nuits-Villages, Nuits-St-Georges and Nuits-St-Georges Vieilles Vignes. Chopin-Groffier Côtes de Nuits-Villages. Bruno Clair Marsannay Longerois; Jean-Jacques Confuron Côtes de Nuits-Villages. Bernard Dugat Gevrey-Chambertin Vieilles Vignes and Gevrey-Chambertin Vieilles Vignes Coeur du Roi. Michel Esmonin Gevrey-Chambertin Vieilles Vignes. Geantet-Pansiot Gevrey-Chambertin Vieilles Vignes. Jayer-Gilles Hautes Côtes de Beaune, Hautes Côtes de Nuits and Côtes de Nuits-Villages. Lécheneaut Chambolle-Musigny and Nuits-St-Georges. Hubert Lignier Gevrey-Chambertin, Morey-St-Denis, and Chambolle-Musigny. Perrot-Minot Chambolle-Musigny and Morey-St-Denis La Riotte.

OTHER CONSISTENTLY OUTSTANDING, VERY EXPENSIVE SOURCES FOR RED BURGUNDY: Domaine Claude Dugat, Domaine Groffier, Dominique Laurent, Domaine Leroy, Domaine Méo-Camuzet, Domaine Denis Mortet, Domaine Mugneret-Gibourg, Domaine de la Romanée-Conti, Domaine Joseph Roty, Domaine Christian Sérafin, Domaine Comte Georges de Vogüé.

═══ CÔTE D'OR WHITE WINES ═══

Tasting Notes

Recommended Producers and Wines

★ ★ ★ ★ **DOMAINE MICHEL COLIN-DELEGER:** Dense, silky, engaging wines with the deep smoky notes and palate-caressing texture that come from frequent stirring of the yeast lees. Archetypal Chassagne-Montrachet. **Look for**: St-Aubin Charmois, Chassagne-Montrachet Chaumées, Chassagne-Montrachet Chenevottes, Chassagne-Montrachet Remilly, Chassagne-Montrachet Morgeot, Chassagne-Montrachet Vergers, Puligny-Montrachet Truffières and Puligny-Montrachet Demoiselles.

★ ★ ★ ★ **DOMAINE LEFLAIVE:** Puligny-Montrachet's most famous name, with the high prices to match. After coasting through the 1980s, Leflaive is once again making extremely concentrated, classy wines that offer an uncanny combination of power, finesse and firm underlying structure. **Look for**: Puligny-Montrachet Combettes, Puligny-Montrachet Pucelles, Batard-Montrachet and Chevalier-Montrachet.

★ ★ ★ ★ **DOMAINE SAUZET:** Along with Leflaive, the other fabled name in Puligny-Montrachet. The style here tends toward generous, powerful, thoroughly ripe wines with clean, complex aromatics and superb delineation of flavor. Prices are rather high. **Look for**: Puligny-Montrachet Referts, Puligny-Montrachet Champs-Canet, Puligny-Montrachet Combettes and Batard-Montrachet.

★ ★ ★ ★ **VERGET:** The *négociant* venture of the four-star Mâconnais producer Jean-Marie Guffens, offering dramatic, full-blown Burgundies from all over the Côte d'Or. The Verget style is marked by deep, complex aromas and flavors, extraordinarily rich mouth feel and uncanny persistence on the palate. These wines offer near-unbeatable quality/price rapport. **Look for**: Meursault Rougeot, Meursault Poruzots, Meursault Charmes, Puligny-Montrachet Sous le Puits, Puligny-Montrachet Enseignères, Chassagne-Montrachet, Chassagne-Montrachet Remilly, Chassagne-Montrachet La Romanée, Corton-Charlemagne and Batard-Montrachet.

★ ★ ★ **DOMAINE GUY AMIOT & FILS:** Fat, rich, juicy wines with early appeal. Often flamboyantly fruity, if not downright exotic, with smoky, leesy qualities and supple texture. **Look for**: Chassagne-Montrachet Champs-Gains, Chassagne-Montrachet Vergers, Chassagne-Montrachet Caillerets and Puligny-Montrachet Demoiselles.

★ ★ ★ **DOMAINE JEAN-MARC BOILLOT:** Clean, bright, spicy wines frequently characterized by tangy orange peel, peach and dried fruit aromas. Typically ripe-verging-on-sweet but with sound balancing acidity. **Look for**: Puligny-Montrachet, Puligny-Montrachet Referts, Puligny-Montrachet Champs-Canet, Puligny-Montrachet Combettes and Puligny-Montrachet Truffières.

★ ★ ★ **DOMAINE BERNARD MOREY:** Full-bodied, rich Chassagnes that offer early pleasure. Generally late harvesting typically yields wines with aromas and flavors of honeyed, exotic fruit and relatively low acidity. Reasonably priced. **Look for**: St-Aubin Charmois, Chassagne-Montrachet Vieilles Vignes, Chassagne-Montrachet Embrazées, Chassagne-Montrachet Vide Bourse, Chassagne-Montrachet Caillerets and Puligny-Montrachet Truffières.

★ ★ ★ **MAISON LOUIS JADOT:** Intensely flavored, sharply focused, ageworthy white Burgundies whose crisp acidity often requires a few years of bottle aging. Aromas tend toward vibrant spiced apple, lemon-lime and minerals. Some Burgundy insiders consider Jadot's white Burgundies even more consistently strong than their reds. **Look for**: Chassagne-Montrachet (Duc de Magenta), Puligny-Montrachet Clos de la Garenne (Duc de Magenta), Meursault Perrières, Puligny-Montrachet Perrières, Corton-Charlemagne and Chevalier-Montrachet Demoiselles.

OTHER EXCELLENT, VERY EXPENSIVE SOURCES FOR WHITE BURGUNDY: Domaine Carillon, Domaine Boyer-Martenot, Domaine Patrick Javillier, Domaine des Comtes Lafon (a superstar, but the wines are scarce), Domaine Marc Morey, Domaine Michel Niellon, Domaine Paul Pernot, Domaine Jacques Prieur (since 1994), Domaine Ramonet.

CHABLIS

TRUE CHABLIS BEARS NO RELATION TO THE INEXPENSIVE WHITE plonk of American jug wines. When grown in the cool, clay-and-chalk soils around the sleepy town of Chablis, on the northern outskirts of the Burgundy region, Chardonnay is transformed into one of the world's most cerebral and distinctive whites. With its flinty minerality, notes of wet stones and new-mown hay and penetrating acidity, Chablis seemingly has more in common with Sauvignon Blanc from the Loire Valley than it does with most Chardonnays from the New World. Chablis is typically more austere and more delicate than white Burgundy from the Côte d'Or, nearly 100 miles to the southeast—and potentially at least as long-lived.

ON THE LABEL: The wine simply labeled Chablis comes from lesser vineyards around the town of Chablis and can usually be drunk young. *Premier* and *grand cru* Chablis, like their equivalents from the Côte d'Or, are from favored vineyard sites.

AT THE TABLE: *Premier cru* Chablis is the ultimate oyster companion: the best Chablis vineyards literally lie on soil made from decomposed oyster shells.

THE BOTTOM LINE: *Le vrai* Chablis is always in short supply, and prices can be high. But at $25–$35 for *premiers crus*, and $40–$60 for *grands crus*, they are about 33–50% less expensive than their counterparts from the Côte d'Or.

Vintage Rating 1994/C+ 1995/A- 1996/A

Tasting Notes

Recommended Producers and Wines:

★ ★ ★ ★ **RENÉ ET VINCENT DAUVISSAT:** My own favorite Chablis producer for consistently high quality. These wines show the concentration and richness that come from low yields, extraordinary aromatic complexity and great longevity. Intensely flavored, incisive wines that are both true to their *terroir* and long on personality. The wines are mostly fermented in tanks and then aged in barrels. Also bottled under the Dauvissat-Camus label. **Look for:** Chablis Sechets, Chablis Vaillons, Chablis Forêt, Chablis Preuses and Chablis Clos.

★ ★ ★ ★ **DOMAINE RAVENEAU:** In the best vintages, often the greatest Chablis. Extremely slow-developing, highly concentrated, intense wines that brilliantly reflect their specific vineyard sites. These unusually rich yet true-to-their-soil, barrel-fermented wines are as ageworthy as any white Burgundies from the Côte d'Or. Americans, unfortunately, must pay a premium for their scarcity in this country. **Look for**: Chablis Butteaux, Chablis Vaillons, Chablis Montée de Tonnerre, Chablis Blanchots, Chablis Valmur and Chablis Clos.

★ ★ ★ ★ **VERGET:** Expressive, rich, layered wines from old vines in the best sites. The Mâconnais *négociant* Jean-Marie Guffens, who began making Chablis from purchased fruit only with the 1994 vintage, is controversial for his extensive use of oak (perhaps appropriate for Chardonnays of the Côte d'Or but excessive for Chablis, say his critics) and active stirring of the lees. But the wines display extraordinary density of fruit and texture and, with a few exceptions, plenty of *terroir* character. Prices are quite reasonable. **Look for**: Chablis Vaillons, Chablis Montée de Tonnerre and Chablis Valmur.

★ ★ ★ **DOMAINE BILLAUD-SIMON:** Bright, minerally wines featuring sharply focused green apple and citrus fruit aromas and flavors; made mostly in stainless steel in a spanking-clean, high-tech winery. Not particularly rich Chablis, but fresh, stylish and capable of extended aging. Much improved following a recent generational change. **Look for**: Chablis Mont de Milieu Vieilles Vignes, Chablis Montée de Tonnerre, Chablis Vaudésir, Chablis Preuses and Chablis Clos.

★ ★ ★ **DOMAINE JEAN-PAUL DROIN:** A style perfectly suited for Chardonnay lovers who find more classic Chablis too austere for their tastes: dense, generously fruity wines with a tendency toward high alcohol and rather exotic aromas. Typically from late-picked fruit, made using a high proportion of small oak barrels, and featuring extensive use of lees contact. Best suited for drinking on the young side. **Look for**: Chablis Tête de Cuvée, Chablis Montmains, Chablis Montée de Tonnerre, Chablis Valmur, Chablis Clos and Chablis Grenouilles (often made in a style verging on late-harvest).

★ ★ ★ **LOUIS MICHEL ET FILS:** Routinely cited as the classic example of Chablis made entirely in stainless steel: minerally, bright, focused wines that frequently show more Chablis character early on than wines aged in oak. They can also reward aging. Widely available at very reasonable prices. **Look for**: Chablis Vaillons, Chablis Montée de Tonnerre, Chablis Vaudésir, Chablis Grenouilles and Chablis Clos.

OTHER CONSISTENTLY RELIABLE SOURCES: Domaine Adhémar Boudin, Domaine Jean Dauvissat, Caves Duplessis, Jean-Pierre Grossot.

CÔTE CHALONNAISE

THE PINOT NOIRS AND CHARDONNAYS MADE IN THIS REGION JUST south of the Côte d'Or tend to be less refined, more immediately accessible and considerably less expensive. Bottles from the most talented growers can offer better value than unexciting wines from the snob villages up north, as international demand for these wines is less frenzied. Pinot Noirs from the Côte Chalonnaise tend to be solidly built; you're more likely to find aromas and flavors of black fruits (black cherry, cassis) than the ineffable, spicy raspberry and strawberry of wines from the Côte d'Or. The best will age gracefully, but they are not in the longevity league of the famous reds to the north. Côte Chalonnaise Chardonnays generally show a firm edge and sometimes a green apple character.

ON THE LABEL: Of the region's four appellations, two (Givry and Mercurey) are best known for their red wines, one (Montagny) for its whites and one (Rully) equally for Pinot Noir and Chardonnay.

AT THE TABLE: Côte Chalonnaise reds pair well with pork chops or veal; the whites complement fish dishes.

THE BOTTOM LINE: Prices have risen recently in the Côte Chalonnaise, but even the best wines are rarely more expensive than simple "village" wines from the more hallowed *communes* of the Côte d'Or.

Tasting Notes

Recommended Producers and Wines:

★ ★ ★ **DOMAINE JOBLOT:** Consistently deeply colored, new-oaky, full-throttle Givry reds whose density and concentration of dark berry fruit virtually transcends the appellation. Generally impressive early on, but capable of aging. *Look for*: Givry Clos de la Servoisine and Givry Clos du Cellier aux Moines.

★ ★ **DOMAINE DeLAUNAY:** Dense, gutsy, traditionally made Mercureys with a structure that demands cellaring. Slightly rustic dark berry and tar aromas. *Look for*: Mercurey Meix Foulot and Mercurey Clos du Château de Montaigu.

★ ★ **DOMAINE MICHEL JUILLOT:** White wines with vibrant, minerally aromas and flavors, and supple reds with uncommon depth and weight for Mercurey. Both whites and reds are unusually ageworthy for the appellation. Prices are reasonable. *Look for*: Mercurey and Corton-Charlemagne among whites, Mercurey Clos des Barraults, Mercurey Champs Martin and Corton-Perrieres among reds.

★ ★ **MAISON FAIVELEY:** Richly fruity, solidly constructed, often slightly meaty Mercureys that are quite refined in the context of the appellation. From the largest vineyard owner in Burgundy, who also makes excellent wines from more than a dozen *premiers* and *grands crus* holdings in the Côte de Nuits. *Look for*: Mercurey Clos du Roi and Mercurey Clos des Myglands.

MÂCONNAIS

IT'S NO LONGER A SECRET THAT THE FINEST WINEMAKERS OF THE Mâconnais region are crafting Chardonnays that can compete against far more expensive examples from the Côte d'Or. The best of these wines are among the world's most compelling values in high-end Chardonnay. In style, Mâconnais whites tend to be a bit leaner and stonier than Chardonnay from the Côte d'Or, with good concentration and sound acidity, but barrel-aged versions can be creamy and mouth-filling.

ON THE LABEL: The basic white wine of the region is simply labelled Mâcon blanc. Mâcon Supérieur, Mâcon-Villages and Mâcon with the name of a village appended (such as Clessé or Viré) are typically better, and more expensive, wines. But note that many mass-produced Mâconnais wines made by cooperatives have climbed to price levels out of step with their quality. The appellation called Pouilly-Fuissé produces a somewhat richer version of Chardonnay, but prices are higher and good values harder to find. The wine called Saint-Véran, on the other hand, is relatively inexpensive and can offer excellent value.

AT THE TABLE: Pour these wines with river fish, shrimp, or crab. Use richer versions as you would California Chardonnay.

THE BOTTOM LINE: A more affordable version of white Burgundy. Mâconnais whites from co-ops are generally around $15, but quality is unreliable. The best growers' wines are more likely to set you back $18–$25, or more, but these wines compare favorably to higher-priced Chardonnays from elsewhere. Pouilly-Fuissé is almost always $30 or higher in today's market, while Saint-Véran is typically $10–$15.

Tasting Notes

Recommended Producers and Wines:

★ ★ ★ **DOMAINE ANDRÉ BONHOMME:** Intensely flavored but never heavy wines that consistently avoid extremes of oakiness, sweetness and alcohol; generally require a bit of bottle aging to blossom. Can approach the class of good Côte d'Or whites. **Look for:** Mâcon-Viré Cuvée Spéciale and Mâcon-Viré Vieilles Vignes.

★ ★ ★ **DOMAINE DE LA BONGRAN/JEAN THÉVENET:** A specialist in super-ripe, often downright honeyed, wines from late-picked grapes. A distinctly idiosyncratic style of Chardonnay, remarkable in the years with noble rot (such as 1994 and, especially, 1995). **Look for:** Mâcon-Clessé Cuvée Tradition and Mâcon-Clessé Le Vrouté.

★ ★ ★ **DOMAINE DU VIEUX SAINT-SORLIN/OLIVIER MERLIN:** Intensely flavored, smoky-rich wines given vivacity by underlying citric and mineral notes. These wines beat the pants off most California Chardonnays that cost twice as much. **Look for**: Mâcon La Roche Vineuse Les Cras and Mâcon La Roche Vineuse Vieilles Vignes.

★ ★ ★ **VERGET:** This *négociant* firm is a terrific source for good value Mâconnais. Fat, silky, but focused wines that offer immediate appeal and have the stuffing to age. **Look for**: Saint-Véran Tête de Cuvée, Mâcon Tête de Cuvée and Pouilly-Fuissé Tête de Cuvée.

OTHER CONSISTENTLY EXCELLENT SOURCES FOR MÂCONNAIS WINE: Domaine Ferret, Château de Fuissé, Domaine Henri Goyard, Domaine Guffens-Heynen, Domaine Robert-Denogent, Domaine Valette.

══════════ BEAUJOLAIS ══════════

BEAUJOLAIS IS A CAPTIVATING, EXPLOSIVELY FRUITY, EASYGOING RED wine with nearly universal appeal. Its fresh acidity, aromas and flavors of cherry, strawberry and raspberry and very mild tannins make Beaujolais ideal for uncritical quaffing. The nouveau Beaujolais that is released each November is just a pale, unaged representation of the finer Beaujolais that will be shipped months later, but, as the first wine of the recent harvest, it is an excuse for celebration.

GRAPES & STYLES: Beaujolais is made from the Gamay grape, a red variety that produces refreshing, fruity wines generally suited for early consumption. Unfortunately, Beaujolais is too often overchaptalized (that is, too much sugar is dumped into the fermenting wine to raise the alcohol level), negating its easy drinkability and dulling its vivid fruit and freshness.

ON THE LABEL: Beyond the early-released Beaujolais Nouveau, there are three major designations:

Beaujolais as an appellation by itself can incorporate wines from anywhere in the region; this accounts for about half of all Beaujolais production.

Beaujolais-Villages comes from a number of favored *communes*, most with granite-based soils, in the hillier, northern part of the region. This accounts for another one-quarter of the total.

Cru Beaujolais includes the top hillside *communes*, which may place their own names on the label: Brouilly, Côte de Brouilly, Chénas, Chiroubles, Fleurie, Juliénas, Morgon, Moulin-à-Vent, Régnié and Saint-Amour. Some of the best *cru* bottlings are made traditionally (rather than by carbonic maceration) and become more complex with a few years of bottle aging.

BEHIND THE SCENES: Today, 90% of Beaujolais production is controlled by *négociants* (firms that buy grapes and/or juice from growers, bottling the wines under their own names), of whom Georges Duboeuf, who buys from more than 400 growers, is king. But the wines of the region's best small domains, though much more difficult to find in the retail market, are often far more distinctive and are worth a special search.

AT THE TABLE: Best drunk chilled, Beaujolais is one of the world's most versatile food wines, pairing well with fish, poultry and meats. In Lyons, which lies just to the south of the Beaujolais region, these wines are perennial favorites with roasted chicken, grilled sausages and charcuterie.

THE BOTTOM LINE: Expect to pay $8–$15 for most Beaujolais. The best *cru* bottlings from smaller growers typically carry prices of between $15 and $20, but these wines can be more interesting, and more fun, than lesser red Burgundies at twice the price.

Vintage Rating 1995/A- 1996/B-

Tasting Notes
Recommended Producers

★★★**HENRY FESSY:** A *négociant*/grower, whose Beaujolais offerings show complex aromatics, spicy fruit and expressive floral tones. *Look for*: Beaujolais-Villages, Brouilly Cuvée du Plateau du Bel-Air, Chiroubles Cuvée Peyraud and Morgon Calot.

★★★**TRENEL:** One of the most reliable *négociants*, producing elegant, silky wines that emphasize vivid fruit flavors. Bottlings offered range from one of the better Nouveaus to top *crus* from old vines. *Look for*: Beaujolais-Villages en Primeur, Chiroubles, Morgon Côte de Py and Moulin-à-Vent Domaine de la Tour du Bief.

WHAT IS CARBONIC MACERATION?

Carbonic maceration is a fermentation technique designed to extract fruit rather than tannins from grapes. Virtually every Beaujolais bottled as nouveau, and most *négociant* Beaujolais, is made this way. Whole clusters of grapes go into the vat unbroken and some or most of the fermentation takes place within the intact berries. The minimal contact between the fermenting juice and the grape skins extracts less tannin and emphasizes the fruity character of the Gamay grape. Many other regions (among them the Côtes du Rhône), have adopted this technique to make a more accessible style of wine.

★ ★ **GEORGES DUBOEUF:** Refreshing, delicious, fruity wines perfectly suited to uncritical quaffing. Many Duboeuf releases have in common a perfumed, candied character and a whiff of banana. Generally more distinctive—and well worth a couple of extra bucks—are the Duboeuf wines bottled and marketed under the names of various individual *domaines*. **Look for**: "Flower-label" Juliénas, Fleurie, Moulin-à-Vent. Chiroubles Château de Javernand, Fleurie Château des Déduits, Fleurie Clos des Quatre Vents, Morgon Domaine des Versauds, Morgon Jean Descombes, Moulin-à-Vent Domaine des Rosiers and Moulin-à-Vent Domaine de la Tour du Bief.

★ ★ **LOUIS JADOT:** Substantial, serious examples of Beaujolais, in many instances sacrificing a bit of up-front fruitiness in favor of more weight and structure. **Look for**: Fleurie, Morgon and Moulin-à-Vent.

SMALL BEAUJOLAIS GROWERS TO SEEK OUT, AND BOTTLES TO BUY

Guy Bréton: Morgon

Domaine Calon: Morgon

Domaine des Champs Grilles: St-Amour

Michel Chignard: Fleurie Les Moriers

Domaine Diochon: Moulin-à-Vent Vieilles Vignes

Domaine Laurent Dumas: Fleurie

Durdilly: Beaujolais Nouveau, Beaujolais Les Grandes Coasses

Jacky Janodet: Moulin-à-Vent

Jean Foillard: Morgon Côte de Py

Domaine du Granit: Moulin-à-Vent

M. Lapierre: Morgon

Domaine de la Madone: Beaujolais-Villages Le Perreon

Domaine Manoir du Carra: Beaujolais-Villages

Yvon Métras: Fleurie

Pierre Meziat: Chiroubles Sélection Vieilles Vignes

Joël Rochette: Brouilly Pisse-Vieilles, Regnié Côtes des Braves

Clos de la Roilette: Fleurie

Michel Tête: Beaujolais-Villages, Juliénas, Juliénas Cuvée Prestige

Jean-Paul Thevenet: Morgon Vieilles Vignes

Georges Viornery: Côte de Brouilly

Domaine du Vissoux: Beaujolais Primeur Pierre Chermette, Fleurie Poncié, Moulin-à-Vent Rochegrès

Domaine de la Voûte: Côte de Brouilly

ALSACE

Here's what you need to know about the wines of Alsace: (1) Virtually all the good stuff is white. (2) Alsace's wines are among the most food-friendly in the world, thanks to fresh fruit flavors unobscured by new oak. (3) Alsatian wine is vastly underappreciated by American wine lovers, perhaps because the bottle shapes and vineyard names are Germanic and many people assume the wines are sweet. In fact, the region's classic wines are dry, with no more impression of sweetness than the average California Chardonnay.

ON THE LABEL: Unlike most French wines, Alsace's wines are labeled by grape variety. You'll find lots of other terms on the label as well, including proprietary names (such as Cuvée Laurence) and the names of the villages or specific vineyards from which the grapes were picked.

Vendange tardive (late harvest) wines are made from late-picked, very ripe fruit and normally carry 13%–15% alcohol. These heady, powerful releases range from completely dry to moderately sweet.

Rare and luxury-priced *sélections de grains nobles* (SGN) wines come from even riper grapes, usually heavily affected by the "noble rot," botrytis cinerea, and are very sweet, even nectarlike.

THE BOTTOM LINE: Though their prices are certainly not bargain-basement, the unfashionableness of Alsatian whites makes them one of the last great quality-for-value secrets in world-class wine.

RIESLING

RIESLING IS THE FINEST EXPRESSION OF ALSATIAN WINEMAKING, AS well as the region's most ageworthy wine. Classic Alsace Riesling is dry and penetrating, often downright austere in its youth, with aromas and flavors of flowers, citrus, apple, pear and minerals. Riesling is prized for its balance and elegance more than for sheer power or weight.

AT THE TABLE: Riesling is a prime partner for delicate fresh-water fish and shellfish and has the acidity to take on cream sauces. A classic duo in Strasbourg is Riesling and onion tart.

THE BOTTOM LINE: Expect to pay at least $12–$15 for a good Riesling, and $25 to $30 (in some cases considerably more) for the best examples from *grand cru* vineyards. Many excellent values can be found in the $15–$20 range.

Vintage Rating 1993/B+ 1994/B- 1995/B+ 1996/A-

GEWÜRZTRAMINER

SPICY, EXOTIC GEWÜRZTRAMINER IS A LOVE-IT-OR-LEAVE-IT VARIETY. Its heady perfume of rose petal, smoked meat, lichee, spice and grapefruit can be immediate and captivating, although some Gewürztraminers suffer from low acidity and high alcohol.

AT THE TABLE: Gewürztraminer marries beautifully with rich dishes like pork or goose, as well as with the exotic spices of Indian, Oriental and Moroccan cuisines. In Alsace, Gewürztraminer is routinely paired with fatty, intensely flavored pâtés and terrines, foie gras and choucroute garnie.

THE BOTTOM LINE: Expect to pay $15–$25 for better wines and up to $40 for single-vineyard, *grand cru* releases.

Vintage Rating 1994/A- 1995/B- 1996/B+

PINOT GRIS

PINOT GRIS (TRADITIONALLY CALLED TOKAY D'ALSACE, A NAME NOW banned by the EU to prevent confusion with the very different Hungarian Tokay), is the third grape of Alsace's blessed trinity and is growing in popularity. It is characterized by exotic aromas and flavors of peach, apricot, orange, butter, spice, earth and honey. Traditional versions are dry or just off-dry, with alcohol in the 13%+ range giving them substantial palate impact and body.

AT THE TABLE: Pinot Gris wines are ideal with pâtés and foie gras, richer fish like tuna, swordfish and salmon, and chicken and pork. In Alsace, Pinot Gris is often served with sausages, red meats and even venison.

THE BOTTOM LINE: Better examples generally begin at $15–$20 and can easily mount to $30 or more.

Vintage Rating 1994/C+ 1995/B+ 1996/B+

PINOT BLANC

OFTEN CALLED THE POOR MAN'S CHARDONNAY, PINOT BLANC IS typically round, soft and generously flavored, with notes of peach, apricot, apple, pear and honey.

AT THE TABLE: Lighter wines complement fish terrines and flounder, while richer ones pair nicely with poultry and pork.

THE BOTTOM LINE: Basic bottlings retail for less than $15. Those from low-yielding vines may well be Alsace's best values.

OTHER WINES

THE BETTER PRODUCERS MAKE EXCELLENT WINES FROM THE NORmally thin Sylvaner and the flowery Muscat. Crémant d'Alsace is a dry, uncomplicated Champagne-method sparkling wine.

Tasting Notes

Recommended Producers and Wines

★ ★ ★ ★ **JEAN-MICHEL DEISS:** Balanced, ageworthy, rather intellectual wines whose harmoniousness is due in part to long aging on the lees. Deiss's wines emphasize the *terroir* character of his many sites rather than their particular grape variety. Serious and rewarding. **Look for**: Pinot Blanc Bergheim, Muscat Bergheim, all Rieslings (especially the *grands crus* Altenberg and Schoenenbourg), Tokay-Pinot Gris Bergheim and the Gewürztraminers St-Hippolyte, Bergheim and Altenberg.

★ ★ ★ ★ **WEINBACH:** Currently undergoing a change in style, from opulent, exotic and somewhat sweet to a bit drier and crisper. The wines of this domaine, often from very late-picked grapes, combine power and finesse and are among the most concentrated of Alsace. Prices are on the high side. **Look for**: Muscat, Pinot Réserve, Riesling Cuvée Théo, Riesling Ste-Cathérine, Riesling Schlossberg Ste-Cathérine, Gewürztraminer Cuvée Théo and Gewürztraminer Cuvée Laurence.

★ ★ ★ ★ **ZIND-HUMBRECHT:** One of the world's greatest wineries, with correspondingly celestial prices. The house style is for remarkably opulent, concentrated, dense wines from very low yields. In recent vintages, most of these wines have been bottled with significant residual sugar; the extremely expensive, extravagantly sweet yet impeccably balanced *vendange tardive* and SGN wines are legends in the making. **Look for**: anything you can find and afford—from basic bottlings to the supernal late-harvest wines from *grand cru* vineyards.

★ ★ ★ **LÉON BEYER:** Serious, uncompromising, ageworthy wines, typically with high alcohol (often approaching 14%) and very little residual sugar—meant to be consumed with food. Perhaps best known for full-bodied but dry Gewürztraminers. **Look for**: Pinot Blanc de Blanc, Riesling Cuvée des Ecaillers, Riesling Comte d'Eguisheim, Gewürztraminer and Gewürztraminer Comte d'Eguisheim.

★ ★ ★ **BOTT-GEYL:** A turnaround story in the making, following a recent generational change. Very pure, rich wines, less sweet than previously. Techniques include risky late harvesting for maximum ripeness, and extensive use of the lees to enrich the wines. Very reasonably priced for the quality. *Look for*: Pinot Blanc Beblenheim, Muscat Riquewihr, Riesling Grafenraben, Gewürztraminer Furstentum and Gewürztraminer and Tokay-Pinot Gris Sonnenglanz.

★ ★ ★ **HUGEL ET FILS:** An impressive array of wines at a range of price points from the most famous Alsace producer. The house style is characterized by firm but supple wines with relatively low residual sugar and considerable aging potential. But note that Hugel is also a specialist in *vendange tardive* and SGN wines, which it occasionally bottles in significant quantities. Prices are fair. *Look for*: the Tradition and Jubilee wines, especially from Riesling and Pinot Gris; also a consistently reliable, inexpensive Gentil.

★ ★ ★ **JOSMEYER:** Subtle, understated wines ideally suited to playing a subservient role to food. In fact, owner/winemaker Jean Meyer is renowned for pairing a dozen or more of his wines with multicourse banquets for some of Europe's top restaurants. *Look for*: Pinot Auxerrois "H" Vieilles Vignes, Riesling Les Pierrets and Riesling and Gewürztraminer from the *grand cru* Hengst.

★ ★ ★ **KUENTZ-BAS:** Refined, slow-to-open, long-lasting wines with dense textures but modest levels of residual sugar. A very good source of *vendange tardive* wines. *Look for*: the very reasonably priced Réserve Personnelle series (including the Muscat) and the *grand cru* Gewürztraminers Pfersigberg and Eichberg.

★ ★ ★ **DOMAINE ANDRÉ OSTERTAG:** Very rich, leesy wines from a trail-blazing producer controversial for making Pinot Gris and Pinot Blanc in new oak barrels. Ostertag's best wines are aromatically complex, minerally and bright but quite dense, with the oak-aged Pinot bottlings rounder and spicier. *Look for*: Sylvaner Vieilles Vignes, Muscat Fronholz, Pinot Blanc Barriques, Riesling Epfig, Riesling Muenchberg, Tokay-Pinot Gris Muenchberg and Gewürztraminer Fronholz.

★ ★ ★ **TRIMBACH:** Focused, powerful wines with crisp citric and mineral character and very low levels of residual sugar. Excellent agers. *Look for*: The Réserve series of bottlings (the basic bottlings offer reasonable value but are generally unexciting); this producer's Riesling Frédéric Émile, Riesling Clos Ste-Hune and Gewürztraminer Seigneurs de Ribeaupierre are justly considered three of Alsace's most famous wines.

★ ★ **LUCIEN ALBRECHT:** Round, supple wines that offer satisfying early drinkability thanks to rather low acidity. Relatively inexpensive for Alsatian wine. *Look for*: Pinot Blanc and Tokay-Pinot Gris (reliable and inexpensive); also Riesling and Tokay-Pinot Gris Pfingstberg, especially when bottled as *vendange tardive*.

OTHER CONSISTENTLY EXCELLENT ALSACE PRODUCERS: Albert Boxler, Ernest Burn, André Kientzler, Marc Kreydenweiss, Albert Mann, Mittnacht-Klack, Rolly-Gassmann, Charles Schleret, Bernard Schoffit.

CHAMPAGNE

Many sparkling wines around the world are made by the traditional "Champagne method," but few if any approach the intensity and complexity of the real article. Although the name has often been borrowed (some might say stolen), true Champagne can only come from the designated Champagne district northeast of Paris.

GRAPES & STYLES: Champagne making is the refined art of blending base wines into a mix that's far more than the sum of its components. The grapes that go into the Champagne blend come from three varieties, the white grape Chardonnay and the black grapes Pinot Noir and Pinot Meunier, and are typically drawn from different villages and vineyards in the region. Champagne styles range from austere and lemony to creamy-rich, toasty and nutty, and from very dry to quite sweet.

VINTAGE & NONVINTAGE CHAMPAGNES: Nonvintage wine accounts for the vast majority of Champagne bottlings, and the reputations of the major firms hinge on the quality of their nonvintage blends, which maintain consistent house styles year in and year out.

In this cool climate, only three or four harvests per decade provide the raw materials to make balanced, complete, vintage-designated wines (1990 and 1985 are the greatest recent vintages on the market).

So-called *têtes de cuvée*, or prestige bottlings (such as Moët & Chandon's Dom Pérignon and Roederer's Cristal) are the finest wines the Champagne houses can concoct. These are vintage wines, made from the best grapes, using labor-intensive, traditional methods, and given extended aging before being put on the market.

AT THE TABLE: The Champenois insist that their wine can be drunk throughout a meal—or at least until the meat course. You may prefer to enjoy Champagne as an aperitif, but it is fine with deep-fried or salty appetizers (squid and shrimp tempura, cheese *gougères*), as well as with fatty fishes or those cooked in rich sauces. Rosé Champagne with sushi is a combination that pleases the eye and the palate.

THE BOTTOM LINE: True Champagne will never be a bargain-priced wine, but many big-name Champagnes are discounted at holiday time or as loss leaders, and a little shopping around can yield very good deals. Happily, the better nonvintage Champagnes are every bit as satisfying as many vintage bottlings—and a lot cheaper. Expect to spend $25–$35 for nonvintage (NV) wines. Vintage Champagnes are generally priced at $35–$60, while prestige cuvées are routinely in the $60–$80 range, and many retail for $100 or more.

Tasting Notes

$25–$35

★★★**LANSON NV ROSÉ BRUT:** Perfumed strawberry and apple nose, with Pinot-like spice and earth notes. Rich, ripe and round; a soft, creamy style of rosé with excellent fruit and just enough crispness.

★★★**GUY LARMANDIER NV PREMIER CRU BRUT:** Fresh, pale, green-tinged color. Pure, bright, penetrating, lemon custard aroma. Round, ripe and pristine in the mouth; intense, pure, youthful flavors of lemon and apple. Lovely sweetness is balanced by ripe acids. Quite dry and long.

★★★**LEGRAS NV GRAND CRU CHOUILLY BRUT:** Chablis-like aromas of stones and lemon grass, plus notes of toast and cut hay. Initially creamy, rich and rather soft, this wine shows better penetration as it opens in the glass. Strong fruit carries through to a long, crisp finish.

★★★**POL ROGER NV BRUT:** Minerally, chalky nose hints at earth and warm bread. Yeasty, complex middle palate offers lovely vinosity and

STYLES OF CHAMPAGNE

The words on a Champagne label describe the dryness (or sweetness) of the wine, and in some instances its grape composition and color.

BRUT, which literally means "raw," signifies a wine that ranges from fairly dry to bone-dry. The overwhelming majority of Champagnes are bruts. Slightly sweet to sweet wines (in order of sweetness) are labeled Sec, Extra Dry, Demi-sec and Doux.

BLANC DE BLANCS is a brut Champagne made entirely from Chardonnay.

ROSÉ Champagne comes in varying shades of pink; it is normally made by adding a small percentage of still red wine to the clear juice.

depth of flavor; the leesy, chalky aspect carries through in the mouth. Unusually brisk, youthful nonvintage brut. Quite dry and fresh.

★ ★ **JACQUESSON NV PERFECTION BRUT:** Discreet aromas of citrus skin, spiced apple and oyster shell. Intensely flavored and ripe but crisp, with attractive midpalate creaminess. Not especially complex but the flavors are clean and firm. Finishes firm and slightly toasty.

★ ★ **MUMM NV CORDON ROUGE BRUT:** Faintly yeasty aroma of baked apple, pear, nutmeg and toast. Round and supple in the mouth; a user-friendly, moderately dry, fruity style of Champagne, with decent length.

★ ★ **PHILIPPONNAT NV ROYALE RÉSERVE BRUT:** Stony, toasty aromas of spiced apple and pear. Fresh and medium-bodied, with pear and spice flavors and Chablis-like notes of chalk and hay. Tangy and expressive in the mouth. Displays very good length, with hints of exotic fruit on the aftertaste.

★ ★ **PLOYEZ-JACQUEMART NV BRUT:** Deep aromas of nuts, coffee and crème brûlée. Ripe, medium-bodied and expressive in the mouth; flavors of toast and vanilla custard. Very harmonious wine with enough acidity to keep it firm and fresh. Lovely finishing fruit.

★ ★ **POMMERY NV ROSÉ BRUT:** Delicate raspberry, strawberry and toast nose. Creamy and easygoing in the mouth; conveys an impression of ripeness. The sweeter side of brut. Tasty, intensely flavored fruit shows modest complexity. Slightly bitter-edged but refreshing finish.

$30–$50

★ ★ ★ ★ **LARMANDIER NV PREMIER CRU ROSÉ BRUT:** Subtle, delicate, minerally nose, with a faintly floral quality. Firm, elegant and dry, with very understated red fruit tones. Offers outstanding clarity and vibrancy of flavor. Very long and refreshingly crisp on the aftertaste.

★ ★ ★ ★ **J. LASSALLE 1992 SPECIAL CLUB BRUT:** Very ripe leesy, yeasty nose offers notes of apple, peach, grilled nuts and toffee. Creamy-sweet and mouth-filling, with outstanding richness and depth. In a full-bodied, rather gentle style, but with lovely supporting acidity. Very strong, long finish. A fairly early release for a prestige cuvée, but already delicious.

★ ★ ★ **BILLECART-SALMON NV ROSÉ BRUT:** Delicate flowery nose. Fresh, creamy red fruit palate offers subtle earth tones, lovely ripeness and excellent texture. Perfect rosé for current drinking.

★ ★ ★ **BOLLINGER NV SPECIAL CUVÉE BRUT:** Copper-tinged straw color. Classic Bollinger aromas of toasted bread, toffee and apple cider. Medium-bodied and quite fresh, with a touch of barrel toast. Just a hint of the maturity suggested by the nose. Very long, very firm, dry finish.

★ ★ ★ **LANSON 1990 BRUT:** Bright, deep aromas of peach, apricot and coffee, plus toasty and floral nuances. Ripe, frothy and intensely flavored; light-to-medium-bodied and fairly dry. The hints of very ripe fruit echo in the mouth. Finishes with good length and a nutty note.

★ ★ ★ **POL ROGER 1988 BRUT:** Musky, stony, truffley nose. Penetrating but rich and ripe stony fruit shows pungent lemon-lime flavor and an herbal nuance, not to mention outstanding intensity of flavor. The brisk finish stains the palate.

★ ★ ★ **TAITTINGER NV ROSÉ CUVÉE PRESTIGE BRUT:** Very fresh lemon, mineral and toast aromas, with a delicate red berry note. Then surprisingly rich in the mouth, with persuasive red fruit flavors and an impression of thorough ripeness. Very subtle and long. Classic Champagne on the nose, distinctly rosé on the palate.

★ ★ ★ **VEUVE CLICQUOT NV DEMI-SEC:** Lemony nose, with a suggestion of warm brioche. Shows a fresh, peachy quality. Serious and stylish. A superb example of the semi-sweet, demi-sec style.

$50–$75

★ ★ ★ ★ **PAUL BARA 1988 COMTESSE MARIE DE FRANCE BRUT:** Deep, highly nuanced nose combines toast, lime, apple, vanilla custard and hints of red berries. Very concentrated and fresh; restrained and quite elegant. Still rather unevolved in the middle palate, but not at all austere. Firmly structured and very long on the back end.

★ ★ ★ ★ **CHARLES HEIDSIECK 1985 BLANC DES MILLÉNAIRES BRUT:** Very pale color. Deep, toasty, Chardonnay aromas of smoke, earth, lemon and mint. Big, rich and creamy in the mouth; a ripe, fairly sweet brut Champagne with terrific depth and intensity of flavor and outstanding vinosity. Toast and caramel flavors open nicely on the finish.

★ ★ ★ ★ **HEIDSIECK MONOPOLE 1989 DIAMANT BLEU:** Complex stony, floral aromas of earth, lemon custard and barrel char. Big, rich and very ripe, yet quite vibrant for the vintage. Great perfume in the mouth. More minerally than yeasty. Boasts terrific depth of fruit and a persistent, ripe finish. At its peak now.

★ ★ ★ ★ **PLOYEZ-JACQUEMART 1989 d'HARBONVILLE:** Brisk mineral and lemon notes, plus a very ripe, maturing, yeasty quality on the nose. Deep and intensely flavored, with steely, lemony, Chardonnay-dominated flavors and intriguing toffee and herbal nuances. Has the vinosity and richness of a topnotch white Burgundy.

★ ★ ★ **DRAPPIER 1989 GRANDE SENDRÉE BRUT:** Lemon, smoke and toast on the nose. Slightly candied fruit in the mouth; bright, juicy flavor shows surprising acidity for this very warm vintage. Concentrated, maturing flavors on the lingering finish.

★ ★ ★ **POL ROGER 1988 CHARDONNAY BRUT:** Lemon and chalk on the nose. Bright and quite fine on the palate; subtle notes of yeastiness and citrus fruits. Lovely balance. Crisp, long and strong on the aftertaste. Dry but not austere. A Blanc de Blancs.

★ ★ ★ **POL ROGER 1988 ROSÉ BRUT:** Pale strawberry color. Pinot-dominated red berry and biscuit nose, with a dash of fresh apple. Intensely flavored, rich and vinous, with vibrant acidity. A rosé with plenty of flavor punch. Finishes very long, with a subtle Pinot Noir spiciness.

★ ★ ★ **VEUVE CLICQUOT 1988 ROSÉ BRUT:** Pale copper-orange. Fruity red berry and chalk aroma. Penetrating and bright. Lovely intensity without excessive weight. Terrific flavor impact. Long, firm finish.

LOIRE VALLEY

T he aromatic, lively wines of the Loire Valley may be the most underappreciated French wines in America. Typically light- to medium-bodied and ready to drink young, Loire wines captivate through sheer vibrancy and food-friendliness.

GRAPES & STYLES: Most Loire Valley wines are made without the influence of new oak barrels; what they offer, first and foremost, are the flavors of fresh fruit. Three grape varieties account for virtually all of the best wines:

Sauvignon Blanc, which makes the perfect summertime white wine—refreshingly brisk and dry—finds its greatest expression in Sancerre (sahn-SAIR) and Pouilly-Fumé (POOEY-fu-MAY).

Chenin Blanc, grown in a variety of sites from Vouvray to Savennières (sah-ven-YAIR), yields wines that range in style from austere, minerally and bone-dry to very sweet. There is even a sparkling wine made from Chenin Blanc. The sweetest (*moelleux*) bottlings of Chenin Blanc are among the longest-lived nonfortified wines.

Cabernet Franc, the chief red of the region, makes a fragrant, juicy wine in ripe years but can be rather green, if not downright underripe, in cooler vintages.

THE BOTTOM LINE: The most famous wines of the Loire are fully priced, and rarely offer exceptional value. But many big names have lesser-known siblings that provide quality at more palatable prices—especially in the exciting 1995 and 1996 vintages.

═══════ SAUVIGNON BLANC ═══════

THE BEST SAUVIGNON BLANC WINES OF THE LOIRE VALLEY ARE characterized by aromas and flavors of herbs, citrus fruits, gooseberries and minerals, and bright, bracing acidity. In less-ripe years the wine's herbacity is more overtly vegetal (tending toward asparagus), making it rough going for drinkers accustomed to rounder wines like New World Chardonnay.

Connoisseurs claim that Sancerre is a bit lighter and finer, Pouilly-Fumé somewhat flintier, even smoky. But for all practical purposes, these two wines, from vineyards on facing sides of the river, are interchangeable. The nearby appellations of Quincy, Reuilly and Ménétou-Salon produce slightly less fine, less concentrated and less expensive versions of Sauvignon. Although the best Loire Valley Sauvignon Blancs are capable of aging, they are generally best consumed within two or three years after the vintage for their youthful fruit and acidity.

AT THE TABLE: Sancerre and goat cheese—both, preferably, from the village of Chavignol—is a classic indigenous pairing. Loire Valley Sauvignon Blanc makes an excellent partner for dishes that would be overwhelmed by richer or oakier wines: shellfish, fresh fish, light poultry dishes, pasta and spring vegetables.

THE BOTTOM LINE: Sancerre and Pouilly-Fumé don't come cheap: Examples lower than $12 generally lack character. Still, relatively few wines exceed $20. The best producers in the lesser nearby appellations often produce good alternatives at prices in the $10 range.

Vintage Rating 1995 /A   1996 /A+

Tasting Notes

UNDER $12

★★★**DOMAINE DÉLETANG 1996 TOURAINE CÉPAGE SAUVIGNON:** Mineral, spice and talc notes on the nose, along with exotic orange peel and mango nuances. Intensely flavored, juicy and delicious.

★★**MAURICE BARBOU 1996 TOURAINE SAUVIGNON:** Refreshingly cool aromas of spearmint and lemon. Very dry and lemony in the mouth, with a grassy character and excellent flavor intensity. Bracing Sauvignon that suggests lemon iced tea with mint.

★★**HENRI BEURDIN 1996 REUILLY:** Pungent aromas of grapefruit, gooseberry, fresh herbs and spearmint. Fresh, grassy and bracing, with excellent fruit intensity and bright lemony acidity. Lean, firm and persistent.

★★**CLOS DE LA ROCHE BLANCHE 1996 TOURAINE SAUVIGNON:** Very ripe aromas of melon and spun sugar. Supple, sweet and textured in the mouth; it has a very ripe, almost honeyed quality to go with hints of orange peel and dried fruit. Broad, fat, easygoing and ripe on the finish.

$12–$20

★★★**BOUCHIÈ-CHATELLIER 1995 POUILLY-FUMÉ LA RENARDIÈRE:** Very ripe aromas of peach, pear and licorice. Bright and sweet on entry, then high-pitched and penetrating; slightly grassy fruit is given focus by strong, racy acidity. Very long, intense finish.

★ ★ ★ **CÉLESTIN BLONDEAU 1995 POUILLY-FUMÉ LES RABICHOTTES:** Vibrant, musky aromas of minerals, lemon oil, melon, mint and licorice. Bracing on entry, then ripe and concentrated, with strong, integrated acidity. Not at all austere. Intensely flavored and nuanced.

★ ★ ★ **A. CAILBOURDIN 1996 POUILLY-FUMÉ LES CRIS:** Sweet, juicy, minty nose hints at grapefruit and flowers. Firm and shapely in the mouth, with intense, creamy fruit and a solid spine of acidity. Strong herbal and minty flavors. Persistent and fresh.

★ ★ ★ **JEAN-CLAUDE DAGUENEAU 1996 POUILLY-FUMÉ:** Knockout aromas of ginger, gooseberry, quinine and curry powder. Supple and juicy, with a layered texture, ripe lemony acidity and intensely flavored, youthfully aggressive fruit. Finishes fresh and ripe, with sneaky length.

★ ★ ★ **RÉGIS MINET 1996 POUILLY-FUMÉ VIEILLES VIGNES:** Pungent, musky aromas of grapefruit, lime and minerals. Bright and sharply focused; strong acidity and distinctly citric flavors give this wine superb thrust. Manages both outstanding clarity and a mouth-filling quality. Long and brisk on the aftertaste.

★ ★ ★ **ANDRÉ NEVEU 1996 SANCERRE LE MANOIR VIEILLES VIGNES:** Grapefruit, fresh herbs and clove on the nose. Creamy-rich and chewy in the mouth; the old vines give this wine great palate presence and depth of flavor. Wonderfully ripe, but with a firm spine of acidity. Very young but already thoroughly appealing.

★ ★ ★ **HENRI PELLÉ 1996 MÉNÉTOU-SALON:** Sweet, deeply pitched tarragon and fennel aromas. Doesn't have quite the stony backbone of a top Sancerre, but structured and penetrating nevertheless, with a solid core of supple fruit, ripe acids and terrific persistence.

★ ★ ★ **HIPPOLYTE REVERDY 1996 SANCERRE:** Pure, bright aromas of lemon and gooseberry. Minerally and fresh with a distinct flavor of grapefruit. Firm but not at all hard; rather gently styled.

★ ★ ★ **LUCIEN THOMAS 1995 SANCERRE CLOS DE LA CRÈLE:** Very subtle aromas of minerals, lime, grapefruit and curry. Intensely flavored, fresh and ripe in the mouth; quite rich, but pristine and bright thanks to lively acidity. Firm, long and solidly built.

★ ★ ★ **VACHERON 1996 SANCERRE:** Stony aromas of muskmelon, lime, herbs, spice and pineapple syrup. Stuffed with ripe, sweet fruit; expansive, accessible and utterly delicious. Terrific juicy acidity gives the wine shape. Dusty, minerally finish is ripe and very long.

CABERNET FRANC

CABERNET FRANC IS A COMPONENT OF MOST WINES OF BORDEAUX, but in the Loire Valley this fruitier, lighter, less solidly structured cousin of Cabernet Sauvignon is used to make fine wine on its own. Loire Valley Cabernet Franc displays aromas and flavors of bitter cherry, raspberry and blackberry, a silky texture in warm years, and a leafy, herbaceous quality that can be excessive in less successful vintages. These wines offer lively acidity, and firm but not especially strong tannins. Chinon (SHEE-nohn), Bourgueil (boor-GUH-ya) and Saumur-Champigny are the most famous appellations. Rosés from Cabernet Franc make for delicious warm-weather drinking.

AT THE TABLE: Loire Valley Cabernet Franc is an excellent choice when a lighter but firm red wine is needed. These wines pair wonderfully with richer fish, poultry and, especially, game birds. They can also work with red meats, as long as the meat flavors are not too intense. With multicourse meals, they provide excellent lead-ins to richer, more powerful reds.

THE BOTTOM LINE: Chinon and Bourgueil are generally priced in the $15–$20 range, where they offer reasonable value in the riper years. St-Nicolas-de-Bourgueil and Saumur are often a few dollars cheaper.

Vintage Rating 1994/C- 1995/A- 1996/A

Tasting Notes

UNDER $10

★ ★ **DOMAINE DU RONCÉE 1995 CHINON:** Tangy cherry, raspberry, smoke and earth nose. Soft, velvety and smooth; a seamless, fruity, pliant Cabernet Franc that finishes with fine-grained tannins.

★ **SAUVION 1996 CHINON:** Juicy cherry-scented nose. Fruity berry flavor; shows the unusual ripeness and solidity of the vintage. Tannins are even and ripe.

$10–$20

★ ★ ★ **PHILIPPE ALLIET 1995 CHINON VIEILLES VIGNES:** Brooding, sappy black fruit, spice and cinnamon aromas. Rich, supple, fat and dense, with nuances of meat and chocolate and subtle oak. Creamy and intensely flavored. Finishes fresh and firm, with substantial tannins.

★ ★ **BERNARD BAUDRY 1996 CHINON LES GRANGES:** Tart cranberry, bitter cherry and licorice aromas. Textured and fairly dense in the mouth, but quite juicy; youthful, very fresh flavors of cranberry and pomegranate. Refreshingly bitter-edged finish.

★ ★ **PIERRE-JACQUES DRUET 1996 BOURGUEIL LES CENT BOISSELÉES:** Deep red-ruby. Dark fruit aromas of black cherry, blackberry and licorice. Soft, lush and fruity; a medium-bodied, slightly herbal wine for early drinking; Finishes quite gentle, with sweet fruit and well-managed, dusty tannins. A lighter bottling from one of the area's great winemakers.

★ ★ **FILLIATREAU 1995 SAUMUR-CHAMPIGNY LA GRANDE VIGNOLLE:** A wine with high-toned cherry and loamy earth aromas. Focused, youthful flavors of tart red cherries and crushed berries. Intensely flavored and quite vibrant. Long on the palate. A terrific Cabernet Franc for the dinner table.

★★ **JEAN GAMBIER 1995 BOURGUEIL TRADITION:** Aromas of perfumed, jammy red fruits complicated by spice, mint and black pepper. Supple, sweet, clean and rather stylish. Fresh and appealing. Finishes with an edge of dry tannins.

★★ **CHARLES JOGUET 1996 CHINON VARENNES DU GRAND CLOS:** Very good dark color. Superripe, expressive aromas of raspberry and spice. Supple, pliant and broad in the mouth, with a flavor of fresh, crushed berries. Ripe acidity frames the intense fruit. Finishes with silky, even tannins. Thoroughly ripe Cabernet Franc, with no green edge.

★★ **CHÂTEAU DE TARGÉ 1995 SAUMUR-CHAMPIGNY:** Red berry, cherry and mint nose, with some alcohol showing. Supple, rather broad cherry fruit, with a hint of green apple. Good texture and ripe acidity. Ripe yet slightly herbal finishing flavor.

CHENIN BLANC

ONLY IN ITS LOIRE VALLEY HOMELAND DOES THIS RATHER UNFASH-ionable grape reach its full, often extraordinary potential, in wines that range in style from austere to supersweet, all with piquant acidity. With 5 to 10 years of bottle aging, even the driest Chenin Blancs take on a honeyed richness.

Depending on the site, the weather and the winemaker's inclination, Vouvray may be dry (sec), off-dry (demi-sec), medium sweet (*moelleux*), or luscious beyond all reason (doux, *liquoreux* or a variety of proprietary names). Underripe Vouvray grapes and those from lesser vineyards are often turned into sparkling wine. The best dry Vouvrays are approachable when young, though high in acidity, and gain in complexity for a decade or more. In the top vintages, and especially in those that benefit from an outbreak of noble rot, outstanding sweet wines are made. Montlouis, across the river from Vouvray, offers a similar range of styles, with the twin advantages of somewhat earlier drinkability and lower price.

From a cool year, a steely, acidic, lemon-limey Savennières is the masochist's wine of choice. But riper, rounder wines are made in top-notch vintages like 1995 and 1996, some with a bit of residual sugar. Excellent sweet wines are also made in nearby Coteaux du Layon, particularly in its favored enclaves: Chaume, Quarts de Chaume and Bonnezeaux.

AT THE TABLE: Dry and off-dry Savennières go swimmingly with river fish of any stripe, as well as with crudités. Vouvray is even more flexible, pairing well with fresh-water fish in lemon-based sauces or lobster with cream sauces. Try demi-sec Chenin Blancs with dishes that feature sweet spices, such as curried chicken salad or ginger shrimp. Moderately sweet Chenins are often paired with foie gras, while *moelleux* bottlings can be desserts in themselves.

THE BOTTOM LINE: Dry and off-dry Vouvrays are reasonably priced at $12–$18; Montlouis is a few dollars less, Savennières a few bucks more. The sweet wines of the Loire are $20 to $30 in good years, but very limited special bottlings from the great botrytis vintages can easily run to $50 or more.

Vintage Rating

DRY CHENIN BLANC	1994/B-	1995/A	1996/A+
SWEET CHENIN BLANC	1994/C-	1995/A-	1996/A

Tasting Notes

$10–$20

★ ★ ★ ★ **DOMAINE DES BAUMARD 1995 SAVENNIÈRES CLOS DU PAPILLON:** Very complex aromas of peach, smoke and minerals, along with spicy oak. Clean, bright, spicy and intensely flavored: orange peel over a foundation of stones. Lovely richness and balance. Very dry, long and firm on the aftertaste. Amazingly smooth for such a stony wine.

★ ★ ★ ★ **FOREAU 1995 VOUVRAY SEC:** Ripe, pure aromas of minerals, lemon and grapefruit. Precise, delineated and uncompromising on the palate; has a strongly floral character and terrific flavor intensity. More than enough fruit to support the penetrating acidity. Firm, classic Vouvray, with a chalky finish.

★ ★ ★ ★ **HUET 1995 VOUVRAY LE MONT SEC:** Pure aromas of spice, lime blossom, honeysuckle and toast. Rich but brisk, with strong lemony acidity; Champagne-like notes of toast, citrus rind and stone, plus exotic orange and peach components.

★ ★ ★ **DOMAINE DES BAUMARD 1995 COTEAUX DU LAYON:** Expressive aromas of honey, apricot and spices. Medium-sweet and very rich, with vibrant acidity and a core of spice giving the wine lovely brightness. Finishes long, spicy and bright, with a flavor of peach. Delicious.

★ ★ ★ **BOURILLON-DORLÉANS 1996 VOUVRAY SEC VIEILLES VIGNES LA COULÉE D'ARGENT:** Cool, minty nose hints at fresh herbs. Lemony, juicy and intensely flavored; a strong mineral quality and rich extract mitigate the penetrating acidity. Dense and tactile. Long, dry aftertaste.

★ ★ ★ **BOURILLON-DORLÉANS 1996 VOUVRAY DEMI-SEC:** Lime, spice, honey and mint on the nose. Fat, easy and slightly sweet, with integrated, ripe acidity framing the fruit. Enticing flavors of white peach and minerals. Very nicely balanced, attractive demi-sec.

★ ★ ★ **DOMAINE DÉLETANG 1996 MONTLOUIS LES BATISSES:** Bright, tangy aromas of peach, tangerine and licorice. Lush and fat, but quite fine, with enticing flavors of peach, pear and lime. Delicious juicy acidity enlivens and extends the fruit. Succulent and beautifully balanced.

★ ★ ★ **PIERRE-YVES TIJOU 1995 SAVENNIÈRES CLOS DES PERRIÈRES:** Precise, understated aromas of lime, honeysuckle, wet stone, minerals and mint. Tightly wound and pristine on the palate; at once delicate and intensely flavored, very dry but pliant. Textbook Savennières.

★ ★ ★ **DOMAINE VIGNEAU-CHEVREAU 1996 VOUVRAY MOELLEUX:** Vibrant aromas of lime, nectarine and honeysuckle. Medium-sweet but not at all viscous; the bracing but harmonious limey acidity gives the ripe nectarine and peach flavors a tangy quality. Lovely balance and cut.

★ ★ **DIDIER CHAMPALOU 1996 VOUVRAY CUVÉE DES FONDRAUX:** Tangy peach, ginger and floral aromas. Medium-sweet, supple and fruity; has a creamy middle but enough lemony acidity to give it a mouthwatering freshness. A fruity, gentle style of Vouvray, with deceptive length.

MUSCADET

MUSCADET, FROM THE MELON DE BOURGOGNE GRAPE, IS MADE around the city of Nantes, where the Loire River empties into the Atlantic Ocean. Muscadet is a crisp, bracing wine, with fairly low alcohol, lively acidity, fresh lemon/lime tones and the saline, minerally scent of the sea. It is a wine to drink in the year or two following the vintage.

ON THE LABEL: Most of the best Muscadets come from the Sèvre-et-Maine region and are labeled *sur lie*. Aging the wine on its lees adds complexity and preserves freshness.

AT THE TABLE: Muscadet is a classic partner for fresh shellfish, especially clams and oysters. Stick to the superb '95s and '96s.

THE BOTTOM LINE: At $8–$12, Muscadet offers good value.

Vintage Rating 1995/A 1996/A+

Tasting Notes

UNDER $10

★ ★ ★ **CLOS DES ALLÉES 1995 VIEILLES VIGNES:** Fat, ripe and enticing on the nose; slight lime nuance. Plump and generous in the mouth, with ripe lemon, lime and mineral flavors and a tangy, spicy character. Sweet and ripe, but bracing acidity gives it solid structure.

★ ★ ★ **DOMAINE DE LA FRUITIÈRE 1995:** Musky mineral and earth aromas. Silky-rich and generous in the mouth; really extraordinarily deep for Muscadet. Has a gentle, ripe, almost Chardonnay-like texture.

★ ★ ★ **CHÂTEAU DE LA MORINIÈRE 1995 DOMAINE DE LA MORINIÈRE:** Musky, saline nose. Ripe and round, with good fat for Muscadet; lemon, spice and stone flavors. Ripe, lingering finishing fruit clings to the palate.

★ ★ **CHOBLET CÔTES DE GRANDLIEU 1995:** Complex mineral and fresh herb aromas, along with a saline nuance. Brisk and very dry in the mouth, with a penetrating lemony quality and lovely fruit intensity.

★ ★ **DOMAINE DE L'ECU 1996:** Subtle lime and grapefruit nose, with herbal and earth notes. Ripe and generous in the middle palate, then finishes with a youthful, refreshingly bitter kick of quinine.

★ ★ **CHÂTEAU DE LA RAGOTIÈRE 1996:** Fresh mineral, lime and spearmint nose. Stony and subtle in the mouth, with citric hints of orange and lemon and sneaky flavor intensity. Still tightly wrapped, but has excellent focus and cut. Classic Muscadet.

NORTHERN RHÔNE

The Northern Rhône Valley is the homeland of the two greatest Syrah-based wines: the brooding, full-bodied, powerful Hermitage and the more perfumed, seductive Côte Rôtie. Both are produced from steep-sloped vineyards in very limited quantities, and the best wines are quickly snapped up by collectors. Lesser Syrah wines of the region—Crozes-Hermitage, St-Joseph and Cornas—are far less expensive, and offer notably better value for everyday drinking.

The Northern Rhône is also the original abode of Viognier (VEE-ohn-yay), an exotically scented and suddenly fashionable white variety currently being planted on several continents. Here, too, prices are high, but few Viogniers from elsewhere can match the best examples produced in Condrieu.

The white wines of Hermitage, Crozes-Hermitage and St-Joseph are blended from Marsanne and Roussanne grapes. While a few of these wines stand out for their quality and longevity (Hermitages from Chave and Chapoutier, for example), few offer compelling value.

CÔTE RÔTIE AND ST-JOSEPH

CÔTE RÔTIE, WHICH MEANS "ROASTED SLOPE," IS ACTUALLY A series of steep hillside vineyards whose terraces date back to the Roman era. Côte Rôtie is typically more accessible than Hermitage early on, and the best wines are deeply colored, with floral, spicy aromas of raspberry, violet, black pepper and smoked meat; suave, velvety texture; and a core of spicy fruit.

St-Joseph, which comes from a much wider area stretching from just south of Condrieu virtually to Cornas, is a leaner, lighter and considerably less expensive version of Côte Rôtie.

BEHIND THE SCENES: In recent years, due in part to a powerful international thirst for Côte Rôtie, the appellation has been significantly expanded to include additional land on the plateau above its fabled slopes, but wine from these vineyards generally lacks the ineffable aromatic complexity and silkiness of the great Côte Rôties.

AT THE TABLE: Côte Rôtie and St-Joseph go perfectly with game birds, rabbit, duck and goose, as well as with a variety of full-flavored red meat dishes, including just about anything cooked on the grill.

THE BOTTOM LINE: At prices generally ranging from $30 to $50, relatively few Côte Rôties can be considered bargains, though the better wines offer at least as much individuality as most Bordeaux or Burgundy at similar prices. Although St-Joseph is rarely as "serious," well-made examples, particularly those from older, well-placed vines, can offer some of the best values in Syrah, as well as earlier drinkability.

Vintage Rating 1994/B- 1995/B 1996/B+

Tasting Notes

UNDER $25

★★ **ROGER BLACHON 1995 ST-JOSEPH:** Blueberry and cracked pepper on the nose. High-pitched dark berry fruit shows a firm acidity. The leaner, fruit-driven, extremely food-flexible side of St-Joseph.

★★ **YVES CUILLERON 1995 ST-JOSEPH L'AMARYBELLE:** Impressive black-ruby color. Violets, blueberry and pepper on the nose. Bright, intense, youthful black fruit flavor. Fine tannins kick in late. Doesn't show much fat, but this subtle wine has very good persistence and structure.

★★ **PIERRE GAILLARD 1995 ST-JOSEPH LES PIERRES:** Floral, scented aromas of woodsmoke and meat. Fleshy and seamless in the mouth; the berry and smoked meat flavors are complicated by a hint of oak spice.

★ ★ **ALAIN GRAILLOT 1995 ST-JOSEPH:** Smoke, raspberry, black currant, and leather on the nose. Supple, juicy and spicy, with a flavor of black currants. Firmly tannic but not particularly hard.

$25–$50

★ ★ ★ **BERNARD BURGAUD 1995 CÔTE RÔTIE:** Floral, spicy nose hints at licorice and mint. Smooth, layered and dense on the palate. Lovely dark berry intensity of flavor. Very young and firm. Finishes with fine-grained tannins and a note of pepper.

★ ★ ★ **PIERRE GAILLARD 1995 CÔTE RÔTIE ROSE POURPRE:** Highly aromatic nose combines violet, smoked meat and toffee. Very rich, smooth and concentrated, with complex flavors of dark berries, minerals, tobacco and spicy oak. Really blossoms in the glass. Finishes with sweet tannins and notes of smoke and pepper.

★ ★ ★ **VINCENT GASSE 1995 CÔTE RÔTIE VIEILLES VIGNES:** Black-ruby color. High-toned, intensely spicy, black cherry, cassis and licorice nose; has a sappy sweetness and a pungent spiciness. Very intensely flavored and dense; unforthcoming and seriously structured. Will require several years of aging.

★ ★ ★ **GUIGAL 1994 CÔTE RÔTIE BRUNE & BLONDE:** Aromas of raspberry, kirsch, and oak spice. Very good intensity and cut, with enticing black fruit and spice flavor and strong acidity. A very successful vintage for this wine, which typically requires several years of aging to harmonize.

★ ★ ★ **JAMET 1995 CÔTE RÔTIE:** Perfumed nose combines violets, raspberry, smoked meat, pepper and woodsmoke. Concentrated, firm and powerful; tightly built and in need of aging due to its solid backbone of acidity and tannin. Dark berry and pepper notes repeat on the palate. Very long, youthfully tannic aftertaste.

★ ★ ★ **MICHEL OGIER 1995 CÔTE RÔTIE:** Highly aromatic violet and bacon fat nose, with a smoky-oaky quality. Dense, spicy, cherry and berry flavors are given clarity by brisk acidity. Finishes long and spicy, with fine, even tannins. A perfect example of the extraordinary perfume of Côte Rôtie.

★ ★ ★ **RENÉ ROSTAING 1995 CÔTE RÔTIE LA LANDONNE:** Wild, perfumed nose of smoked meat, black plums and licorice. High-pitched and very concentrated; flavors of black fruits, iron and pepper. Very long and suave on the aftertaste, with even tannins.

Splurgeworthy:

★ ★ ★ ★ **RENÉ ROSTAING 1995 CÔTE RÔTIE CÔTE BLONDE:** Black-ruby to the rim; deeply pitched black raspberry, licorice and tar aromas, along with a floral top note; a huge, extremely concentrated wine of great finesse and character, with a real palate-saturating aftertaste.

★ ★ ★ **JEAN-MICHEL GERIN 1995 CÔTE RÔTIE LES GRANDES PLACES:** Crushed small berries, violets, spice, pepper and an oaky pungency on the nose; very sweet and dense in the mouth, but the dark berry flavors are fresh and sharply defined; has the acid and tannin structure for long development in bottle.

CONDRIEU

VIOGNIER MADE IN THE TINY APPELLATION OF CONDRIEU IS MADdeningly inconsistent; too many examples are disappointingly thin or overwhelmingly alcoholic. The best, though, show extraordinarily perfumed aromas of flowers, apricot, peach, tangerine and violet. And, although they offer a seductively glyceral richness in the mouth, these utterly unique wines also manage to convey a sense of delicacy. Viognier is not generally a wine for aging—most bottles should be consumed within three years of the vintage.

AT THE TABLE: Serve Condrieu alongside melon as an appetizer or with river fish. Locally it is enjoyed with snails.

THE BOTTOM LINE: Good Condrieu is scarce and very expensive, typically in the $30–$50 range. Viogniers made from vineyards just outside the Condrieu appellation or from young Condrieu vines (and thus not allowed to be labeled Condrieu) are generally less pricey but frequently lack distinction.

Vintage Rating 1995/B 1996/B

Tasting Notes

UNDER $35

★★★**PIERRE GAILLARD 1996 CONDRIEU:** Aromas of lime blossom and mint. Smooth and rich. Quite fresh and spicy, with the fruit/acid balance of a ripe peach. Bright mineral tones and a hint of apricot add complexity. Firm, spicy aftrtaste.

★★★**GUIGAL 1995 CONDRIEU:** Fresh, citric nose. Rich and pure; dense yet delicate and very well-delineated. Holds its shape on the aftertaste. Notes of lemon and grapefruit. This is firm, long and still youthful.

★★★**YVES CUILLERON 1996 CONDRIEU LA CÔTE:** Complex aromas of apricot, peach, mint and acacia honey. Fairly rich, even opulent, in the mouth, but lively acidity gives this wine a firm shape; bright apricot and mint flavors. Finish is subtle and long.

HERMITAGE AND CROZES-HERMITAGE

THE VINEYARDS OF HERMITAGE STRETCH OVER A GRANITE-RICH hillside above the town of Tain l'Hermitage. Hermitage, historically referred to as France's most "masculine" wine due to its deep color and massive structure, is also one of the longest-lived. A top Hermitage offers aromas of black currant, plums and spices and a solid acid and tannin backbone. Though full-bodied and mouth-filling, it should not be heavy or coarse.

Crozes-Hermitage, which comes from a wide variety of vine-yard sites north and south of Tain, aspires to be a junior version of Hermitage. Only the very finest examples really compare to Hermitage in concentration or character, but then Crozes sells for about half the price. And many Crozes-Hermitages are drinkable at a much younger stage.

AT THE TABLE: Red Hermitage is the ultimate red meat and game wine. It is traditionally served with robust, full-flavored fare like T-bone steaks, wild boar or saddle of hare, which take the edge off the wine's tannic bite. Strong Syrah wines like Hermitage also go well with mature, aggressively flavored cheeses. Crozes-Hermitage pairs successfully with game ter-rines and game birds, as well as with meat stews.

THE BOTTOM LINE: Prices for Hermitage are generally in the $30–$60 range due to limited production. For everyday drink-ing, the lighter Crozes-Hermitage, typically priced between $15 and $25, is a better bet.

Vintage Rating 1994/B 1995/A- 1996/B+

Tasting Notes

UNDER $25

★ ★ ★ **ALBERT BELLE 1995 CROZES-HERMITAGE CUVÉE LOUIS BELLE:** Very saturated purple color. Sweet, stony, blackberry-scented nose. Fresh and sharply delineated, but has an unevolved, grapey quality. Long, very strong finish. Has the fruit intensity to stand up to the firm tannins. Should reward aging.

★ ★ ★ **ALAIN GRAILLOT 1995 CROZES-HERMITAGE LA GUIRAUDE:** Very deep ruby color. Spicy, floral, blackberry-scented nose. Rich and dense; sweet and fleshy. Already displaying a lot of personality but then this bottling is typically harmonious early in its development. Long, tannic finish.

★ ★ ★ **JABOULET 1995 CROZES-HERMITAGE THALABERT:** Superripe, port-like nose of sappy cassis, chocolate, smoke and damp earth, plus an intriguing vegetal complexity. Tightly knit but delineated. A strong, young wine that's very much like a junior version of Hermitage, with the balance to age. Finishes with ripe tannins.

★ ★ ★ **TARDIEU-LAURENT 1995 CROZES-HERMITAGE:** Black-ruby to the rim. Aroma of crushed berries and licorice, with floral and spice notes. Similar flavors in the mouth; juicy, dense and powerfully structured. Hints at spicy depths. Quite tannic.

★ ★ **ALBERT BELLE 1995 CROZES-HERMITAGE LES PIERRELLES:** Deep, black-ruby in color. Smoky nose complicated by an aroma of roast meat. Juicy, intensely flavored and well-delineated. Not fleshy, but pure, firm and long. Less powerfully structured than the above, and a better bet for impatient drinkers.

★ ★ **FERRATON 1995 CROZES-HERMITAGE LA MATINIÈRE:** Complex smoke, rust and leather aromas; rustic and somewhat high-toned yet reasonably fresh. Supple and sweet, with good density and texture. Spice and pepper notes. Finishes with dusty but even tannins. Serious, artisanal Crozes.

★ ★ **ALAIN GRAILLOT 1995 CROZES-HERMITAGE:** Saddle leather, smoke, spice and licorice on the nose, plus a suggestion of cooked fruit. Juicy and pure in the mouth, with more red fruit flavor than black. Nicely delineated. Should drink well early.

$25–$50

★ ★ ★ **ALBERT BELLE 1995 HERMITAGE:** High-pitched blueberry and spice aroma. Dense and juicy, with very good texture and underlying sweetness. Broad on the finish. Still, this is quite tight and peppery today.

★ ★ ★ **MICHEL FERRATON 1995 HERMITAGE CUVÉE DES MIAUX:** Deep ruby color. Rather cool aromas of cassis, blackberry, shoe polish and pepper, plus high-toned pine and floral nuances. Sweet, intensely flavored and dense, but brooding and virtually impenetrable today. Finishes with tough tannins and a note of licorice.

★ ★ ★ **JABOULET 1995 HERMITAGE LA CHAPELLE:** Superripe, portlike aromas of crushed black currants, pepper, chocolate and damp earth. Intense, well-defined flavors are very tightly wound. Finishes with a powerful blast of tannins. Should develop in bottle for many years, and may ultimately merit four stars.

Splurgeworthy:

★ ★ ★ ★ **JEAN-LOUIS CHAVE 1995 HERMITAGE:** Perfumed dark berry and game aromas. Smooth, dense and very concentrated, with brisk acidity lending clarity to the sweet flavors; subtle and extremely persistent—a great Hermitage.

★ ★ ★ **CHAPOUTIER 1995 HERMITAGE LA SIZERANNE:** Still very tight and unevolved aromas of blackberries and blueberries, leather and spice; fat, sweet, dense and sharply defined. Finish is very long and spicy, with fine tannins.

CORNAS

THANKS TO GENTLER VINIFICATION, CORNAS TODAY IS LESS FORBIDding in its youth than the legendarily tough wines of a generation ago. Still, most of the top wines of Cornas will be more satisfying after six to eight years of bottle aging. Expect to find aromas of black currant, black olive and leather, with sound acidity and good concentration.

AT THE TABLE: Cornas complements rustic fare, such as meat pies and beef bourguignon.

THE BOTTOM LINE: Cornas generally retails in the $25–$30 range, where it offers limited value.

Vintage Rating 1994/B 1995/B- 1996/B

Tasting Notes

UNDER $30

★★★ **NOËL VERSET 1995 CORNAS:** Black and blue fruits and black olive on the nose. Dense, sweet and unevolved; hints of licorice and iron. Actually rather tame for a Cornas from this outstanding traditional producer. Classic Cornas from very low-yielding vines; built to age.

★★ **DUMIEN-SERETTE 1995 CORNAS:** Black currant, black cherry and black olive on the nose. Sweet, supple and fruit-oriented; not a particularly tough style of Cornas but already displays good inner-mouth complexity. Should drink well fairly early but has the structure to age.

★★ **JABOULET 1995 CORNAS:** Deep ruby-red color. Brooding, high-toned black currant and licorice nose, with notes of herbs and a hint of alcohol. Dense and tightly wrapped; possesses good acidity but is not yet displaying its personality. This will require at least a few years of bottle aging.

Splurgeworthy:

★★★ **CLAPE 1995 CORNAS:** Roasted black cherry and cassis nose; dense, minerally, tightly wound and serious, but with plenty of lurking richness. Finishes with very firm but fine tannins.

★★★ **JABOULET 1995 CORNAS DOMAINE DE SAINT-PIERRE:** Brooding aromas of black currant, black olive, licorice and pepper. Very ripe and very concentrated black fruit and licorice flavor; has a solid acid and tannin backbone for extended aging.

SOUTHERN RHÔNE

The vast Southern Rhône region is an extraordinarily rich vein of full-flavored red wines that share a distinctly warm, ripe flavor but range widely in style: from fruity, easygoing Côtes du Rhônes (many under $10), to powerfully spicy, meaty Châteauneuf-du-Papes (many $20–$25) capable of improving in bottle for a decade or two. Although the Southern Rhône also produces white wines, its reputation rests on its reds.

GRAPES & STYLES: The region's red blends are typically

dominated by Grenache, but wineries are making increasing use of more oxidation-resistant varieties like Syrah and Mourvèdre to add backbone and aging potential. Southern Rhône reds are often flamboyant, lushly fruity wines with medium-full to full body and substantial alcohol levels.

THE BOTTOM LINE: Though not the sensational values they were as recently as the late 1980s, southern Rhônes are still well-priced given their quality.

CHÂTEAUNEUF-DU-PAPE

THIS IS THE UNDISPUTED STAR OF THE SOUTHERN RHÔNE VALLEY, and a world-class red wine in a mouth-filling, robust style. Its minimum legal alcohol content, at 12.5%, is the highest in France, and in warm vintages these wines routinely approach 14%.

There is no "typical" Châteauneuf-du-Pape, owing to the region's varied soil types, vastly different winemaking methods (ranging from ultratraditional to carbonic maceration) and the fact that 13 different grape types are permitted in the blend. Even the most ageworthy wines can usually be enjoyed early on, thanks to the sheer sweetness of their fruit and the absence of harsh tannins.

The current vintage, 1995, is the best since the great 1989s and 1990s, though the wines rarely show the same roasted ripeness as the wines from those drought years.

AT THE TABLE: Châteauneuf-du-Pape pairs well with robust dishes like full-flavored game and garlic-rich, Provençal-style leg of lamb. It can also be served with aggressively flavored, hard cheeses such as aged Cheddar.

THE BOTTOM LINE: A place to look for quality, not bargains.

Vintage Rating 1993/B- 1994/B 1995/A- 1996/B-

Tasting Notes

UNDER $30

★ ★ ★ ★ **CLOS DES PAPES 1995:** Pungent, youthful aromas of cassis and spice. Dense black currant fruit; large-scaled, intensely flavored and persistent. Ripe tannins and brisk acidity provide structure for aging.

★ ★ ★ **LES CAILLOUX 1995:** Complex raspberry, cassis and smoke aromas. Juicy and penetrating, with subtle hints of smoke, earth and pepper. Firm tannins and sound acidity give this wine excellent structure for aging. Stylish for Châteauneuf.

★ ★ ★ **Château Fortia 1995:** Superripe cherries, leather and menthol on the nose. Sweet, sensual and layered in the mouth. Long, spicy, very ripe finish, with fine tannins.

★ ★ ★ **Domaine de la Janasse 1995 Chaupin:** Reticent, slightly minty nose. Deep flavor of crushed blackberries and spice; lovely restrained sweetness and shape. The persistent finish features smooth tannins.

★ ★ ★ **Domaine de Marcoux 1995:** Flamboyant scents of red currant, raspberry, cassis and spicy, nutty oak, along with floral and violet nuances. Expansive and tangy on the palate, with strong oak and red-currant flavor. Finishes with substantial dusty tannins and flavors of oak and black cherry.

★ ★ ★ **Clos du Mont-Olivet 1995:** Reserved nose of raspberry, spice and smoke. Round and rich, with intense red fruit flavor, but rather closed in the early going. Still, this finishes long, with smooth tannins.

★ ★ ★ **Domaine de Monpertuis 1995 Cuvée Classique:** Expressive aromas of black cherry, blueberry, mint and spice. Intense, fresh dark berry and floral flavor offers attractive sweetness. Has sound acidity and firm tannins for aging.

★ ★ ★ **Château Mont-Redon 1995:** Nuanced aromas of black cherry, dark berries, spice and leather: classic Châteauneuf-du-Pape. Rich, supple and sweet, with a sappy quality and excellent flavor definition. Firmly tannic and unevolved.

★ ★ ★ **Domaine de la Mordorée 1995:** Vibrant floral, black fruit nose, with a spicy component. Rich, layered and beautifully delineated. Lovely restrained sweetness and subtle oak spice. A very stylish, fresh, youthful wine.

★ ★ ★ **Château La Nerthe 1994:** Complex, warm aromas of game, iron, woodsmoke and fresh herbs. Smooth and mouth-coating, with notes of iron and truffle. Flavors are nicely focused. Quite solidly structured. Finishes with restrained cherry and smoky oak sweetness.

★ ★ ★ **Domaine Saint-Benoit 1995 Cuvée de Grande Garde:** High-toned raspberry, oak, spice and smoke aromas, with notes of leather and game. Sweet, supple and very concentrated; strong tobacco, leather and earth tones. The flamboyantly ripe side of Châteauneuf.

★ ★ ★ **Vieux Donjon 1995:** Slightly rustic aromas of leather, earth and black cherry. Concentrated, dense and peppery, with good flavor definition. This wine's firm tannic structure will require some aging.

★ ★ ★ **Vieux Télégraphe 1995:** Very youthful aromas of spicy black cherry and licorice. Strong, superripe red fruit flavor on the palate. Silky-sweet, large-scaled and very concentrated. Substantial tongue-coating tannins are balanced by sheer depth of fruit.

Splurgeworthy:
★ ★ ★ ★ **1995 Chateaux de Beaucastel:** Kirsch, licorice, herbal nose, with a chocolatey ripeness; velvety, thick and sweet in the mouth; very concentrated, deep and long; ripe tannins are buried in sweet fruit.

★ ★ ★ **DOMAINE DE MARCOUX 1995 VIEILLES VIGNES:** Liqueurlike cassis and raspberry aromas with a penetrating herbal quality; sappy, creamy and impressively concentrated; a superripe wine with a very long resiny, oaky aftertaste balanced by intense fruit.

GIGONDAS

CHÂTEAUNEUF'S LITTLE BROTHER, FROM A VILLAGE A FEW MILES TO the northeast, is a similarly sturdy, spicy red wine with high alcohol and mouth-filling texture. Gigondas (JEE-gawn-doss) may lack the cachet of Châteauneuf, but the better bottles (many retailing for $15–$20) certainly rival it. Grenache is the dominant grape, but increasing use of Syrah and Mourvèdre is resulting in higher-quality, fresher wines. As a rule, Gigondas is best suited for drinking within 6 to 10 years after the vintage.

AT THE TABLE: Use as you would Châteauneuf-du-Pape.

Vintage Rating 1993/C   1994/C+   1995/A   1996/B-

Tasting Notes

UNDER $20

★ ★ ★ **JABOULET 1995 PIERRE AIGUILLE:** Deep, superripe aromas of black currant, raspberry, licorice and smoked meat. Large-scaled, sweet and peppery in the mouth, with substantial alcohol. Finishes quite long, with lush, tongue-coating tannins and a wave of fruit.

★ ★ **DOMAINE DU GOUR DE CHAULÉ 1994:** Black cherry, pepper, smoke and a deep spiciness on the nose. Fairly dense and sweet, but very fresh and vinous. Not at all overripe. Finishes with fine-grained tannins and lingering, peppery fruit.

★ ★ **GUIGAL 1994:** Cherry, raspberry, plum and pepper aromas. Superripe to the point of raisiny and quite brawny in the mouth; sweet, thick Grenache fruit has a pepper complexity and good freshness. Finishes with fine, tongue-dusting tannins.

CÔTES DU RHÔNE AND OTHER WINES OF THE SOUTHERN RHÔNE VALLEY

THE ENTIRE RHÔNE VALLEY IS COMMONLY REFERRED TO AS THE Côtes du Rhône, but this is also the name of a generic appellation covering more than 100 *communes* in the region. Until a decade ago, when quality in France's Midi began to skyrocket, the Côtes du Rhône was *the* source of red wine values from southern France. It still offers a trove of well-priced, straightforward red wines with lush, peppery, berrylike fruit. The white wines are generally of less interest.

A number of villages hold the right to call their wines Côtes du Rhône-Villages, or to append their actual village name (like Rasteau or Cairanne). These wines are usually a step up in quality and in price (typically $12–$16 versus $8–$12 for a simple Côtes du Rhône), and they must possess higher minimum alcohol content (which means that the grapes must be picked riper) and come from lower-production vines.

Côtes du Ventoux reds are typically lighter in body and less expensive than Côtes du Rhône. The reds of Vacqueyras and Lirac are generally priced in line with Côtes du Rhône-Villages.

AT THE TABLE: Ideal for everyday drinking with red meats and lighter game dishes, as well as stews and casseroles.

THE BOTTOM LINE: One of France's top sources for bargain reds.

Vintage Rating 1994/B- 1995/B+ 1996/B

Tasting Notes

UNDER $10

★ ★ ★ **DOMAINE LA GARRIGUE 1995 CÔTES DU RHÔNE CUVÉE ROMAINE:** Dark ruby color. Syrah-like aromas of dark berries, chocolate, woodsmoke and eucalyptus. Velvety, spicy and very intensely flavored; dense and juicy. Complex finish features notes of leather, pepper and spice. Amazing Côtes du Rhône.

★ ★ **DOMAINE D'ANDÉZON 1996 CÔTES DU RHÔNE VIEILLES VIGNES:** Pleasing aroma of barbecue sauce: ketchup, molasses, liquid smoke. Supple and smoky in the mouth, with strong black fruit character. Substantial and textured, with sound framing acidity.

★ ★ **DANIEL BRUSSET 1995 CAIRANNE CÔTES DU RHÔNE-VILLAGES:** Dark berries and spice on the nose, along with floral and pepper notes. Silky and peppery in the mouth; shows enticing sweetness and healthy acidity. Lightly tannic but firm, berry-flavored aftertaste.

★ ★ **CHAPOUTIER 1995 BELLERUCHE CÔTES DU RHÔNE:** Cherry, plum and herbs on the nose; showed a liqueurlike raspberry quality with aeration. Round, gentle and shapely, thanks to nicely integrated acidity. A bit less roasted and more serious than most Côtes du Rhônes; shows complex tobacco, leather and earth notes.

★ ★ **DOMAINE DE FENOUILLET 1995 CÔTES DU RHÔNE-VILLAGES, BEAUMES DE VENISE:** Floral aromas of black cherry, dark berries and licorice. Black cherry fruit offers very good intensity. Brisk acidity. Finish is firm, with a peppery nuance.

★ ★ **DOMAINE AU GRAND PRIEUR 1996 CÔTES DU RHÔNE:** Cherry and black pepper on the nose. The sweet and agreeable, silky red fruit has solid underlying structure. Finishes with soft tannins. A gently styled, easy-drinking Côtes du Rhône.

★★ **GUIGAL 1994 CÔTES DU RHÔNE:** Plum, leather and pepper aromas. Lush, sweet and generous in the mouth; easygoing flavors offer surprising depth. Finishes with dusty, ripe tannins.

★★ **DOMAINE DE MAROTTE 1995 CÔTES DU VENTOUX:** Flamboyant, deep aromas of raspberry, cherry, meat and pepper; tangy and complex. Soft, rich and chewy in the mouth; red fruit flavors are bright and complex. Finishes with dusty but ripe tannins. A lot of flavor for the price.

★★ **DOMAINE DE LA MORDORÉE 1996 CÔTES DU RHÔNE:** Blackberry, black pepper and exotic spices on the nose. Peppery and intensely fruity; not especially fleshy but fresh and firm. Spicy, brisk finish.

★★ **VIGNERONS D'ESTEZARGUES 1995 CUVÉE DU VENT AXE NORD CÔTES DU RHÔNE:** Meat, cherry and pepper scents. Supple, silky and sweet; cherry flavor of noteworthy depth. Has a juicy greenness that carries through to the firmly tannic finish.

★ **JABOULET 1995 PARALLEL 45 CÔTES DU RHÔNE:** Smoke, earth and black fruit aromas. Dense and fruity in the mouth, with notes of pepper and earth. Finishes with rich, dusty tannins. Contains an unusually high 60% Syrah.

★ **DOMAINE SANTA-DUC 1995 CÔTES DU RHÔNE:** Black fruits, herbs and earth on the nose. Chewy, ripe fruit has good texture and underlying structure. Firm, moderately tannic finish.

Splurgeworthy:

★★★ **DOMAINE DE MARCOUX 1995 CÔTES DU RHÔNE:** Deep aromas of raspberry, smoke and leather; rich, lush and sweet; meat and pepper nuances complement smoky berry flavor; lovely balance of fruit, acidity and tannins; quite long on the palate.

PROVENCE

Mediterranean France enjoys a wonderfully dry, sunny climate, with less vintage variation than anywhere else in France. In Provence, the sunshine translates into rich, spicy red wines and crisp rosés (the white wines too often lack freshness). Many Provençal reds show the influence of *garrigue*, the wild and pungently spicy brush that dots rocks and hillsides along France's Mediterranean coast. A *garrigue* element is often detectable in the wines of the region in aromas of thyme, rosemary, basil, sage, lavender, wild mint and fennel.

The rosés, drier and more sophisticated than most American blush wines, are among the most seductive pink wines made anywhere.

GRAPES & STYLES: With the exception of the Mourvèdre-based wines of Bandol, Provençal reds have traditionally relied on classic southern French grape varieties like Grenache, Carignan and Cinsault. But today, the more interesting bottles are increasingly based on Syrah and Cabernet Sauvignon.

AT THE TABLE: These assertive wines might easily overpower subtle dishes, but they are perfectly suited to the regional cuisine, which is dominated by garlic, fresh herbs and spices and grilled preparations.

THE BOTTOM LINE: The expensive hotels and restaurants of Provence draw waves of well-heeled, international tourists, which may explain why there are so few good, cheap bottles to be found. But while there's very little wine worth looking for under $10, Provence does offer some very good values in the $12–$20 range.

BANDOL

THIS SMALL APPELLATION, LOCATED ON THE MEDITERRANEAN coast southeast of Marseilles, makes what are arguably southern France's finest and most serious red wines. Bandol is the only wine-growing region in France where the late-ripening Mourvèdre achieves reasonable ripeness in most years. In strong vintages, the red wines of Bandol offer notes of black fruits, licorice, leather and woodsmoke and a tannin structure that demands cellaring.

AT THE TABLE: Assertively flavored, tannic Bandol goes especially well with roast duck or duck confit, as well as with roast lamb and game dishes.

THE BOTTOM LINE: Most Bandols today retail for at least $20 in the U.S., and some special old-vine or vineyard-designated bottlings can reach $30 or more. But these prices are actually fair given the fine quality and long aging potential of the Bandol wines.

Vintage Rating 1993/A 1994/B- 1995/B+ 1996/B+

Tasting Notes

UNDER $25

★ ★ ★ CHÂTEAU PRADEAUX 1991: High-toned, meaty aromas of black fruits, *garrigue* spices, iron and coffee. Initially quite closed in the mouth, but opens to show rich, dense fruit and an unusual smoothness for a wine from this domaine. A big wine that will repay aging.

★ ★ LA BASTIDE BLANCHE 1994 VIEILLES VIGNES: Deep, warm aromas of blackberry and bitter chocolate. Crushed berry and spice flavors in the mouth; creamy texture and acidity still need to harmonize. Has decent structure for aging. Finishes spicy, with dusty tannins.

★ ★ DOMAINE TEMPIER 1994 CUVÉE SPÉCIALE: Wild aromas of blackberry, meat and tobacco. Creamy, spicy blackberry flavor shows a restrained sweetness. A flamboyant wine, but with good texture and balance. Slightly dry-edged finish features a leathery nuance.

═══════════ ROSÉ WINES ═══════════

MORE THAN HALF OF THE WINES MADE IN PROVENCE ARE ROSÉS, and the best are the finest in the world. Provençal rosés are crisp and bright, with subtle hints of strawberry and raspberry fruit and refreshing acidity. Bandol rosés can benefit from a couple of years of bottle aging, but most Provençal rosés are best suited to drinking within the year following their release.

AT THE TABLE: Chilled Provençal rosé is perfect with garlicky, salty or oily fish preparations (it's *de rigueur* with bouillabaisse in the local restaurants) or with grilled poultry, but it also goes well with lighter meat dishes flavored with garlic or fresh herbs.

THE BOTTOM LINE: Better bottles often go for $15 or more.

Tasting Notes

UNDER $12

★ ★ ★ DOMAINE RICHEAUME 1996 ROSÉ, CÔTES DE PROVENCE: Expressive, floral red fruit aroma has a slight candied aspect. Fruity yet delicate flavors of raspberry, strawberry, mint and spices. Firm and lively on the lingering finish. Delicious.

★ ★ CHÂTEAU MARAVENNE 1995 GRANDE RÉSERVE, CÔTES DE PROVENCE: Pale copper-tinged salmon color. Delicate aromas of tangerine, flowers and mint, plus a faint yeasty quality. Supple and easygoing, with subtle strawberry flavor and just enough acidity. Very ripe aftertaste.

★ ★ COMMANDERIE DE PEYRASSOL 1996 ROSÉ CUVÉE EPERON D'OR, CÔTES DE PROVENCE: Pale salmon color. Reticent red berry aroma. Supple entry, then very dry, fresh and stony, with delicate cranberry and strawberry flavors and excellent cut. An understated style of rosé.

$12–$20

★ ★ ★ CHÂTEAU PRADEAUX 1996 ROSÉ, BANDOL: Complex, earthy nose hints at honeysuckle. Supple and creamy on the palate, with impressive texture and depth for a rosé; ripe flavors are given clarity by fresh acidity. Notes of honeydew and cantaloupe on the firm, lingering aftertaste.

★ ★ ★ DOMAINE TEMPIER 1996 ROSÉ, BANDOL: Complex strawberry, orange peel and earth aromas. Ripe and silky in the mouth; has the palate-caressing texture of a red wine from southern France. Quite stylish and shapely. Lingering, subtle finish.

★ ★ MAS DE GOURGONNIER 1996 ROSÉ, LES BAUX DE PROVENCE: Subtle cherry and thyme aromas. Fresh, bright and juicy; a faintly citric note gives the intense fruit terrific cut. Very firm without being austere. Subtle, classic Provençal rosé that should be flexible at the dinner table.

CÔTES DE PROVENCE, COTEAUX VAROIS, COTEAUX D'AIX-EN-PROVENCE, ═══ LES BAUX DE PROVENCE ═══

COOLER SPOTS WITHIN THE WARM PROVENÇAL REGION PRODUCE wines with a shade more finesse and precision of flavor. The Coteaux Varois, for example, generally covers cooler sections within the more generic Côtes de Provence appellation, while Les Baux, where the harvest frequently does not begin until the first of October, is home to the renowned, ageworthy Domaine de Trévallon, a blend of Cabernet Sauvignon and Syrah.

THE BOTTOM LINE: Prices are generally in the $10–$20 range for reds in these appellations, and good values abound.

Vintage Rating 1993/B+ **1994**/B **1995**/B+ **1996**/B+

Tasting Notes

UNDER $10

★ ★ COMMANDERIE DE PEYRASSOL 1996, CÔTES DE PROVENCE: Highly aromatic nose combines cherry, raspberry, black pepper and roasted herbs. Juicy, bright and on the lean side, but pure and light on its feet. Not as complex as the nose suggests, but the brisk raspberry and pepper flavor makes for a refreshing drink.

★ COMMANDERIE DE BARGEMONE 1995, COTEAUX D'AIX-EN-PROVENCE: Cherry, red berries and an herbal nuance on the nose. Broad but rather dry cherry and raspberry fruit; a tart cranberry note carries through to the finish. A somewhat clenched wine that needs a bit of bottle aging.

$10–$20

★ ★ ★ COMMANDERIE DE PEYRASSOL 1992 CUVÉE MARIE-ESTELLE, CÔTES DE PROVENCE: Perfumed, sappy aromas of black currant, black raspberry, coffee and roast meat. Vibrant crushed berry flavor is complicated by notes of pepper and tar; intensely flavored and sharply delineated yet supple and layered. Fruit flavors are quite persistent.

★ ★ ★ **MAS DE GOURGONNIER 1994 RÉSERVE DU MAS, LES BAUX DE PROVENCE:** Wild aromas of raspberry, leather, pepper and game. Rich and lush in the mouth; brambly raspberry fruit offers lovely sweetness and a silky, pliant texture. The leather note repeats on the persistent, ripely tannic finish.

★ ★ **MAS DE GOURGONNIER 1995, LES BAUX DE PROVENCE:** Initially leathery nose shows a raspberry quality with aeration. Plump and juicy in the mouth, with cherry and currant flavors that grow stronger and fruitier as the wine opens in the glass. Finishes with soft, slightly dry tannins.

★ ★ **CHÂTEAU REVELETTE 1995 LE GRAND ROUGE DE REVELETTE, COTEAUX D'AIX EN PROVENCE:** Highly aromatic, slightly briary cherry/berry nose is brightened by floral and oaky scents. Cool, lively, cherry, cranberry and pepper flavors. Not a weighty wine but one with very good intensity and a firm structure. Note of cracked black pepper on the lightly tannic finish.

Splurgeworthy:
★ ★ ★ ★ **DOMAINE DE TRÉVALLON 1994:** Very dark color. Extravagant, superripe aromas of crushed raspberry, game, leather and black olive. Lush berry flavor has terrific concentration and strong acidity. Finishes with furry tannins and a note of Provençal herbs. This huge wine was denied its Les Baux de Provence appellation by the authorities for being atypical, and was bottled as VdP des Bouches du Rhône.

LANGUEDOC-ROUSSILLON

This sun-drenched, crescent-shaped region hugs the Mediterranean from the Rhône River delta to the Spanish border. Wine production here has undergone a rapid upgrade in the past decade, and improvements in quality have far outpaced increases in price. Today the Languedoc-Roussillon (longa-DOC roo-see-YOHN) offers more delicious red wine for under $12 than any other grape-growing zone in the world, plus easy-drinking rosés.

Behind the surge in quality: the indigenous, often bland Carignan grape continues to be replaced by noble varieties like Syrah, Cabernet Sauvignon and Merlot, resulting in wines that are darker, stronger and finer. At the same time, many grape growers who previously sold their fruit to industrial-scale cooperatives are investing heavily in modern equipment in order to make and bottle their own proprietary wines.

GRAPES & STYLES: Reds range from rustic blends based on Carignan, Grenache and Cinsault to finer, Syrah-based wines from cooler, inland spots; there are also new plantings of Cabernet Sauvignon and Merlot. Virtually all examples offer considerable youthful appeal. White wines from indigenous varieties lack fruit and freshness, but recent plantings of Chardonnay, Sauvignon Blanc and Viognier bear watching. The region's reasonably priced rosés make for delicious early drinking.

THE BOTTOM LINE: The Languedoc-Roussillon is the mother lode for rich, assertive red wine under $12.

AT THE TABLE: The red wines of this region pair best with hearty foods that can stand up to their assertive flavors. They work well with grilled red meats, robust stews and full-flavored or mature cheeses.

Vintage Rating 1994/B+ 1995/A- 1996/B

COTEAUX DU LANGUEDOC, FAUGÈRES, ST-CHINIAN

THE COTEAUX DU LANGUEDOC IS A CLUSTER OF GRAPE-GROWING areas stretching over nearly 75 miles, many of them situated on hillsides far enough inland to be protected from hot winds off the Mediterranean Sea. Particularly favored villages such as Faugères and St-Chinian have been granted their own appellations, while others, such as La Clape, Montpeyroux and Pic-St-Loup, simply append their names to the basic Coteaux du Languedoc appellation.

GRAPES AND STYLES: The Carignan and Cinsault grapes dominate here, but Mourvèdre and especially Syrah have made strong inroads.

THE BOTTOM LINE: Some of the top Syrah-based wines here can be compared to the better Syrahs from the Rhône and sell for a fraction of the price.

Tasting Notes

UNDER $10

★★ **CHÂTEAU GRANDE CASSAGNE 1996, COSTIÈRES DE NÎMES:** Deep purple to the rim. Brooding, slightly floral, blueberry and blackberry aromas. Silky-sweet and stuffed with dark berry flavor. Pure, clean and fresh. Superb intensity and balancing acidity. Finishes with firm tannins.

★★ **CHÂTEAU PUECH-HAUT 1995 CUVÉE TRADITION ST-DRÉZÉRY, COTEAUX DU LANGUEDOC:** Floral, bitter cherry aromas, with hints of licorice, coffee, herbs and grilled meat. Fat, supple and harmonious; sweeter in the mouth than on the nose. Finishes with ripe, smooth tannins and very good length.

★★ **CHÂTEAU PUECH-HAUT 1996 ROSÉ ST-DRÉZÉRY, COTEAUX DU LANGUEDOC:** Pale cherry red. Fruit aromas of cherry, strawberry and apricot complicated by stony, earthy nuances. Fresh and silky in the mouth, with fairly complex flavors of apricot, pear and mint. Large-scaled for rosé. A bit of alcohol shows on the finish.

★★ **CHÂTEAU DE VALCOMBE 1995, COSTIÈRES DE NÎMES:** Penetrating aromas of black cherry, currant, tobacco and Provençal herbs. Spicy and bright, but with good underlying density. Fresh acids give the wine lovely clarity of flavor. Finishes firm and fresh, with light tannins.

★★ **CHÂTEAU DE VILLESPASSANS 1994, ST-CHINIAN:** Dark ruby-red color. Perfumed blackberry aroma. High-pitched and grapey in the mouth, with violet and blackberry flavors. A very fruity style of wine with modest flesh and underlying structure.

★★ **CHÂTEAU VIRANEL 1994, ST-CHINIAN:** Raspberry, cocoa, toffee and leather aromas. Sweet, spicy and pliant; strong coffee and oak tones in the mouth. Finishes with a peppery note.

★★ **CHÂTEAU VIRANEL 1996 ROSÉ, ST-CHINIAN:** Pale silver-tinged salmon color. Delicate fruit skin and fruit pit aromas call to mind rosé Champagne. Fresh, lively, lean and stylish; very understated and dry. A model southern French rosé in an austere style.

$10–$20

★★★ **DOMAINE D'AUPILHAC 1995, MONTPEYROUX:** Highly nuanced nose of cassis, black cherry, cola, smoke, mocha and tarragon. Sweetly pungent dark berry and sassafras flavors. The wine's dense texture is given definition by lively acidity.

★★★ **DOMAINE LÉON BARRAL 1994 FAUGÈRES:** Perfumed, Pinot Noir-like aromas of raspberry, strawberry, cherry and spicy oak, plus a minerally undertone. Bright and delineated; dry yet silky. Flavors of red fruit and spice. Finishes firm and peppery, with obvious oak tones.

★★★ **DOMAINE DE LAVABRE 1995 CHÂTEAU LE LAVABRE, PIC ST-LOUP:** Flamboyant aromas of raspberry, violet, chocolate and smoky oak; reminiscent of a Côte Rôtie costing four times as much. Rich and sweet in the mouth, but the lively fruit shows excellent clarity and backbone. Long, violet-tinged finish, with plenty of fruit to stand up to the tannins.

★ ★ ★ **MAS JULLIEN 1995 LES DEPIERRE, COTEAUX DU LANGUEDOC:**
Brooding raspberry nose has a sappy, liqueurlike quality. Rich, pliant
and warm in the mouth; a generous wine with the fat and extract to
balance the alcohol. Finishes with smooth, ripe tannins.

★ ★ **GILBERT ALQUIER 1995 FAUGÈRES:** Aromas of blackberry, coffee and
herbs. Rich, deep and layered, but tightly wrapped and crisp. Intense
tart berry flavor is complemented by a floral nuance. Nicely focused
right through to the bright, strong finish.

★ ★ **CHÂTEAU DE FLAUGERGUES 1995, COTEAUX DU LANGUEDOC LA
MÉJANELLE:** Deep red-ruby color. Vibrant, floral aroma of violet, cassis
and toast. Juicy, penetrating, floral and dark berry flavor. Has density
but is not yet showing its flesh or underlying sweetness. Blackberry and
mineral notes on the firm finish.

★ ★ **DOMAINE L'HORTUS 1995 GRANDE CUVÉE, PIC-ST-LOUP:** Dark
berries, roasted meat and alluring oak notes of smoke, clove and coffee.
Smooth and generous in the mouth, with a pliant texture and enough
balancing acidity to give clarity to the fruit.

★ ★ **CHÂTEAU DE LASCAUX 1994 LES NOBLES PIERRES, PIC-ST-LOUP:**
Coffee and caramel oak notes currently dominate red berries on the
nose. Juicy and tight in the mouth; not a fat wine but one with excellent flavor intensity and delineated red berry flavors.

★ ★ **CHÂTEAU LA ROQUE 1996 PIC-ST-LOUP:** Perfumed aromas of black
currant, violet pastille, black pepper, tree bark and flowers. Intensely
flavored and thick, but fresh acidity gives the wine very good delineation. Very young, fruity and fresh. Finishes with a slightly dry edge
and a peppery quality. From very old Mourvèdre vines.

★ ★ **CHÂTEAU LA ROQUE 1995 CUPA NUMISMAE, PIC-ST-LOUP:** Black
raspberry, black currant and tobacco aromas. Bright and delineated in
the mouth, with juicy currant and dark berry flavors. Quite vibrant and
structured for a Languedoc red. Finishes with firm but sweet tannins.

Splurgeworthy
★ ★ ★ **DOMAINE PEYRE ROSÉ 1993 CLOS DES CISTES:** Flamboyantly
sweet aromas of black raspberry, framboise and chocolate. The extravagant, concentrated, portlike superripe fruit still comes across as bright
and well-defined.

═CORBIÈRES, MINERVOIS & ROUSSILLON ═

CARIGNAN AND GRENACHE ARE THE BACKBONE OF MOST OF THESE
blends, but higher Syrah and Mourvèdre content is now contributing freshness and aromatic complexity to what were previously more rustic wines. Although these appellations are similar,
Minervois lies farther from the heat of the Mediterranean coast
than most of Corbières, and its wines are frequently somewhat
finer. Dry reds from the very warm Roussillon region, not far
from the border with Spain, are also rapidly improving.

THE BOTTOM LINE: The prices for better Corbières and Minervois—rarely higher than $12—are extremely low for their quality. The wines of Côtes du Roussillon-Villages can be indistinguishable from Corbières and Minervois and are usually even cheaper.

Tasting Notes

UNDER $10

★ ★ ★ **CHÂTEAU D'OUPIA 1995 MINERVOIS:** Deep ruby red. Explosive red berry, smoked meat and pepper aromas. Lush and seamless, with bright acidity. Really stuffed with fruit. Finishes with tongue-coating tannins and lingering berry and spice flavors.

★ ★ ★ **DOMAINE DES MURETTE 1995 MINERVOIS CLOS DE L'OLIVIER:** Deep ruby-red color. Rather reticent cassis and clove nose reveals a faintly floral quality. Supple-textured, rich and generous; ripe berry and pepper flavors verge on sweetness. A fleshy wine that finishes with even tannins.

★ ★ **DOMAINE BAILLAT 1996 ROSÉ CORBIÈRES:** Scented cherry, strawberry and floral nose. Easygoing and charming; intense cherry flavor has a fresh citrus edge that keeps it crisp and firm. Quite dry on the finish, with a suggestion of strawberry gelato.

★ ★ **BOYER-DOMERGUE 1994 CAMPAGNE DE CENTEILLES MINERVOIS:** Very ripe raspberry, spice and coffee nose. Silky and supple in the mouth; tangy red fruit flavors are fresh and nicely delineated. Firmly tannic.

★ ★ **COL DES VENTS 1995 CORBIÈRES:** Nose combines dark berries, smoked meat, pepper and a floral nuance. A sweet, supple midweight with a juicy quality and an appealing shape. Quite ripe and creamy on the finish, with a peppery note; firmly tannic but not at all hard.

★ ★ **CHÂTEAU DU DONJON 1994 CUVÉE TRADITION MINERVOIS:** Aromas of black currant, game, earth, iron and tobacco. Intensely flavored, nicely focused currant and raspberry fruit; not especially fleshy but offers good vinosity. The raspberry flavor expands on the finish, covering the wine's ripe tannins.

★ ★ **CHÂTEAU DE JAU 1995 CÔTES DU ROUSSILLON-VILLAGES:** Jammy raspberry and pepper aromas. Superripe on the palate, but the spicy, peppery fruit maintains its shape and freshness. Strong flavor carries through to the spicy finish.

★ ★ **CHÂTEAU MARIS 1995 COMTE CATHARE MINERVOIS:** Impressively dark color. Floral-scented nose combines raspberry and a hint of truffle. Tangy, high-pitched berry fruit; thick yet juicy and bright thanks to harmonious acids. Very ripe on the aftertaste, with slowly building tannins.

★ ★ **DOMAINE MARIS 1995 CARTE NOIR CUVÉE SPÉCIALE MINERVOIS:** Aromas of blackberry and cherry eaux-de-vie, along with floral and smoky nuances. Fat on entry, then peppery and firm. Intensely flavored, with a faint green edge that repeats in the finish.

$10–$15

★ ★ ★ Château Mansenoble 1995 Réserve du Château Corbières: Floral cassis and licorice nose offers noteworthy purity. Intensely flavored and dense, but high-pitched and tight. Oak spice brightens the flavors. Fresh, youthful and delineated, and quite long on the palate.

★ ★ Château Belle Évêque 1995 Corbières: Knockout nose features tangy raspberry, sandalwood and a peppery note. Sweet but fresh; young and serious. Flavors of bitter cherry and pepper are bright and delineated. Finish is slightly dry but juicy.

★ ★ Les Palais 1994 Randolin Vieilles Vignes Corbières: Deep red-ruby color. Multifaceted nose combines cassis, chocolate, licorice, cinnamon and a briary hint of Provençal herbs. Thick and serious in the mouth, but pliant and juicy; complicating notes of herbs and spices.

VINS DE PAYS

A MAJORITY OF FRANCE'S SIMPLE "COUNTRY WINES"—LABELED *vins de pays* (van de PAYEE)—come from the vast Languedoc-Roussillon area. These are generally quite inexpensive and intended for immediate consumption; the best of them are among the world's most extraordinary red wine values. France's most frequently seen country wine is Vin de Pays d'Oc.

The recent trend toward planting "international" varieties such as Cabernet Sauvignon, Merlot, Chardonnay and Sauvignon Blanc has yielded some bottlings that, for sheer value, beat the pants off inexpensive varietal wines from most New World growing areas. But buyer take note: There are also a number of thin and weedy *vins de pays* on the market.

THE BOTTOM LINE: A budget wine shopper's paradise.

Tasting Notes

UNDER $10 VINS DE PAYS (VDP) WHITE WINES

★ ★ Domaine des Aires Hautes 1996 Sauvignon, VdP d'Oc: Gooseberry, melon and herbs on the nose: the essence of Sauvignon Blanc. Concentrated and tactile in the mouth; lovely ripe fruit offers excellent depth. Well-integrated acidity. Long, strong finish. An impressive wine for the price.

★ ★ Domaine Capion 1996 Marsanne-Roussanne, VdP de l'Hérault: Complex, vibrant aromas of smoke, fig, citric fruit, herbs and mint. Rich, spicy and layered; ripe, floral flavor is given clarity by lemony acidity. Concentrated and enticing.

★ ★ Domaine de Coussergues 1996 Sauvignon Blanc, VdP d'Oc: Musky, pungent, grassy nose. Ripe and grassy, with herbal and pineapple notes. Very good intensity and focus. Juicy, bracing and persistent.

★**J&F Lurton 1996 Chardonnay, VdP d'Oc:** Delicate peach and apricot aromas. Bright lemon and peach flavor, along with a suggestion of flower blossom. Fresh framing acidity. Finishes clean and persistent.

★**Domaine des Salices 1996 Viognier, VdP d'Oc:** Very pale straw color. Delicate mint, floral and peach aromas. Good flavor intensity and focus; leanish and penetrating, with crisp lemony acidity.

★**Val d'Orbieu 1996 Chardonnay Réserve St. Martin, VdP d'Oc:** Peach, mint, and celery on the nose. Crisp, clean, peach-flavored fruit offers good intensity and juicy acidity. Fresh Chardonnay made without oak, perfect for warm-weather drinking.

★**Val d'Orbieu 1996 Viognier Réserve St. Martin, VdP d'Oc:** Lemon, grapefruit and mint aromas. Juicy, fresh and crisp, with a firm shape. Not a particularly fleshy or rich Viognier, but pure and fresh.

UNDER $10 VINS DE PAYS (VDP) RED WINES

★★**Domaine de L'Arjolle 1995 Cuvée de L'Arjolle Vdt des Côtes de Thongues:** Enticingly sweet aromas of black raspberry, tree bark and licorice. Concentrated, spicy blackberry flavor offers excellent delineation thanks to juicy acidity; nuances of tobacco and Provençal herbs. Strong dark berry, herb and pepper aftertaste.

★★**Domaine Capion, VdP d'Oc:** Very ripe aromas of dark berries, licorice, chocolate and herbs, plus hints of toast. Dense cassis-flavored fruit shows a portlike superripeness, yet maintains a juicy character thanks to sound acids. A faintly meaty Syrah note adds to its complexity. Finishes with substantial mouthcoating tannins.

★★**Ch. Mansenoble 1995, VdP des Coteaux de Miramont:** Impressive ruby red. Vibrant cassis and blackberry aromas. Intense, pure dark berry flavor, with harmonious acidity. Slightly dry finish, with notes of cranberry and loganberry. Impeccable fruit/acid balance.

★★**Domaine St. Martin de la Garrigue 1995 Cuvée Réservée, VdP des Coteaux de Bessilles:** Dark ruby red. Aromas of red currants, dried flowers and fresh herbs call to mind an Italian wine. Deep fruit hides a solid tannic structure. Has a truly uncanny sweetness of flavor for a dry wine.

★**Domaine de Gournier 1996 Merlot, VdP des Cévennes-Uzège:** Black raspberry, cassis and mint on the nose. High-pitched berry fruit offers good intensity and sweetness, as well as juicy acidity. A brisk, firm style of Merlot, with little extra fat but convincing flavor.

★**Domaine de Serame 1995 Syrah, VdP d'Oc:** Pepper, violets, raw meat and a candied note on the nose. Good texture and sweetness give the wine impressive palate presence. Smooth raspberry fruit.

$10-$15

★★★**Mas des Bressades 1995 Cabernet-Syrah, VdP du Gard:** Impressive ruby-red color. Brooding black fruit, licorice and spice aromas. Supple, velvety and impressively concentrated. Finishes with ripe tannins and a burst of berry flavor.

Your Personal Tasting Journal

ITALY

ITALY IS THE WORLD'S LARGEST PRODUCER AND EXPORTER OF wine. Vineyards blanket the country from the Alpine north to the baking plains of the south, creating a bewildering array of wine styles and local specialties. A revolution in vineyard management and winemaking quality has swept the country over the past 20 years and a new generation of talented winemakers has come to the fore. Although not all of Italy's wineries have caught the wave by any means, your chances of finding an exciting wine in an Italian bottle have never been better. And, of course, Italy's finest wines have long ranked with the world's best.

WINE GEOGRAPHY: Tuscany and Piedmont remain the focal points for great Italian red wine, while the Northeast corner of the country produces the top white wines. As a general rule, the temperate, more continental climate of the northern half of Italy offers good conditions for making structured, ageworthy, complex wines of finesse, while the hotter south is a reliable source of straightforward but inviting wines for uncritical quaffing.

ON THE LABEL: Italian wine can be a complicated subject for consumers to grasp because Italian wineries use such a vast assortment of French, German and indigenous grapes. And, although a sizable percentage of the country's wines are labeled by grape varietal (as Chardonnay, for example), many of Italy's most famous wines are labeled by traditional place-names. It is hardly surpris-

ing, therefore, that wine consumers abroad have consistently clung to a handful of familiar names like Chianti, Soave, Orvieto and Valpolicella. But these wines barely hint at the riches Italy has to offer today.

THE BOTTOM LINE: Italy's most sought-after wines (such as the Killer Bs: Barolo, Barbaresco and Brunello di Montalcino) are priced on par with the costliest bottles from France, and offer true value only to collectors with unlimited budgets. But for the consumer willing to do a little digging, Italy is one of the world's richest sources of distinctive wines at modest prices.

NORTHWEST ITALY

The Piedmont region of northwest Italy is the home of Nebbiolo, Italy's noblest variety. Like Pinot Noir and Syrah, the late-ripening Nebbiolo is extremely sensitive to soil and site, producing aromatically complex and ageworthy wines in the best spots but less distinguished bottles elsewhere. The greatest examples of Nebbiolo—Barolo and Barbaresco—rank among the world's great red wines and are priced accordingly. The Piedmont is also home to two lighter reds, Barbera and Dolcetto, that typically need little or no cellaring time and are some of Italy's most food-friendly wines.

BAROLO AND BARBARESCO

BAROLO, ALONG WITH ITS LITTLE BROTHER BARBARESCO, IS THE greatest expression of the Nebbiolo grape, from the Langhe hills around Alba, Italy's white truffle capital. The best wines are made in small quantities on mostly south-facing ridges perched above the frequent October fog (*nebbia*). Barbaresco is a marginally less powerful but often more elegant wine than Barolo, but the similarities between the two generally outweigh the differences.

ITALY'S DOC SYSTEM

Denominazione di Origine Controllata (DOC) laws—Italy's counterpart to France's AOC laws—were established in the 1960s to define standards, improve quality and guarantee the authenticity of Italy's wines. Unfortunately, this system has had only mixed success, and labeling remains somewhat chaotic. DOC regulations are often so rigid as to stifle experimentation and prevent needed improvements. Many of Italy's most progressive producers have rejected the DOC as a hindrance to quality, instead producing proprietary wines that do not satisfy DOC requirements and are simply labeled Vino da Tavola (VdT), or "table wine." The most visible examples of these are the new-wave "Super-Tuscans" (such as Sassicaia), which are among the finest and most expensive wines of Italy, typically commanding prices higher than their region's officially "permitted" wines.

For much of this century, Barolo was an austere, macho monster whose fierce tannins made it virtually unapproachable in the first decade of its life in bottle. But wines, like fashions, change with the times, and a revolution in winemaking technique is producing Barolos and Barbarescos that can be enjoyed sooner.

GRAPES & STYLES: Nebbiolo grown in Barolo and Barbaresco produces wine with strong acidity and a firm tannic spine. However, largely in response to changing consumer tastes, the trend in Barolo and Barbaresco in recent years has been toward less energetic extraction of harsh tannins through shorter fermentation and less aging in barrel.

These smoother new-wave wines preserve the fresh fruit character of the Nebbiolo—the dried flower and violet nuances and the notes of cherry, raspberry and strawberry—while minimizing the hard, dry tannins that might otherwise overwhelm the fruit. The modern-style Barolos and Barbarescos are still powerful, full-bodied wines capable of a decade or two of development in the bottle, but they are far more accessible in their youth.

AT THE TABLE: Barolo and Barbaresco are a classic match for roast meats and game, especially venison. They are also ideal with aged and smoked cheeses. But note that the new-wave wines are more flexible accompaniments to today's cuisines than the older style, whose leather, tar and truffle character and mouth-puckering tannins demand strongly flavored red meat and game dishes.

THE BOTTOM LINE: Quantities of the best Barolos and Barbarescos are very limited, and strong worldwide demand has pushed prices up sharply in recent years. Even basic bottlings are typically $30 or more, while vineyard-designated releases are more often $40 to $60, and some are considerably higher. (Note that the 1995 Barbarescos can't be legally released until 1998, the 1995 Barolos until 1999.)

Vintage Rating

1990/A   1991/B   1992/C-   1993/B   1994/C+   1995/A-

Tasting Notes

Recommended Producers and Wines

★ ★ ★ ★ **ELIO ALTARE:** Perfumed, silky Barolos from a leader of the modernist school. Wines of impressive clarity and depth of flavor that are easy to drink upon release as their ripe, smooth tannins are typically covered by explosive fruit. *Look for*: Barolo and Barolo Arborina.

★ ★ ★ **DOMENICO CLERICO:** Harmonious, ripe, intensely fruity Barolos aged in a high percentage of new oak. These wines typically have the stuffing to support substantial tannins. Not surprisingly, they offer both early appeal and a track record for graceful aging in bottle. One of the first of the new-wave Barolo producers. *Look for*: Barolo Ciabot Mentin Ginestra and Barolo Pajana.

★ ★ ★ **ALDO CONTERNO:** Marvelous Barolos that provide an uncanny combination of *terroir* character and rich, dense, inviting fruit. Conterno has shortened the contact between the grape juice and the skins to avoid extracting bitter tannins but refuses to use small French barrels in the belief that the aromas of oak would overwhelm the delicate Nebbiolo aromas. The perfect example of an enlightened traditionalist. Prices are high. *Look for*: Barolo Bussia Soprana, Barolo Bussia Soprana Vigna Colonello and Barolo Bussia Soprana Vigna Cicala.

★ ★ ★ **ANGELO GAJA:** Progressively styled wines that command the highest prices in the region, from a relentlessly innovative, perfectionist winemaker. Gaja's Barbarescos are highly concentrated, seamless wines that show extraordinary complexity and precision of aromas and flavors. While firmly tannic and eminently ageworthy, they are rarely tough or dry. *Look for*: Barbaresco, Barbaresco Costa Russi, Barbaresco Sorì Tildin, Barbaresco Sorì San Lorenzo and Barolo Sperss.

★ ★ ★ **LUCIANO SANDRONE:** Remarkably sweet, fresh wines with flamboyantly perfumed aromas (flowers, tar, kirsch, toffee) and layers of fleshy fruit. Tannins are firm enough to give the wines excellent structure for aging but are rarely astringent. *Look for*: Barolo Cannubi Boschis and Barolo Le Vigne.

★ ★ ★ **CANTINA VIETTI:** Robust, complete wines with impressive levels of extract, powerful tannic structure and superb aging potential, from an open-minded traditionalist who does not hesitate to take advantage of modern techniques. This estate's several Barolos and Barbarescos accurately reflect their markedly different sites. *Look for*: Barbaresco Masseria, Barolo Brunate, Barolo Lazzarito and Barolo Rocche.

★ ★ **MAURO MASCARELLO:** Very rich, traditionally made Barolos that frequently show an almost exotic floral perfume upon release but require extended bottle aging to resolve their tannins. The great Monprivato bottling is an immensely rich, sweet, yet stylish wine whose wave of fruit often hides its substantial tannins in the early going. *Look for*: Barolo Santo Stefano, Barolo Bricco and Barolo Monprivato.

★ ★ **PRUNOTTO:** Elegant, supple Barolos, with good depth and backbone. Some wines of the '80s seemed a bit too tannic for their underlying material, but under new ownership maceration of the grape skins has been shortened and many of the winery's older casks have been replaced. *Look for*: Barbaresco Montestefano, Barolo Bussia and Barolo Cannubi.

★ ★ **RENATO RATTI:** Sweetly fruity Barolos whose silky textures and aromas of red fruits, truffle, smoke and earth call to mind red Burgundy.

The Ratti wines can be approached early but also age well. Renato Ratti originally created the modern style of Barolo back in the 1960s. **Look for**: Barolo Marcenasco and Barolo Marcenasco Rocche.

★ ★ ★ **ALBINO ROCCA:** Supple, lush, fruit-driven wines (cherry, cassis, raspberry) that frequently offer an ineffable violet perfume. The Barbaresco Bric Ronchi is made entirely in small French *barriques*. A rising star in Barbaresco. **Look for**: Barbaresco Vigneto Bric Ronchi and Barbaresco Vigneto Loreto.

★★★ **PAOLO SCAVINO:** Remarkably rich, often quite oaky wines, with tangy black cherry, dark berry and spice aromas and superb generosity of flavor. Another modern-style producer whose use of gentle, slow extraction of tannins allows him to avoid the toughness that makes so many traditional Barolos impossible to enjoy for a decade or more after bottling. A reliable performer in difficult vintages. May soon merit a fourth star. **Look for**: Barolo Bric del Fiasc, Barolo Cannubi and Barolo Rocche.

OTHER CONSISTENTLY EXCELLENT PRODUCERS: Brovia, Ceretto, Michele Chiarlo, Cigliutti, Conterno-Fantino, Corino, Giacomo Conterno, Bruno Giacosa, Manzone, Marcarini, Bartolo Mascarello, Moccagatta, Parusso, Giuseppe Rinaldi, Seghesio, Roberto Voerzio.

═══ OTHER NEBBIOLO WINES ═══

MOST BAROLO AND BARBARESCO PRODUCERS BOTTLE AND RELEASE a lighter version of Nebbiolo (labeled simply Nebbiolo d'Alba) that offers much of this variety's complexity and character in a more accessible and far less expensive package. In addition, the Piedmont region produces several other Nebbiolo wines from sub-Alpine climates north of Alba, where the grape goes by the name of Spanna. Gattinara and Ghemme are Nebbiolo wines with the earthy perfume of the variety, but they very rarely compete with Barolo and Barbaresco for freshness or sheer palate impact. As with Barolo and Barbaresco, other Nebbiolos of the region range widely in style, with more modern versions accenting sweet, fresh fruit.

AT THE TABLE: In addition to pairing wonderfully with meat dishes, lighter-weight Nebbiolo goes well with sharp cheeses. Try a fruitier-styled Nebbiolo with mushroom risotto; the earth notes of the wine marry perfectly with the forest floor scents of the mushrooms, while the fresh, sweet fruit of the young wine harmonizes with the Parmesan and butter in the dish.

THE BOTTOM LINE: At prices generally in the $15–$30 range, the best Nebbiolo bottlings offer considerable complexity and character for the price.

Tasting Notes

UNDER $30

★ ★ ★ **CANTALUPO 1989 GHEMME COLLIS BRECLEMAE:** Autumnal aromas of dark berries, loam, mocha, cinnamon and smoke. Then surprisingly fresh and penetrating in the mouth, with tart berry flavor and strong acidity. Finishes slightly dry but not particularly tannic.

★ ★ ★ **ICARDI 1995 NEBBIOLO SURÌSJVAN NEBBIOLO LANGHE:** Delicately scented nose combines berries, flowers and smoke. Rich, supple and sweet, with a suave, seamless texture reminiscent of red Burgundy and complex, subtle flavors of cherry, strawberry, mocha and tar. This is a very stylish Nebbiolo.

★ ★ ★ **PRUNOTTO 1995 NEBBIOLO D'ALBA OCCHETTI:** Sweet aromas of roses, loam, oak spice and licorice. Sweet and harmonious, with lovely freshness and volume in the mouth. Has the spicy red fruit character and silky texture of Burgundy. Finishes with dusty, ripe tannins.

★ ★ ★ **TRAVAGLINI 1990 GATTINARA RISERVA:** Pale brick color. Ethereal aromas of dried flowers, cranberry, prune and tar, plus a suggestion of autumn leaves. Then startlingly sweet and alive in the mouth, with a supple texture and bright plum and currant fruit flavors. The finish is brisk and long.

═══ DOLCETTO AND BARBERA ═══

ALTHOUGH THE PIEDMONT STAKES ITS CLAIM TO VINOUS GREATNESS on its Barolos and Barbarescos, its lighter-bodied reds, Dolcetto and Barbera, actually cover far more vineyard acreage and provide delicious, affordable options for everyday drinking.

GRAPES & STYLES: Dolcetto is an easygoing, supple, intensely fruity wine with healthy, deep color and significant alcohol, generally best consumed young. Though sometimes described as the Italian version of Beaujolais because of its fruit intensity and charm, Dolcetto is actually less candied and more complex. Barbera is a lighter-bodied but more penetrating wine that relies almost entirely on its acidity, rather than its tannins, for structure and cut.

AT THE TABLE: Thanks to its tart acidity and bracing flavors of bitter cherry and cranberry, Barbera is a perfect palate-cleanser with rich foods, especially fatty meats. It's also well-suited to pizza, pasta in tomato-based sauces and beef cooked in red wine sauces. Dolcetto makes an ideal companion for aged cheeses or simply prepared dishes such as roast chicken and grilled meats. It is also popular in the Piedmont alongside fritto misto, a dish of lightly breaded and fried vegetables.

THE BOTTOM LINE: Barbera is normally a sound value in the $12–$18 range; considerably more expensive special bottlings aged in small French oak barrels rarely justify their premium prices. Dolcetto is generally a dollar or two less.

Vintage Rating 1994 /C+   **1995** /A-   **1996** /A

Tasting Notes

UNDER $15

★ ★ ★**ICARDI 1996 DOLCETTO D'ALBA ROUSORI:** Dark berries and smoke on the nose, plus floral and spice notes. Very rich, deep, currant, plum, cherry and meat flavors coat the palate. Finishes very long and subtle, with the juicy fruit flavor outlasting the moderate tannins.

★ ★ ★**ALBINO ROCCA 1996 DOLCETTO D'ALBA VIGNALUNGA:** Aromas of blackberry, cassis, violet, licorice and oak spice. Tightly wrapped, very intense black fruit, violet and mint flavor in the mouth; strong acidity gives the wine excellent thrust. Long, firm and spicy on the aftertaste, with the blackberry and licorice flavors repeating.

★ ★**FRANCESCO BOSCHIS 1996 DOLCETTO DI DOGLIANO:** Reticent black cherry and herbal aromas. Firm, fresh and youthful; fairly intense cherry and raspberry flavors are given clarity by good acidity. A rather minerally, dry Dolcetto, finishing with dusty tannins.

★ ★**COPPO 1995 BARBERA D'ASTI L'AVVOCATA:** Scented floral and berry nose. Juicy, fruity and pure, with lovely cut and flavor intensity. Firm and stylish.

★ ★**ATTILIO GHISOLFI 1995 DOLCETTO D'ALBA:** Violet pastille, licorice and spice on the nose. Very intense black cherry and licorice flavor, complicated by a slight menthol quality. Bracing acidity gives this wine a racy finish.

★ ★**MARCARINI 1996 CAMERANO BARBERA D'ALBA:** Pungent, tangy aromas of cherry, raspberry and spice. Juicy and crisp in the mouth, with flavors of boysenberry and blackberry. Despite very firm acidity, there are no rough edges. An excellent Barbera.

★ ★**PRUNOTTO 1996 BARBERA D'ASTI FIULOT:** Excellent deep ruby toned color. Superripe cherry and raisin nose. Terrific, very lively cherry and raspberry fruit has a primary grapey character. Brisk but harmonious acidity.

★ ★**ALBINO ROCCA 1995 BARBERA D'ALBA:** Black currant, licorice, violet and smoky oak on the nose. Juicy and dry but supple, with creamy dark berry and pepper flavors. A lively floral component adds complexity. Subtle oak spice softens the wine's tannins without dominating its flavors. Very graceful Barbera.

$15–$20

★ ★ ★**COPPO 1995 CAMP DU ROUSS BARBERA D'ASTI:** Plum, currant, barrel char and hints of exotic fruits on the nose. Sweet and velvety in the mouth; has uncanny body and texture along with the brisk underlying acidity of Barbera. Gutsy, structured wine with a sweet aftertaste.

★ ★ ★ **ICARDI 1995 SURÌ DI MÙ BARBERA D'ALBA:** Knockout nose of minerals, smoke, meat, bitter cherry and toast. Very intensely flavored but silky and supple; despite being youthfully tight, even tart, there are no rough edges. The bitter cherry flavor repeats on the brisk finish. Quintessential food-friendly Barbera.

★ ★ ★ **PARUSSO 1996 DOLCETTO D'ALBA:** Lively, scented cherry/berry and spice aromas. Bright, high-pitched, dark berry, violet and licorice flavors offer remarkable intensity and a penetrating quality; already shows lovely perfume. Bracing acidity and firm tannins give this serious Dolcetto excellent backbone.

★ ★ ★ **RIVETTI 1996 CA' DI PIAN BARBERA D'ASTI:** Vibrant violet, licorice and bitter cherry nose, with a floral topnote. Intense, spicy cassis flavor verges on jammy, but fresh acidity keeps the fruit brisk and firm. Superb Barbera for the dinner table.

★ ★ ★ **PAULO SCAVINO 1996 DOLCETTO D'ALBA VIGNETO DĔL FIASC:** Deep red-ruby color. Dark berries and licorice on the nose. A vibrant floral component enlivens unusually concentrated, sappy black cherry flavor. Strong but harmonious acidity gives the wine a juiciness and a firm, bright finish. Long on the palate.

WHITE WINES OF NORTHWEST ITALY

GAVI, THE AREA'S MOST SERIOUS WHITE WINE, IS MADE FROM THE Cortese grape. It is crisp and, in the best examples, fruity. Arneis yields a perfumed, softer wine for early consumption. Muscat is responsible for the low-alcohol Asti Spumante, the popular, sweet sparkling wine of the Piedmont, as well as for a host of other light, grapey Moscatos. Franciacorta, from the Lombardy region, is Italy's best sparkling wine, though it offers little value in the U.S. marketplace.

Tasting Notes

UNDER $12

★ ★ **SARACCO 1996 MOSCATO D'ASTI:** Lime blossom and peach schnapps on the nose. Sweet and oily in the mouth, with fruity flavors of peach and lime. Not especially spritzy. Very good length.

★ **ICARDI 1996 CORTESE L'AURORA:** Aromas of pineapple, grapefruit, lemon and spice. Good intensity of flavor; slightly high-toned. Easy-drinking wine with a dusty aftertaste.

$12–$25

★ ★ ★ **ALBINO ROCCA 1996 LA ROCCA, LANGHE:** Extraordinarily complex aromas of peach, smoke, marzipan, mint and curry powder. Thick in the mouth, but bright acidity gives this wine terrific freshness and clarity of flavor. Exotic hint of orange peel. Very long aftertaste features subtle, spicy oak notes. A dramatic Cortese wine.

★ ★ ★ **VALDITERRA 1996 GAVI:** Perfumed, floral aromas of pineapple, lemon and herbs. Lovely sweetness of fruit and density in the mouth; quite concentrated and rich. Firm, lingering finish avoids hardness. An impressive Gavi.

★ ★ **STEFANO MASSONE 1996 GAVI VIGNETO MASERA:** Aromas of lemon, herbs and caramelized banana. Juicy, dry and laid-back on the palate, with lemon and mint flavors. Very good but not outstanding intensity.

★ ★ **RIVETTI 1996 LA SPINETTA BRICCO QUAGLIA MOSCATO D'ASTI:** Beguiling aromas of peach nectar, lime, honeysuckle and apple. Flavors of melon, peach and honeysuckle are lifted by a floral nuance. Briskly bubbly. Creamy and supple yet fresh and firm. Lingers on the palate. Classic Moscato.

NORTHEAST ITALY

The generally temperate climate of northeast Italy, a region that includes Friuli-Venezia Giulia, Veneto and Trentino-Alto Adige, is ideal for making fresh, fruity white wines. In recent years a number of producers here have taken their wines to another level by dramatically reducing yields, harvesting later for maximum ripeness and aging the wines on their lees (spent yeast cells) to get more texture, richness and flavor intensity. Don't expect copycat versions of international-style Chardonnays or Sauvignon Blancs à la California or France. Instead, look for expressive, individual wines with a racy fullness and style all their own.

WINE GEOGRAPHY: The hillier eastern side of Friuli—the Collio and Colli Orientali del Friuli—provides superb soils and microclimates for Italy's most important white wines. A multitude of mostly white grape varieties—of French, German and Italian origin—are permitted here.

Trentino-Alto Adige is the Germanic part of Italy. This region features many of the same white varieties as Friuli, plus indigenous reds like Lagrein and Teroldego. Trentino is generally the warmer half of the region, producing fuller wines, while the sub-Alpine vineyards of Alto Adige yield more scented, vivacious whites.

The temperate Veneto produces a sea of wine, but only a small percentage of it is worthy of note. This is the home of dilute Soave and weak red Valpolicella and Bardolino, from flat vineyards that yield huge crop levels. Only in recent years have quality-oriented producers begun to revitalize these wines by planting low-yielding vines in the best hillside locations. Look for the word "Classico" on the label (as in Soave Classico or Valpolicella Classico). At a minimum, this indicates that the wines come from their zones' best vineyard sites.

The Veneto is also the home of *recioto* wines, sweet reds and whites made using grapes that have been dried to concentrate their sugar content. Amarone (ama-ROW-nay) is a dry red version of this style, with all of its sugar fermented to alcohol, resulting in a portlike wine with head-spinning alcoholic content.

GRAPES & STYLES: In Friuli, the stars are primarily Pinot Bianco (Pinot Blanc), Pinot Grigio (Pinot Gris), Sauvignon Blanc and Tocai Friulano. In recent years, growers have cut their vine yields and used more small oak barrels to make increasingly interesting and flavorful Merlots and Cabernets. The best white wines from Alto Adige can rival Friuli's for flavor intensity and true varietal character. The Veneto's Soave is a softer style of white wine; the better versions depend primarily on the Garganega grape, using less of the innocuous Trebbiano. Similarly, the finest Valpolicellas rely almost entirely on the Corvina grape, the best of the three permitted varieties.

AT THE TABLE: Northeast Italy's subtly flavorful whites go perfectly with the delicate sea creatures native to the Adriatic, which might be swallowed up by big, oaky Chardonnay. Serve these wines with antipasti, shellfish and finfish. The region's reds can be served with meat antipasti like salami, prosciutto and liver, and with veal dishes or lamb served at room temperature.

THE BOTTOM LINE: The northeast is the finest source of intensely flavored, refined white wine in Italy, but prices can be high, particularly for wines from the Collio. Still, there are sound values to be found in the $12–$20 range.

Vintage Rating 1994/B+ 1995/B 1996/B

Tasting Notes

WHITE WINES UNDER $12

★★**SUAVIA 1996 SOAVE CLASSICO SUPERIORE:** Inviting aromas of muskmelon, lemon and smoke. Spicy and pliant in the mouth; still has a slight spritz. The melony character follows through on the palate. A fruity rather than minerally style of Soave, and very attractive.

★★**TIEFENBRUNNER 1996 PINOT GRIGIO ALTO ADIGE:** Pear and herbal aromas. Clean, fruity, fairly intensely flavored peach, melon and citrus flavors offer good depth. Firm, fresh finish.

★**CAVALCHINA 1996 BIANCO DI CUSTOZA:** Floral pear and apple nose, with a smoky nuance. Easygoing, slightly sweet but very fresh, with a creamy middle palate and lively flavors of pear and mint. Brisk and flavorful. A superb, inexpensive country wine, from a blend of varieties.

★**NINO FRANCO 1995 RUSTICO PROSECCO DI VALDOBBIADENE:** Chalky, lemony nose, with notes of flowers and herbs. Lemony and quite dry, with good fruit intensity and a clean aftertaste. Prosecco is the popular sparkling wine served in the wine bars of Venice.

★**ENO FRIULIA 1996 PINOT BIANCO:** Youthful aromas of pear, lemon, herbs and mint. Fat and supple, but with solid underlying structure. An accomplished wine for Pinot Bianco in this price range.

★**ENO FRIULIA 1996 PINOT GRIGIO:** Perfumed aromas of white flowers, peach and creamed corn. Lemony, fresh and nicely concentrated; ripe acidity gives the wine lovely vinosity. A Pinot Grigio with good palate presence and a lemony, herbal aftertaste.

WHITE WINES $12–$25

★★★**LA CADALORA 1996 PINOT GRIGIO VALLAGARINA:** Fresh, floral aromas of orange, pear and spice. Intensely flavored and tangy in the mouth; strong acidity gives the wine a refreshing briskness. Juicy, firm and quite dry, but very dense; conveys an impression of strong extract.

★★★**GINI 1996 SOAVE CLASSICO SUPERIORE LA FROSCA:** Subtle, complex orange peel and peach nose, with a whiff of coconut. Vibrant and intensely flavored; currently tightly wrapped due to lively acidity. Finishes unusually long for Soave.

★★★**RENATO KEBER 1996 PINOT BIANCO:** Flamboyant nose combines honeydew, tangerine, fennel and a hint of earth. Very concentrated and creamy in the mouth; a large-scaled, somewhat exotic and thoroughly satisfying Pinot Bianco with bright acidity and terrific length.

★ ★ ★ **RENATO KEBER 1996 PINOT GRIGIO:** Knockout aromas of oak char, orange blossom, lime and fresh herbs, plus a Champagne-like yeasty nuance. Ripe, juicy and very concentrated, with intense, pure mandarin orange and spice flavors. Very long, dusty finish.

★ ★ ★ **PECORARI 1996 TOCAI FRIULANO:** Aromas of almond, smoke and snap peas, along with a stony element. Creamy and full yet quite firm in the mouth; lively acids give the wine terrific thrust on the aftertaste.

★ ★ ★ **POJER E SANDRI 1996 TRAMINER DI FAEDO:** Extroverted aromas of smoke, lichee, honey and mint. Dense and mouth-filling, with superb depth of flavor; conveys a very sweet impression thanks to its terrific body and thickness, but this is actually a dry wine. Has excellent acidity for a wine that's mostly Gewürztraminer. Very long, strong finish.

★ ★ ★ **POJER E SANDRI 1996 SAUVIGNON ATESINO:** Herbs, mint, gooseberry and pear on the nose. Dense, very ripe and quite concentrated, but strong, harmonious acidity gives this wine excellent clarity of flavor. Multilayered. Finishes ripe and very long.

★ ★ ★ **ALDO POLENCIC 1996 PINOT BIANCO:** Reticent nose suggests lime and mint. The wine is almost shockingly intense in the mouth, with razor-sharp, ultrafresh lemon and mineral flavors that carry through to a vivid finish. Manages superb fruit intensity without excess weight. Brilliant food wine: a real high-wire act.

★ ★ ★ **VIE DE ROMANS 1995 PIERE SAUVIGNON:** Bracing minty, stony nose. Thick and fairly full in the mouth, but impeccably delineated and pure. Has a dusty, palate-coating texture. A very subtle, complex Sauvignon Blanc, not at all pungent or aggressive. Spicy and persistent.

★ ★ ★ **ZENATO 1995 CHARDONNAY RISERVA SERGIO ZENATO:** Very ripe, toasty aromas hint at fresh herbs and vanilla. Full, rich and layered in the mouth. Has a strong palate presence and lovely sweetness of fruit. Sound acidity gives the wine a harmonious quality. Very long.

★ ★ ★ **ZENATO 1995 LUGANA RISERVA SERGIO ZENATO:** Distinctive aromas of honey, nut, ginger and orange peel. Lovely, sweet ginger and peach flavor, with nicely integrated oak spice. Plenty of palate presence. Long and subtle on the aftertaste. Has concentration and style.

★ ★ **ABBAZIA DI NOVACELLA 1996 SYLVANER:** Floral, minty nose has an almost oily richness. Dense, ripe and somewhat earthy in the mouth. The wine is perked up by lively mint and green apple notes. Has good texture and length. Amazing for a Sylvaner made outside Germany.

★ ★ **GIROLAMO DORIGO 1996 PINOT GRIGIO VIGNETO MONTSCALPADE:** High-toned mineral, citrus, hazelnut and hay aromas. Full and expansive in the mouth, with a nutty nuance. The acidity is nicely integrated. Ripe and generous on the finish.

RED WINES UNDER $12

★ ★ **ACINUM 1995 VALPOLICELLA CLASSICO SUPERIORE:** Floral aromas of dried cherry and raspberry; slight hint of exotic fruit. Supple, floral and fruity; juicy, youthful and attractive. Very fresh Valpolicella.

★★**Cavalchina 1995 Bardolino Superiore Santa Lucia:** Pale cherry red. Notes of bitter cherry, iron, flowers, earth and smoke on the nose. Soft and spicy, with a thoroughly seductive sweetness supported by lively acidity. Has noteworthy intensity of flavor and freshness for Bardolino. Firm finish.

★**Allegrini 1996 Valpolicella Classico:** Perfumed, cherry-scented nose. Soft but bright and juicy in the mouth. Possesses just enough middle-palate texture for the slightly tart acidity.

★**Zenato 1994 Valpolicella Classico Superiore:** Almond, raisin and a floral nuance on the nose. Fresher in the mouth than on the nose: fat and layered, but vibrant thanks to flavors of apple and mint.

RED WINES $12–$25

★★★**Allegrini 1994 La Grola:** A single-vineyard Valpolicella. Dark ruby color. Complex, deep aromas of black raspberry, plum and smoky oak. Full, sweet and very concentrated in the mouth; dense and velvety. Nicely integrated acidity. Finishes with tongue-dusting, thoroughly ripe tannins.

★★★**Hofstätter 1995 Merlot:** Currant, raspberry and suggestions of leather and earth on the nose. Then very intensely flavored and firm in the mouth, with vivid flavors of spicy raspberry and herbs. Supple and compellingly sweet, but quite shapely thanks to brilliantly integrated acidity. Fresh, young and very long.

★★★**Vignalta 1995 Rosso Colli Euganei:** Saturated ruby-red color. Seductive aromas of kirsch, red currant, toast and tobacco. Highly concentrated, lush and creamy, with an almost confectionery sweetness. A tart but ripe pomegranate note gives the wine a firm shape and a vibrant finish. Goes straight to the pleasure center of the brain.

★★**Brigaldara 1995 Il Vegro Valpolicella Classico Superiore:** Red currant, dried rose, apple and toffee on the nose. Concentrated, intensely flavored and refreshing, with flavors of bitter cherry and cranberry given shape by brisk acids. A slightly tart, very fresh wine that shines with food.

★★**Foradori 1996 Teroldego Rotaliano:** Fruity aromas of bitter cherry, dark berries, leather and herbs. Juicy, dry and tart-edged; a leaner-styled, very refreshing wine with brisk, sharply delineated flavors and a firm finish. Still quite young, but already approachable.

★★**Mazzi 1994 Valpolicella Classico Superiore Vigneto Poiega:** Superripe nose combines spicy red currant, cherry and dried flowers. Fat, silky and mouth-filling; gives an almost chewy impression of extract. Subtle oak is in harmony with the wine. Finishes long and complex, with a distinct peppery quality. Long on personality.

Splurgeworthy:

★★★**Allegrini 1991 Amarone Classico Superiore:** Complex nose combines raspberry, truffle, dried fruits and a woodsy nuance; big, rich and sweet, with soft, palate-caressing texture; an easy-drinking Amarone that has both weight and elegance.

★★★**MASI 1993 AMARONE:** Portlike black cherry, chocolate, herb and raisin aromas. Dense, lush and mouth-filling, but not at all heavy handed. The lovely red fruit expands on the powerful finish.

★★★**ZENATO 1990 AMARONE DELLA VALPOLICELLA:** Exotic smoke, dried fruit and green apple nose; very rich and intensely flavored, with vibrant acidity framing the fruit and keeping it remarkably fresh; very long, firm finish features moderate tannins.

TUSCANY

If the Piedmont resembles Burgundy, with its small estates producing limited quantities of wine from favored hilltop vineyards, then Tuscany is more like Bordeaux. Here castles and villas, many owned by wealthy families from outside the region, have achieved the grandeur of Bordeaux châteaux. The late-ripening Sangiovese (san-jo-VAY-zay) grape, the most widely planted variety in Italy, is the foundation for nearly all of the best Tuscan reds.

CHIANTI

THE HEART OF TUSCANY—AND ITALY'S SINGLE MOST IMPORTANT wine area—is Chianti, a region covering the hilly countryside between Florence and Siena. As recently as the early 1980s, much Chianti was undistinguished, even pallid red wine. But in 1984 regulations were changed to cut back permitted yields and sharply reduce the required percentage of white grapes in the blend. The result has been fresher, more concentrated, more serious wines, even if basic Chianti is still intended for pleasurable early drinking.

WINE GEOGRAPHY: The Chianti Classico area is the center of the Chianti zone and, following the revival that began in the late 1970s, Italy's most reliable source of high-quality wine. Chianti Rufina, east of Florence, produces a less dense but equally fine version of Chianti. Less frequently seen in the U.S. are Chianti Colli Fiorentini, Chianti Colli Senesi and Chianti Colli Aretini, named after the hills surrounding Florence, Siena and Arezzo, respectively.

GRAPES & STYLES: Sangiovese is the backbone of Chianti, which has traditionally been blended with up to three other grapes, including small percentages of white Malvasia and Trebbiano. Today, in order to make more serious, ageworthy wines, the best producers add little or no white juice.

Chianti has moderate alcoholic weight and a dry but flavorful character. The better wines show tart, spicy, cherry and plum fruit, nuances of tar, dried flowers and woodsmoke and a firm spine of tannin and acidity. Chianti can be enjoyed young for its fresh fruit but can also age gracefully in bottle for a decade or more. Note that Chiantis labeled *Riserva* have been aged longer in barrel prior to bottling. These wines are, at least in theory, from the estate's best grapes in the strongest vintages.

AT THE TABLE: With the medium weight of red Bordeaux and even firmer acidity, Chianti is at least as versatile with food. In the restaurants of Tuscany, it is frequently paired with *osso buco*, *bistecca alla fiorentina*, *bollito misto* and stuffed peppers, as well as with Parmigiano-Reggiano. Chianti is also perfect with mixed grills and hamburgers and with pastas in red sauce.

THE BOTTOM LINE: On release, most basic Chiantis will fall between $12 and $18, with Chianti Classicos normally a couple of bucks more. *Riserva* bottlings command prices up to $30.

Vintage Rating
1990/A+ 1991/B- 1992/C- 1993/B+ 1994/B- 1995/A+ 1996/B

Tasting Notes

UNDER $15

★ ★ ★ **LE CORTI 1995 CHIANTI CLASSICO:** Saturated deep red color. Sweetly aromatic nose combines fruit scents of cherry, raspberry, plum and cassis with a smoked meat nuance. Sweet, lush and concentrated; very deep fruit flavor accentuates the wine's remarkable sweetness. At once fat and juicy. Very long finish, with tannins buried in fruit.

★ ★ **LE BOCCE 1995 CHIANTI CLASSICO:** Tart cherry, flowers and spice on the nose, plus a dusty nuance. High-pitched cherry/berry fruit offers good intensity and sweetness; firm underlying acidity keeps it fresh. Finishes with supple tannins and good length.

★ ★ **CASTELLO DI FARNATELLA 1995 CHIANTI COLLI SENESI:** Perfumed bitter cherry and raspberry nose shows an ethereal floral component. Supple, sweet and juicy, with easygoing cherry and raspberry flavor. A refreshing wine in a lighter style, but one with plenty of intensity.

★ ★ **FATTORIA DI VETRICE 1995 CHIANTI RUFINA:** Fresh floral, appley, spicy aromas. Tart cherry and berry flavors offer a notable intensity without much weight. A textbook example of the lighter but elegant Chianti Rufina style.

★★ROCCA DELLE MACÌE 1995 CHIANTI CLASSICO: Spicy black cherry nose. Fresh, supple, round and ripe in the mouth, yet juicy and nicely delineated. Offers impressive length for the price range.

★★VILLA CAFAGGIO 1995 CHIANTI CLASSICO: Fruity cherry and gunflint nose. Bright, very ripe and succulent, but has a firm edge. Aromas and flavors of fresh fruits. A Chianti in a style reminiscent of California reds.

$15–$25

★★★CASTELLO DI RAMPOLLA 1995 CHIANTI CLASSICO: Complex plum, chocolate and tobacco nose. Big, sweet and unusually approachable for this wine: lovely sweetness over a serious structure. Really packed with fruit. Finishes with tongue-coating but thoroughly ripe tannins.

★★★FELSINA 1995 CHIANTI CLASSICO: Brooding, liqueurlike aromas of black cherry, mint, herbs and tar. Sweet, fat and deep; shows its superb fruit already but built for the long haul. Finish is subtle and long, with substantial palate-dusting tannins.

★★★FONTODI 1995 CHIANTI CLASSICO: Sappy, deep aromas of bitter cherry, black currant and pepper. Very rich and approachable on the palate; black cherry flavor plus an exotic suggestion of raspberry eau-de-vie. Highly concentrated fruit is given clarity by fresh acidity. Finishes quite long, with dusty, even tannins.

★★★ROCCA DI MONTEGROSSI 1995 CHIANTI CLASSICO: Floral aromas of bitter cherry and grilled nuts. Very rich and concentrated; round, generous and mouth-filling. Sweet cherry/berry and licorice flavors are complicated by a subtle note of toasty, spicy oak. Crisp acidity gives the wine brilliant clarity.

★★★RUFFINO 1993 CHIANTI CLASSICO RISERVA DUCALE: Flamboyant roast meat, plum, coconut and spice aromas. Quite expansive in the mouth, with coffee, plum and cedar notes and a silky texture. Rather developed for a '93 Chianti *riserva*, but its enticing fruit and richness are perfect for near-term drinking.

★★ANTINORI 1993 CHIANTI CLASSICO RISERVA BADIA A PASSIGNANO: Brooding black cherry and violet nose. Thick, supple and concentrated; fat and sweet. Superripe notes of plums and raisins are lifted by a floral quality. Fairly tannic but not hard.

★★BADIA A COLTIBUONO 1995 CHIANTI CLASSICO: Cherry and smoke aromas, complicated by a mineral pungency. Juicy, intensely flavored and elegant; not fleshy but smooth and suave. Has a solid spine of acidity and a bright mineral character. The finish is long, with firm and slightly dry tannins.

★★CASTELLO DI AMA 1995 CHIANTI CLASSICO: Complex aromas of cranberry, blackberry, smoke, herbs and eucalyptus, Dense and chocolately in the mouth, with ripe, intense berry flavor.

★★ **BARON RICASOLI 1994 CASTELLO DI BROLIO CHIANTI CLASSICO RISERVA:** Lavish aromas of blackberry, cassis, cherry, coffee and grilled nuts. Lush, fat and stuffed with fruit; juicy and appealing thanks to bright acidity. Finishes very long, with thoroughly integrated tannins.

★★ **CASTELLO DI VOLPAIA 1993 CHIANTI CLASSICO RISERVA:** Fruit-driven aromas of cherry, plum and raspberry. Intense spicy plum flavor. Finishes firmly tannic but not at all dry, with subtle, lingering fruit.

★★ **NOZZOLE 1993 CHIANTI CLASSICO RISERVA:** Nose initially dominated by tobacco and iron; shows plum, raspberry and licorice nuances with aeration. Dense, ripe and young; the iron note repeats. Finishes quite firm, with slightly tough tannins. Needs patience.

Splurgeworthy:

★★★ **ROCCA DI CASTAGNOLI 1993 CHIANTI CLASSICO RISERVA POGGIO A FRATI:** Slightly high-toned plum and black currant nose; impressively rich, spicy black currant and plum flavors are complicated by a mellow wood note. Has a strong backbone for aging. Very long and deep.

OTHER SANGIOVESE-BASED DOC
WINES OF TUSCANY

BRUNELLO DI MONTALCINO, SOUTH OF SIENA, MAKES A VERY concentrated, full-bodied, slow-aging version of Sangiovese that is considered one of Italy's greatest reds. Vino Nobile di Montepulciano is a Sangiovese wine closer in weight to Chianti than to Brunello. (Both Montalcino and Montepulciano produce lighter, earlier-bottled versions of their top wines, simply called Rosso, or red—i.e., Rosso di Montalciano, Rosso di Montepulciano.)

Carmignano, a small zone northwest of Florence, broke off from Chianti in the 1970s due to the desire of its producers to blend some Cabernet Sauvignon with their Sangiovese. Carmignano is typically a rounder, richer wine than Chianti, with slightly softer acidity.

AT THE TABLE: Brunello can handle more assertively flavored red meat and game and also goes well with aged but not especially pungent cheeses. Serve Rosso di Montalcino, Rosso di Montepulciano and Carmignano with game birds or lighter beef dishes.

THE BOTTOM LINE: Brunello di Montalcino is the most expensive wine of Tuscany and among Italy's most overpriced reds. Only the premier wines from the best vintages justify their high prices. Tariffs generally begin at $25–$30 and can easily reach $50 or more. There is little of interest on the shelves at present since the current vintage, 1992, is a weak one. Vino Nobile di

Montepulciano is less expensive than Brunello, though rarely compelling. But Rosso di Montalcino, and occasionally Rosso di Montepulciano, can provide quite a mouthful for $12–$20. Carmignano tends to be undervalued—expect to pay about $15 for basic wines and up to $30 for *riserva* bottlings.

Tasting Notes

UNDER $20

★ ★ ★ **CIACCI PICCOLOMINI D'ARAGONA 1995 ROSSO DI MONTALCINO:** Inviting aromas of roast meat, currants and tobacco. Lush, sweet and deep; rather soft acidity gives the wine a harmoniousness and a very supple texture. Pure black cherry flavor. Finishes ripe and long, with sweet tannins.

★ ★ ★ **TENUTA FRIGGIALI 1995 ROSSO DI MONTALCINO:** Red currant and cherry notes emerge with aeration. Silky yet penetrating. A fruit-driven, creamy wine that builds nicely in the mouth.

★ ★ ★ **PERTIMALI (L. SASSETTI) 1995 ROSSO DI MONTALCINO:** Highly nuanced nose combines red currant, plum, dried flowers, leather and smoke. Lush and rich but sharply delineated; a gamy nuance adds to its complexity. A rather powerful underlying structure with tongue-coating tannins.

★ ★ **FATTORIA LA BRACCESCA 1995 ROSSO DI MONTEPULCIANO:** Expressive aromas of raspberry and smoke. Sweet and dense in the mouth; has real baby fat, but sound acids lend focus to the red fruit flavors. Finishes with firm, ripe tannins.

★ ★ **LISINI 1995 ROSSO DI MONTALCINO:** Red currant, plum, cherry and spice aromas, plus a leathery nuance. Sweet, lush and seamless; palate-staining, primary cherry fruit. Deep and ripe. Finishes with dusty, even tannins and strong fruit flavor.

★ ★ **MORIS FARMS 1994 MORELLINO DI SCANSANO RISERVA:** Deep ruby-red hue. Sappy, chocolatey-sweet aromas of raspberry against a background of toasty oak. Dense, creamy and superripe on the palate; red currant and plum flavors verge on sweet, but the wine has just enough acidity to keep its balance. A very rich wine that is perfect for early drinking.

$20–$30

★ ★ ★ **AMBRA 1994 CARMIGNANO RISERVA LE VIGNE ALTE:** Scented nose combines plum, black currant, dried rose and tobacco notes with spicy, nutty wood tones. Intense, spicy flavors of cassis and licorice. Supple, sweet and satisfying. Finishes very long, with fine-grained tannins and deep smoky oak.

★ ★ ★ **DEI 1993 VINO NOBILE DI MONTEPULCIANO RISERVA:** Plum, black cherry and leather on the nose. Densely packed and solidly structured, but a floral perfume and an almost confectionery sweetness of fruit give this wine considerable appeal.

★ ★ ★ **FULIGNI 1995 GINESTRETO ROSSO DI MONTALCINO:** Red currant and cherry aromas, with a whiff of vanillin oak. Creamy and rich on the palate, with enough raspberry and bitter cherry flavor to support the considerable oak component. Floral and toffee notes add to the wine's complexity.

Splurgeworthy:

★ ★ ★ **AVIGNONESI 1993 VINO NOBILE DI MONTEPULCIANO RISERVA:** Spicy plum, cherry and marzipan aromas; full, sweet and thoroughly ripe, with fruity flavors of raspberry, cherry and plum.

SUPER-TUSCANS

ANTINORI'S TIGNANELLO WAS THE FIRST "SUPER-TUSCAN," A wine from the Chianti Classico zone that was not allowed to be labeled Chianti because it was made with 100% red grapes (at that time, a minimum of 10% white grapes was required) and aged in small French *barriques* rather than the traditional large old casks. Since the early 1970s, scores of other estates in the region have created their own *vini da tavola*, using varying percentages of Cabernet Sauvignon (or Cabernet Franc or Merlot) and aging in small French barrels to craft bold, attention-grabbing wines. While some traditionalists believe that the herbaceous character of Cabernet Sauvignon overwhelms the more delicate Sangiovese, there's no arguing with the immense popularity of these wines.

THE BOTTOM LINE: Super-Tuscans vary tremendously in price, with the most sought-after wines often priced more for their rarity than for their quality (many of these bottles now sell for $50 or more). Although there are some very good wines in the $20–$30 range, this is not normally a place to look for value.

Tasting Notes

UNDER $15

★ **FONTERUTOLI 1995 MAZZEI POGGIO ALLA BADIOLA:** Cherry and licorice nose. Juicy, nicely delineated cherry flavor in the mouth; leaner in style, but clean, brisk and food-friendly. No shortage of flavor.

$15–$25

★ ★ ★ **TENUTA DELL'ORNELLAIA 1995 LE VOLTE:** Highly perfumed aromas of strawberry, raspberry and nutmeg. Sweet red fruit flavors are simultaneously lush and brilliantly delineated. Notes of dill and thyme add piquancy. A wine with the enticing juicy texture of a Pinot Noir.

★ ★ **PUIATTI 1994 CAPETINO:** A Merlot *vino da tavola* that is soft enough to drink with tonight's dinner. Aromas of charred oak, tar and black fruits. The wine is full and creamy, with a firm, minerally underpinning.

$25–$40

★ ★ ★ ★ **FELSINA 1993 FONTALLORO:** Saturated deep red. Ripe black cherry, currant, chocolate, tar and roasted nuts on the nose. Lush, intensely flavored and highly nuanced; a mineral character gives this powerful but suave wine a firm edge. Very subtle oak treatment. Finishes very long and strong, with dusty tannins.

★ ★ ★ **BOSCARELLI 1994 VINO DA TAVOLA:** Lively mineral, floral and cedary new oak aromas. Cherry-flavored fruit offers excellent ripeness and intensity. A medium-bodied, stylish wine with a very persistent finish and plenty of fruit to balance its tannins.

★ ★ ★ **CASTELLARE 1993 I SODI DI S. NICCOLO:** Warm aromas of plum, red berries, meat and chestnut. Juicy and tight in the mouth, with a solid spine of acidity and an intriguing tobacco nuance. Finish is subtle and long; needs some bottle aging.

★ ★ ★ **CASTELLO DI FONTERUTOLI 1993 CONCERTO:** Dark ruby red. Black cherry, cassis and licorice scents. Tightly wound yet velvety on the palate, with intense berry flavors and an enticing floral quality. Very concentrated and solidly structured. Finishes firm, juicy and quite long.

★ ★ ★ **DEI 1995 SANCTA CATHARINA:** Reserved, somewhat floral cassis, black cherry and licorice aromas. Elegantly styled and rather understated; subtly intense rather than particularly rich, but quite suave, with flavors of tobacco, coffee and herbs.

★ ★ ★ **FATTORIA DEL BUONAMICO 1993 IL FORTINO:** Highly nuanced nose combines raspberry, currant, chocolate, saddle leather and herbs. Silky-sweet and shapely, with subtle but penetrating flavor and good body. Fine-grained tannins are balanced by persistent finishing flavor.

★ ★ ★ **MICHELE SATTA 1995 PIASTRAIA, BOLGHERI:** Expressive aromas of black cherry, plum, red currant and smoky oak. Exuberant, intensely flavored berry fruit shows a toasty nuance. Fat, rich and mouth-filling; the spicy oak gives the fruit excellent definition. Stylish and persistent.

OTHER WINES
OF CENTRAL ITALY

Like Tuscany, the rest of Central Italy is best known for its red wines, but most of these are lesser versions of Sangiovese that cannot compete with the better examples from Chianti or Montalcino. Here are the wines you're most likely to find in the United States, presented by region:

EMILIA-ROMAGNA: A flood of lightweight Sangiovese, and often vapid, characterless white wines made from Trebbiano. Also the home of Lambrusco, which exists in export markets mostly in the form of a fizzy, rather sweet, low-alcohol wine in a screw-top bottle.

ABRUZZI: Home of easygoing, rather soft Montepulciano d'Abruzzo (blended from the local Montepulciano grape and Sangiovese), but only the exceptions have real concentration and density. Also white Trebbiano.

MARCHE: Dry white Verdicchio, in the process of being rescued from oblivion by a handful of conscientious producers. Only the best have real intensity, but prices are reasonable for this fish-friendly white.

UMBRIA: Best known for Orvieto, a sometimes slightly sweet white blend with substantial palate impact. Like Verdicchio, Orvieto is being revitalized by growers with vineyards in the most favored spots. Umbria also features some good varietal wines, including Grechetto, Chardonnay and Sauvignon Blanc. This region offers significant potential for further improvement.

LATIUM: Bland Frascati, based on yet another incarnation of the Trebbiano grape—a wine that typically offers more texture than actual flavor intensity.

AT THE TABLE: Orvieto and Verdicchio are ideal with shellfish, while the softer Frascati may be better as an aperitif. Lighter Sangiovese wines go well with quail and chicken, while more rustic Montepulciano d'Abruzzo is delicious with grilled, peppery steak or grilled Portobello mushrooms.

THE BOTTOM LINE: Prices are generally quite reasonable, but only the better examples in each category merit the interest of discriminating drinkers.

Tasting Notes

WHITE WINES UNDER $15

★ ★ ★ **BUCCI 1995 VERDICCHIO DEI CASTELLI DI JESI:** Bright orange peel and honey nose, with a suggestion of tropical fruits. Intensely flavored and dense, but quite dry and fresh. Thick and juicy. The strong kernel of spicy fruit carries through to the finish.

★ ★ ANTINORI 1996 CASTELLO DELLA SALA CHARDONNAY: Subtly complex aromas of smoked meat, spiced apple, lemon, peppercorn and mint. Vibrant and brisk; focused and very youthful. The oak influence is nicely restrained. Very fresh aftertaste.

★ ★ BOCCADIGABBIA 1996 GARBÌ BIANCO: Fascinating aromas of peat, heather, earth and lemon. Spritzy, steely and intensely flavored; fresh, crisp lemony fruit has a complex musky nuance and real snap.

★ ★ LA CARRAIA 1996 ORVIETO CLASSICO POGGIO CALVELLI: Floral, lemony, honeyed nose has a juicyfruit freshness. Honey and lemon flavors in the mouth; supple and textured. Lovely balance of fruit and harmonious acidity. Very good length.

★ ★ CATALDI MADONNA 1996 TREBBIANO D'ABRUZZO: Lemon and apple on the nose. Supple, intense apple and spice flavors offer good thrust thanks to harmonious acidity. Dry but flavorful. Firm, lingering finish.

★ ★ PALAZZONE 1996 ORVIETO CLASSICO TERRE VINEATE: Tangy aromas of grapefruit, orange peel and minerals. Intensely flavored and thoroughly ripe, with the vibrant citric notes repeating. Very tart and fresh in the mouth, yet supple and generous in the aftertaste.

★ ★ SARTARELLI 1996 VERDICCHIO CLASSICO DEI CASTELLI DI JESI: Aromas of nuts and lemon. Supple and stylish, with spiced apple flavor, good lemony acidity and decent texture in the mouth. Persistent finish.

★ ★ TERRA D'ALIGI 1995 TREBBIANO D'ABRUZZO: Aromas of hay, melon, herbs and lime. Bright and intensely flavored, with a spritz of CO_2. Dry, vivid and light on its feet. An understated wine with a crisp finish.

RED WINES UNDER $15

★ ★ ARNALDO CAPRAI 1995 MONTEFALCO ROSSO: Aromas of black cherry, plum, licorice, leather and smoke. Silky cherry/berry and tobacco middle-palate flavors lead to a firm, dry-edged finish featuring a bittersweet note of cranberry. Shows lovely restrained sweetness and light tannins.

★ ★ CATALDI MADONNA 1995 MONTEPULCIANO D'ABRUZZO: Very deep red-ruby color. Superripe but subdued aromas of berries and licorice. Sweet berry flavor is expressive but has strong underlying structure.

★ ★ COVIO 1994 FANTASIE DEL CARDETO VdT DELL'UMBRIA: Raspberry and ripe tomato on the nose; has a portlike roasted character. Sweet, ripe, large-scaled and a bit rustic, with just enough acidity for balance. Finishes with robust, chewy tannins.

★ ★ FALESCO 1996 VITIANO: Very dark color. Aromas of plum, black raspberry, leather, tar and truffle. Plump and ripe; a bit rustic but in a slightly roasted, inviting way. A fat, uncomplicated wine with soft tannins and rather low acidity. A blend of Cabernet Sauvignon, Merlot and Sangiovese.

RED WINES $15–$30

★ ★ ★ BOCCADIGABBIA 1994 AKRONTE VdT, MARCHE: A Cabernet Sauvignon wine with currants, licorice, tobacco and menthol on the nose, plus a floral nuance. Perfumed berry and mineral notes with a hint of chocolate. Has a lush, smooth texture. An elegant, very complex, deeply flavorful wine that finishes with a smoky, roasted quality and superb length.

★ ★ ★ **LA CARRAIA 1995 FOBIANO:** Superb Merlot. Very deep ruby red. Dark berries, minerals, tar and a truffle note on the nose. Fat and smooth; sweet flavors of chocolate, dark berries and coffee. The baby fat currently covers the wine's powerful backbone. Finishes quite firm, with vanillin, smoky oak.

★ ★ ★ **FALESCO 1995 MONTIANO:** Another impressive Merlot. Complex, Bordeaux-like black fruit and mineral aromas, complicated by notes of tobacco, herbs, earth and toffee. Supple and very rich; has the sheer concentration to support its substantial oak treatment. Sound acids frame the flavors nicely. Finishes with firm but ripe tannins.

★ ★ ★ **PIEVE DEL VESCOVO 1995 LUCCIAIO:** Plums and tobacco on the nose. Full-bodied and ripe; has an almost roasted black fruit character, superb sweetness and depth of flavor and excellent intensity. Tongue-dusting tannins are quite fine. Very long and subtle.

Splurgeworthy:

★ ★ ★ **LA PALAZZOLA 1995 RUBINO:** A serious Cabernet-Merlot blend for aging. Saturated dark ruby; wild aromas of black fruits, charred oak, licorice, leather and iron; full-bodied, dense and plummy, with terrific acidity and a solid tannic spine.

SOUTHERN ITALY

T he southern third of Italy offers a number of distinctive wines from mostly indigenous varieties, as well as significant untapped potential for both reds and whites. Grape farmers in southern Italy face the same challenge as their colleagues in other hot regions: getting enough buildup of fruit flavors before grape sugars soar and the grapes turn to raisins. They accomplish this by planting vines on cooler hillsides or in areas open to the moderating influence of the sea. Rain during the growing season is rare in southern Italy, and vintage variation is less significant here than up north.

GRAPES & STYLES: Apulia produces more wine than any other region of Italy, though most of it is cheap bulk wine for blending. Salice Salentino is Apulia's most important wine, a full-bodied, roasted red from the Negroamaro grape. Campania is the source of southern Italy's most serious wines, beginning with Taurasi, a concentrated, high-acid, long-lived red from the late-ripening Aglianico. This region is also the source of two distinctive dry white wines: the rather rich, almond-scented Greco di Tufo and the somewhat more delicate Fiano di Avellino. Both are unusually ageworthy for white wines from southern climes. The Basilicata region is the home of the tannic, slow-aging Aglianico del Vulture.

Sicily has a long history as a source of dessert wines, including Marsala, made by a variant of the Madeira method, and sweet wines based on versions of the Muscat grape. But increasingly fresh and satisfying—and aggressively priced—table wines are coming from the island, thanks to more sophisticated winemaking and more careful matching of local varieties to the right soils and microclimates.

Most of Sardinia's indigenous varieties are Spanish in origin. Here, too, great strides have been made in the last 20 years. White wines include the light Vermentino; red wines are produced mainly from the Carignan, Grenache and Mourvèdre varieties.

AT THE TABLE: Greco di Tufo goes well with shellfish pastas, while Fiano di Avellino works with antipasti, grilled fish, and white meats, including chicken in tomato-based sauces. White wines based on Vermentino can be served with antipasti, pasta and grilled fish. Red wines based on Aglianico complement roast or lightly grilled meats and game, while the larger-scaled reds of Sardinia are locally favored with roast, herb-suffused meats, especially lamb.

THE BOTTOM LINE: Southern Italy is just beginning to deliver on its potential to offer the best quality/price rapport of any of Italy's major wine zones.

Tasting Notes

WHITE WINES UNDER $12

★ ★ **ARGIOLAS 1996 BIANCO:** Bright lemon and spice nose, with hints of green apple and chalk. Reasonably intense white peach and lemon flavors. Not fat or sweet but quite refreshing. Persistent, clean finish.

★ ★ **FEUDI DI SAN GREGORIO 1996 ALBENTE:** Floral, appley aroma. Penetrating and fresh in the mouth, with a distinct rose-petal note. Nicely delineated and nuanced. Brisk, appley aftertaste.

★ **DI MAJOR NORANTE 1996 FIANO:** Floral, appley, minty nose. Supple in the mouth, with flavors of apple, honey and fresh hay. Shows a faintly candied note. Finishes quite dry.

WHITE WINES $12–$20

★ ★ ★ **COLLI DI LAPIO 1996 FIANO DI AVELLINO:** Highly aromatic nose of honey, lemon, licorice and tarragon, plus a saline, brothy character. Strong acidity and concentrated, piquant flavors of citrus rind and minerals give this very impressive yet somehow delicate wine great intensity. Finishes very long and firm.

★ ★ **CANTINE LENTO 1996 GRECO BIANCO, LAMEZIA:** Honey, resin, pear, lemon and spice on the nose. Fat and gentle in the mouth, with flavors of honey and melon and good texture. Finishes with a lemony freshness.

★ ★ **FEUDI DI SAN GREGORIO 1996 FIANO DI AVELLINO:** Aromas of hazelnut, honey, apple, pear and apricot. The fruitier side of Fiano, but quite dry and brisk. Has good weight in the mouth. Understated and very versatile at the table.

★ ★ **MASTROBERARDINO 1995 GRECO DI TUFO:** Spice, honey, butterscotch pear and peach pit on the singular nose. Lemony and brisk, with a note of almond and a bracing texture.

★ ★ **P.L.D. 1996 GRECO DI TUFO:** Delicate apple and floral aroma. Fresh, supple citric and floral fruit of very good intensity. Finishes with sneaky length.

★ ★ **REGALEALI 1995 NOZZE D'ORO:** Yeasty, nutty aroma. Not at all grassy or herbal despite its Sauvignon Blanc component. Silky in the mouth; understated earthy flavors are nuanced and intriguing. The finish is quite dry. This substantial wine can stand up to white meats.

RED WINES UNDER $12

★ ★ **CANTELE 1995 PRIMITIVO:** Briary berry and chocolate nose. Sweet, lush and attractive; fruity, appealing and intensely flavored, like a California Zinfandel. Gulpably delicious, if not particularly complex. Has the structure to develop in bottle.

★ ★ **LIBRANDI 1995 CIRÓ ROSSO CLASSICO:** Red currant, roasted herbs and exotic notes of orange peel and cinnamon on the nose. Sweet, spicy and concentrated; flavors of dried fruits and leather. No shortage of personality. Has good acidity and slightly dry tannins.

★ ★ **TAURINO 1994 SALICE SALENTINO:** Tar, almond skin, herbs, raisins, and a woodsy note on the nose. Penetrating, very dry floral-herbal flavor. Finishes with firm tannins and a slight bitter edge. Quintessential southern Italian red wine.

★ **ARGIOLAS 1995 PERDERA:** Ripe plum, currant and licorice aromas. Fat and broad on the palate; low in acidity but ripe and substantial.

★ **REGALEALI 1994 ROSSO:** High-toned, superripe aromas of dark berries and grilled nuts; almost portlike. Soft and sweet; a bit rustic, mouth-filling. Has very good acidity and somewhat drying tannins.

RED WINES $12–$25

★★★ **LIBRANDI 1991 DUCA SAN FELICE:** Complex aromas of figs, dates, flowers, raspberry, marzipan and roast meat. Very sweet on entry, then a bit tough due to strong acidity and chewy tannins. Slightly rustic but deep flavors of roasted herbs, meat and spices. A lot of wine here.

★★ **D'ANGELO 1994 AGLIANICO DEL VULTURE:** High-toned floral, cherry and black pepper aromas. Floral and fruity; hints of superripe fruit. Quite dry. Slightly tough tannins call for a bit of patience.

★★ **CANTELE 1994 CERBINARE ROSSO DEL SALENTO:** Plum and cinnamon aromas, with a suggestion of exotic fruits. Intensely flavored, spicy, and deep; rich fruit is supported by sound acidity. Firm, oaky finish.

★★ **MURGO 1994 TENUTA SAN MICHELE:** A Cabernet Sauvignon. Dark ruby red. Berries and menthol on the nose. Supple and smooth, with enticing berry flavors. A slight edge of bitterness leavens the wine's sweetness. Not especially dense but fresh and firm.

★★ **TAURINO 1990 NOTARPANARO:** Licorice, tobacco, fresh herbs and smoke on the nose, along with a suggestion of exotic fruit. Sweet and sappy in the mouth; a fresh appley quality and bracing acidity give the wine a penetrating briskness. Tannins are in balance with the fruit.

Splurgeworthy:

★★★ **FEUDI DI SAN GREGORIO 1993 TAURASI:** Raspberry, leather and oak spice on the nose; full and sweet but quite firm thanks to strong acidity; flavor of dark berries in the mouth and vanillin oak and leather on the finish; a serious, juicy wine whose rather tough tannins call for aging.

SPAIN

SPAIN IS THE WORLD'S THIRD-LARGEST WINE PRODUCER, after France and Italy, and a rich source of bargains. Until the early 1980s, exports of fine wine from Spain were dominated by Rioja (ree-OH-hah) and sherry. Since then, previously obscure regions, whose large cooperatives once produced undistinguished wines for local consumption, have been totally transformed, and a host of quality-conscious smaller producers have emerged. Many of today's wines are improved versions of traditional blends, but others are the familiar varietals or varietal blends demanded by the international market.

GRAPES & STYLES: Red wine rules in this mostly warm country. Many of the best (including most Riojas) are based on the Tempranillo grape, which produces wines with deep color, good acidity and a firm tannic structure for aging. Garnacha (Grenache in France) is also widespread, and Cabernet and Merlot are increasing in acreage. Nowadays, Spain also offers a growing number of intensely flavored white wines, as well as the sparkling wine called cava and some fine rosés. Spain's southern Andalusia region is the home of sherry, probably the world's most underappreciated great wine.

WINE GEOGRAPHY: Spain encompasses a vast range of climates, from the wet, Atlantic-influenced northwest, to the arid, blazing Mediterranean east. As in the south of France, vintage variation is less significant in the warmer parts of Spain than in more northerly wine regions,

where cool weather can prevent fruit from ripening fully, and harvest-time rains can cause grapes to rot.

THE BOTTOM LINE: Cavas and rosés number among the top values from Spain, but there are a wealth of terrific bargains in red and white table wine as well. The best Rioja and Ribera del Duero wines rank with the world's great reds, but their popularity has driven prices higher in recent years. Sherry remains remarkably underpriced.

RIOJA

The red wines of Rioja are a perfect choice for wine-loving carnivores in an age of instant gratification. The most prized Riojas are fragrant, mellow wines that derive much of their character from patient aging in small oak barrels; they are not generally released until they are deemed ready to drink. Riojas are easier on the head and stomach than most of the world's other serious reds, with more flavor and complexity than would seem possible from wines carrying a moderate 12%–12.5% alcohol.

GRAPES & STYLES: The finest Riojas are blends based on Tempranillo, with some jammy Garnacha included for alcoholic strength, Mazuela for acidity and Graciano for aromatic delicacy. The longer the wines age in small barrels, the more their fruit flavors of black cherry, black currant and plum are softened and augmented by notes of tobacco, cinnamon, roast coffee, cedar and vanilla. Tannin levels tend to be light and the wines are generally ready to be consumed upon release. White Riojas are popular in the Spanish market, but their tendency toward excessively oaky, rather oxidized aromas makes most of them a hard sell in the United States.

AT THE TABLE: Riojas are drunk in Spain with roast meats, which are the specialty of the Riojan restaurants called *asadores*. They also go well with meat and chicken stews, lighter game birds and barbecued ribs. Mature Rioja has a mellow quality that perfectly complements filet mignon.

THE BOTTOM LINE: Rioja prices zoomed upward following Spain's entry into the European Economic Community. But the devaluation of the Spanish peseta in the early 1990s, combined with pricing restraint on the part of producers, has provided consumers with a number of very affordable Riojas in the *crianza* and *reserva* categories.

Vintage Rating	1990/B-	1991/B+	1992/C
	1993/C-	1994/A	1995/A-

READING THE RIOJA LABEL

*C*rianza (kree-AHN-zah) and *reserva* wines are aged in small oak casks, or *barricas*, for at least a year, and then are further aged in the bottle. The *crianza* wines cannot be released by the winery until the third year after the vintage, the *reservas* until the fourth. *Gran reservas*, usually made from the finest grapes of the best vintages, spend at least two years in *barricas* and an additional three or more in the bottle. The top Rioja producers exceed these minimum aging requirements. Today, however, even the staunchest traditionalists are bottling earlier to reduce the dominance of oak and to preserve the aromas and flavors of fresh fruit.

Tasting Notes

UNDER $10

★ ★ **BODEGAS BERBERANA 1990 RESERVA:** Leather, plum, nuts and a hint of marzipan on the nose. Smoky, plummy fruit is supple and firm; vegetal and cinnamon notes add to the wine's flavor interest.

★ ★ **BODEGAS SIERRA CANTABRIA 1994 CRIANZA:** Pungent, oaky nose features cinnamon, coconut and vanilla. Fat, sweet and easygoing; strong flavors of spicy cherry and tobacco. Nicely balanced and fresh.

★ **R. LÓPEZ DE HERÉDIA 1993 VINA CUBILLO:** Tart cherry/raspberry nose, with notes of gunpowder and earth. Supple, juicy and lean, with tasty, bracing cherry fruit. Tangy acids give the wine a vibrant quality. Finishes with light tannins. Classic young Rioja.

★ **BODEGAS MONTECILLO 1994 VINA CUMBRERO:** Roasted plum, smoke and herbs on the nose. Tangy and lean in the mouth, with nicely delineated plummy fruit. A drier-styled, food-friendly wine that offers intensity of flavor without much weight. Finishes with light tannins and notes of earth and black olive.

★ **BODEGAS SIERRA CANTABRIA 1996:** Aromatic cherry and leather nose. Bright and fruity (cherry, raspberry), with a complicating earth note.

$10–$20

★ ★ ★ **VIÑEDOS DEL CONTINO 1991 RESERVA:** Mellow wood tones, roasted plum and a hint of smoked meat on the nose. Similar plum-based flavors in the mouth. Seamless and rich, but also bright and intensely flavored. Finishes with fine tannins and very persistent flavor.

★ ★ ★ **BODEGAS MARQUÉS DE MURRIETA 1992 RESERVA:** Extroverted, slightly meaty nose of cherry, raspberry, bitter chocolate and coconut. Packed with succulent, intense plum and dark berry fruit. Herbal and cedary notes add to this medium-bodied wine's complexity. Very long finish features notes of thyme and oregano.

★ ★ ★ **BODEGAS MONTECILLO 1989 RESERVA:** Classic Rioja aromas of smoked meat, currant, plum and mocha. Smooth, ripe and plummy, with an almost velvety texture and excellent intensity of flavor. Sound acidity gives the wine a juicy quality and a firm edge. Finishes with dusty tannins and a cedary nuance.

★ ★ ★ **REMELLURI 1994 CRIANZA:** Deep red-ruby color. Currants and leather on the nose. Very concentrated and creamy, but bright acids give the fruit excellent definition. Suave and powerfully structured. Firmly tannic and very persistent. A superb Rioja, and great value.

★ ★ **MARQUÉS DE CÁCERES 1994 CRIANZA:** Smoky raspberry, cherry and plum aromas, plus a note of tangy oak spice. Juicy, leanish and flavorful; fruity, delineated and quite stylish. Still youthfully tight. Finishes with dusty, even tannins.

★ ★ **BODEGAS MARTINEZ BUJANDA 1994 CONDE DE VALDEMAR CRIANZA:** Superripe black cherry, coffee and cedar nose. Silky-smooth and lush in the mouth, with an almost tomato-ey ripeness and a hint of crème de cassis to go with its plummy flavor. An easygoing, mouth-filling wine that finishes with very soft tannins.

★ ★ **BODEGAS MUGA 1992 RESERVA:** Complex aromas of red currant, smoke, tobacco, coconut and saddle leather. Supple, sweet and gentle; expansive in the mouth. Rather low acidity makes this an easy drink today. Very good length.

Splurgeworthy:

★ ★ ★ **MARQUÉS DE MURRIETA 1987 CASTILLO YGAY GRAN RESERVA ESPECIAL:** Amazingly complex, maturing Rioja aromas of plum, dark berries, cedar, orange peel and cinnamon. A pungent mineral quality along with brisk acidity gives this stylish wine terrific freshness and intensity; very strong aftertaste.

RIBERA DEL DUERO

The Ribera del Duero (ree-BAIR-ah dell DWAIR-oh) region of Spain has capitalized on international tastes for deeply colored, aggressively fruity, tannic red wine. In contrast to the practice in Rioja, winemakers in Ribera del Duero bottle and release their wines earlier to retain youthful fruit. They use their small oak barrels to tame the tannins and acidity of their wines rather than to add flavor. Think of Rioja as Bordeaux-like in style, with Ribera del Duero more akin to California Cabernet.

GRAPES & STYLES: Ribera del Duero reds are generally based on Tempranillo, sometimes with Cabernet Sauvignon and Merlot thrown into the blend. They are generally fuller-bodied and more tannic than Riojas.

AT THE TABLE: The reds of Ribera del Duero can stand up to more assertively flavored or seasoned meats than Rioja. They go especially well with roasted lamb, the specialty of the region.

THE BOTTOM LINE: Unfortunately, the region's better red wines are rarely cheap, due both to the scarcity of well-situated, older Tempranillo vines and to strong demand from

Spanish consumers. But there are excellent values to be found at every quality level.

Vintage Rating 1993/C- 1994/A 1995/A- 1996/A-

Tasting Notes

UNDER $12

★★ **GRANDES BODEGAS 1996 MARQUÉS DE VELILLA, RIBERA DEL DUERO:** Raspberry, game and a whiff of oak on the nose. Sweet, fat and creamy; packed with pliant, sweet fruit. Long, fruity finish features even, dusty tannins. 100% Tempranillo.

★ **IBERNOBLE 1996 COSECHA:** Aromas of smoke, game and berries. Sweet, fruity and smooth, with rather Zinfandel-like briary dark berry flavors. Not especially nuanced but smooth and attractive. Finishes with sweet tannins.

$12–$25

★★★★ **BODEGAS ALEJANDRO FERNÁNDEZ 1994 TINTO PESQUERA:** Pungent, minerally nose combines grilled meat, raspberry, coffee and chestnut. Very concentrated, urgent fruit boasts great freshness and complexity; notes of raspberry, coffee and subtle oak. A compelling, tongue-staining wine with superb flavor definition and great backbone for aging.

★★★ **BODEGAS ISMAEL ARROYO 1994 VALSOTILLO:** Black currant, smoky oak, mocha, and a meaty component on the nose. Fat, sweet and very ripe; a large-scaled, very concentrated wine whose velvety fruit currently covers its rather powerful structure. Finishes very long, with chewy tannins.

★★★ **BODEGAS ARZUAGA 1994 CRIANZA:** Red fruits, vanilla and nutty oak on the nose. Mellow, pliant and stylish in the mouth. A lighter-styled but already very attractive Ribera wine that finishes with light tannins. Has the complex, soft wood tones of a Rioja.

★★★ **BODEGAS CANDADO DE HAZA 1995 TINTO:** Superripe raspberry, plum, and chocolate aromas. Lush, sweet, and concentrated; has a silky texture and superb depth of flavor. Harmonious acids carry the fruit. Finishes with notes of spice, vanilla and toffee.

★★★ **BODEGAS REYES 1994 TÉOFILO REYES:** Perfumed cassis and black raspberry nose, with notes of smoke, iron, tobacco and mocha. Sweet, fat and oaky; really urgent fruit intensity. Suave, claretlike texture. Finishes very long, with firm but sweet tannins.

═══ OTHER SPANISH RED WINES ═══

WINES MOST LIKELY TO BE ENCOUNTERED IN U.S. RETAIL SHOPS include those from Navarra (Navarre), where Tempranillo and Garnacha dominate, but where Cabernet and Merlot often figure prominently, and from Catalonia, especially the warm Penedès region just south of Barcelona. In recent years, the hot, dry Priorato area of Catalonia has emerged with a handful of superrich blockbusters reminiscent of Châteauneuf-du-Pape, but these wines tend to be very expensive.

Tasting Notes

UNDER $10

★ ★ **BODEGAS AGAPITO RICO 1996 CARCHELO MONASTRELL, JUMILLA:** Dark ruby red. Perfumed aromas of blueberry, boysenberry, and cinnamon. Lush, layered and spicy; juicy, pure, peppery berry flavor is sweet and refreshing. Ripely tannic finish. Mourvèdre with some Merlot.

★ ★ **BODEGAS GUELBENZU 1996 JARDÍN GARNARCHA:** Superripe cherry and currant nose, with a slight raisiny nuance. Lively fruit offers good concentration and a peppery note. Has good texture and palate presence. The finish has a mildly drying quality but is not especially tannic.

★ ★ **BODEGAS GUELBENZU 1995 TINTO, NAVARRA:** Aromas of black raspberry, tar and oak. Raspberry, smoke and game flavors; velvety, dense and palate-caressing. Firmly structured but not at all hard. Finishes very long, with soft, tongue-coating tannins. A blend based on Cabernet, Tempranillo and Merlot.

★ ★ **BODEGAS INVIOSA 1994 LAR DE BARROS RESERVA, EXTREMADURA:** Ripe, deep aromas of red currant, plum, leather, smoky oak and spices. Sweet, easy and stuffed with ripe fruit; complicated by notes of loam and tobacco. Complex, fairly full-bodied, and utterly seamless.

★ ★ **BODEGAS NEKEAS 1995 VEGA SINDOA CABERNET-TEMPRANILLO, NAVARRA:** Very dark red-ruby color. Blueberry, cassis, spice and leather on the nose. Bright cassis flavor of noteworthy intensity. Finishes with firm tannins. A serious wine that should improve in bottle, and a steal at the single-digit price.

★ ★ **BODEGAS NEKEAS 1995 VEGA SINDOA MERLOT, NAVARRA:** Creamy, floral aromas of raw crushed dark berries. Very sweet blackberry and black currant flavor in the mouth; concentrated, silky and delineated. Finishes long and sweet, with palate-dusting tannins. Outstanding under-$10 Merlot.

★ **VÍNICOLA DEL PRIORAT 1995 ONIX VI NEGRE:** Spicy currant aroma. Rather dry cherry flavor, with brisk acids and chewy, slightly tough tannins. An unusually inexpensive if somewhat rustic wine from the suddenly fashionable Priorato region.

$10–$20

★ ★ **TORRES 1993 GRAN SANGRE DE TORO, PENEDÈS:** Spicy, red fruit aromas of cherry and strawberry. Very ripe on the palate, with flavors of black cherry, plum, smoked meat, leather and clove. A gutsy yet shapely wine with strong fruit and a rather easygoing finish.

★ ★ **TORRES 1995 LAS TORRES MERLOT, PEÑEDÈS:** Aromas of cherry, raspberry and vanillin oak. Sweet, supple and easygoing, with generous, fresh, red berry flavors. Finishes with soft tannins. Uncommonly lush and satisfying for Merlot in this price range.

ROSÉ WINES

AFTER SOUTHERN FRANCE, SPAIN IS THE WORLD'S BEST SOURCE OF drier style, character-filled rosé (*rosado* in Spanish). The top source is Navarra, but excellent rosés are also made in Rioja and Ribera del Duero. Many of the best wines are based on Garnacha, but Tempranillo, Cabernet and Merlot are also widely used. Compared to the rosés of Provence, examples from Spain tend to be fuller on the palate and more pliant, often giving an impression of sweetness even though they are technically dry.

AT THE TABLE: These dry but fruity wines are perfect with tapas, ham, fish soup and *salade niçoise*. In Spain, rosé is served virtually anytime a white wine is called for.

THE BOTTOM LINE: At prices that rarely exceed $12, Spain's finest rosés offer remarkable value.

Tasting Notes

UNDER $12

★ ★ ★ **BODEGAS JULIAN CHIVITE 1996 GRAN FEUDO ROSÉ, NAVARRA:** Pale strawberry color. Tangy raspberry, mineral and wintergreen aromas. Supple and dense, with intense raspberry flavor and an uncommonly silky texture for a rosé. Very fresh and firm on the aftertaste.

★ ★ **MARQUÉS DE CÁCERES 1995 ROSE, RIOJA:** High-toned aromas dominated by spicy oak. Then dry and delicate in the mouth, with perfumed strawberry and raspberry flavors and a minerally underpinning. Gentle but quite dry, thanks to harmonious acids. A very clean, understated rosé that's not at all austere.

★ ★ **BODEGAS MUGA 1996 ROSADO, RIOJA:** Ripe strawberry and a hint of charred oak on the nose. Big, rich and mouth-filling; has the texture and concentration of a red wine and sound balancing acidity.

★ ★ **BODEGAS OCHOA 1996 ROSADO DE LAGRIMA, NAVARRA:** Raspberry and fresh mint on the nose. Intense, vivid strawberry/raspberry flavor; ripe, supple and big for rosé but a refreshing dry edge gives this wine shape. The strawberry-flavored aftertaste is long and strong.

★ **BODEGAS SIERRA CANTABRIA 1996 CODICE ROSADO, RIOJA:** Very pale watermelon color. Bright, fruity, strawberry and raspberry nose; has an almost candied sweetness. Soft and supple in the mouth, with lovely fruit intensity. A fresh wine of modest complexity.

WHITE WINES

NORTHWESTERN SPAIN, WITH ITS COOL ATLANTIC CLIMATE, IS THE source of Spain's freshest white wines. Galicia, on the coast just above Portugal, produces a vibrant, pure wine from the Albariño grape, the same variety used to make Portugal's Vinho Verde. Similarly crisp but somewhat more substantial wines come from Rueda and its indigenous Verdejo grape, which makes spicy, lemony wines with nutty undertones.

AT THE TABLE: The dry white wines of northwest Spain, particularly Albariño, go perfectly with fish and seafood.

THE BOTTOM LINE: As one of Spain's most-sought-after wines, Albariño is not cheap, but the best are reasonably priced for their high quality. Whites from Rueda, on the other hand, are generally great bargains.

Vintage Rating 1995/A- 1996/B

Tasting Notes

UNDER $10

★★ **BODEGAS BRETÓN 1996 LORIÑON BLANCO, RIOJA:** Spicy lemon aroma shows a toasty aspect. Supple and fruity; ripe and creamy but thoroughly dry. Has the fruit to support the oak treatment. Subtle, lingering, lemony aftertaste.

★★ **MARTINSANCHO 1996 VERDEJO, RUEDA:** Floral aromas of lime blossom, minerals, pineapple, grass and mint. Silky and medium-bodied, with very good depth of flavor and bright limey acidity. Finishes brisk and fresh.

★ **BODEGAS NEKEAS 1996 CHARDONNAY VEGA SINDOA, NAVARRA:** Oaky clove and cinnamon nose. Sweet and spicy in the mouth, with fairly intensely flavored, fat fruit to support the oak treatment. The finish is brisk and firm

★ **BODEGAS PIRINEOS 1996 MONTESIERRA MACABEO, SOMONTANO:** Lemon, green apple, herbs and mint on the nose. Juicy green apple and lime flavors in the mouth; offers good flavor intensity. Manages to be fairly dense without being weighty. Refreshingly bitter lime edge. Bracing, aperitif-style wine.

★ **BODEGAS TELMO RODRIGUEZ 1996 BASA, RUEDA:** Musky, expressive grass and gooseberry nose. Supple, intensely flavored and fresh, with bright vegetal notes, good body and subtle length. A blend dominated by its Sauvignon Blanc component.

★ **TORRES 1996 VIÑA ESMERALDO, PENEDÈS:** Jasmine and honeysuckle aromas. Lemon-lime and Granny Smith apple flavors; juicy, floral and refreshingly tart. Modest intensity but a good, acidic spine.

★ **BODEGAS DE VILARIÑO-CAMBADOS 1996 BURGANS ALBARIÑO, RIAS BAIXAS:** Bright aromas of lemon and banana; nuances of grass and honey. Fat, supple and broad, with enticing sweetness. A bit of CO_2 keeps it fresh. Great value for Albariño, Spain's classic shellfish wine.

$10–$20

★★★ **LUSCO 1996 ALBARIÑO, RIAS BAIXAS:** Smoke, minerals, green apple, citric skin and chicken broth on the nose. Musky, intense lemon, pear and mint flavors, plus a floral nuance. Dense and shapely; a classy, brisk Albariño with very firm grip.

★★ **BODEGAS NEKEAS 1996 VEGA SINDOA CHARDONNAY CUVÉE ALLIER, NAVARRA:** Peach and cinnamon on the nose. Fat, ripe and concentrated. This has the silky texture—and suave oak aging treatment—of a more expensive Chardonnay. Sweet, very long aftertaste, with the peach flavor returning.

★★ **BODEGAS DE VILARIÑO-CAMBADOS 1996 MARTIN CODAX, RIAS BAIXAS:** Spicy but delicate lemon, green apple and peach nose, with a faint minty quality. Fat, lush, ripe and fruity; offers impressive flavor intensity. Nice balance of fruit sugars and harmonious acidity. Firm, lingering finish. 100% Albariño.

===== CAVA =====

MUCH OF THE VINEYARD LAND IN THE PENEDÈS IS GIVEN OVER TO the native white grapes—and increasingly to plantings of Chardonnay—that go into cava, the popular sparkling wine of the region. Here, as elsewhere in Spain, improvements in wine-making technology are yielding cleaner and fresher wines, as well as greater consistency of quality.

AT THE TABLE: Cavas are less fine than Champagne and thus less suitable for drinking by themselves. Serve them alongside spicy tapas, fried appetizers, garlicky shrimp and seviche.

THE BOTTOM LINE: The best cavas are rarely priced higher than $12 in the United States, where they rank among the world's great bargains in sparkling wine.

Tasting Notes

UNDER $12

★★ **MONT-MARÇAL 1993 BRUT:** Complex nose combines herbs, melon, honeysuckle and a yeasty, smoky nuance. Substantial but quite dry in the mouth; flavors of pear, melon, honey and spice. A laid-back cava of noteworthy finesse. Subtle, crisp aftertaste.

★★ **PALAU NV BRUT:** Brisk, clean aromas of apple and ginger. Dry, very fresh lemon and apple flavors, with a faint toasty nuance. Offers unusual richness and depth of flavor for cava, yet maintains a lightness of touch. Extraordinary value in sparkling wine.

★ ★ **SEGURA VIUDAS NV ARIA ESTATE BRUT:** Slightly high-toned, fruity aromas of lime, minerals and honey. Ripe and mouth-filling; low-toned smoke and butterscotch flavors complement the wine's pungent minerality. Rich and gentle, but with enough supporting acidity. In texture, seems halfway between a still wine and a bubbly.

★ **CODORNÍU NV BLANC DE BLANCS:** Fresh peach and apple nose, with a slightly candied quality. Refreshing and understated in the mouth; offers modest flavor intensity but is quite dry and firm. In comparison, the Codorníu Brut is a bit cloying.

★ **CRISTALINO NV BRUT:** Highly aromatic nose of minerals, mint and apple. Pungent mint, floral and fresh herb flavors in the mouth. Juicy and flavorful, with very good cut.

★ **FREIXENET NV CORDON NEGRO:** Brisk lemony aroma. Clean, reasonably intense lemony flavor. A bit lacking in personality, but well-made and satisfyingly dry and firm on the finish.

★ **SUMARROCA NV EXTRA BRUT:** Green apple, mint, lemon, lime and chalk on the nose. Fairly dry lemon-lime flavor has a dusty, gingery component. Finishes brisk, but with a suggestion of residual sugar.

SHERRY

SHERRY-STYLE WINES ARE PRODUCED IN A NUMBER OF COUNTRIES, but the real article comes from the area of Andalusia around Jerez de la Frontera, between Cádiz and Seville. No other wine-producing region has been able to match the sherries of Spain for complexity and balance. Versatile, amazingly underpriced and underappreciated, sherry spans a range of styles, from crisp and bone-dry to lusciously sweet.

GRAPES & STYLES: The best sherries are made from the Palomino grape grown on pale chalky soil called *albariza*. In theory at least, the finest raw materials are reserved for the drier sherries: fino (FEE-no), manzanilla (mahn-tha-NEE-yah) and amontillado (ah-mon-tee-YAH-doh). These dry wines get little or no fortification with grape spirits to boost their alcohol levels and are not sweetened. Some wine lovers find the driest sherries too uncompromising, while others find them habit-forming. Sweetened olorosos and cream sherries may be the best introduction for newcomers.

With few exceptions, sherry is an amalgam of vintages, produced through a blending and aging process called the *solera* system, in which more mature barrels are continually topped up with younger wines of the same sort to ensure a continuity of style and quality for the various sherry types offered by each *bodega*, or winery.

AT THE TABLE: Depending on the style and sweetness, sherry can serve as a revivifying aperitif, an ideal accompaniment to hors d'oeuvres, soups and starters or as the perfect dessert wine—or dessert substitute. Manzanilla with boiled shrimp is a favorite combination at the seafood restaurants of Sanlúcar de Barrameda. At the other extreme, the sweetest sherries can stand up even to chocolate.

THE BOTTOM LINE: Many of the best sherries are incredibly underpriced; few sell for more than $15 a bottle.

Tasting Notes

MANZANILLA UNDER $12

★ ★ ★ ★ **HIDALGO FINA LA GITANA:** The delicate nose of this lighter-style sherry suggests fresh bread and almonds. Very rich, intense wine of pungent freshness and great subtlety. Has an ineffable yeasty quality. Perhaps the perfect aperitif.

★ ★ **HARTLEY & GIBSON FINE VERY PALE EXTRA DRY SHERRY:** Nutty, yeasty aroma, with a resiny nuance. Silky and rich for manzanilla, with substantial flavor interest. Easy to drink for such a dry sherry.

STYLES OF SHERRY

FINO is a light, subtly almond-scented, dry wine generally carrying 16%–18% alcohol. Particularly delicate examples come from the area around El Puerto de Santa María, while fuller-bodied fino is produced in Jerez itself.

MANZANILLA is an even more delicate, though bracing, sherry aged in the port town of Sanlúcar de Barrameda.

AMONTILLADO is basically an aged fino that develops greater body and flavor.

PALO CORTADO combines the nutty aromas of amontillado with the deeper color and fuller body of oloroso. Most found in the U.S. market are slightly to moderately sweet

OLOROSO is made from base materials that are not as refined as those used for fino but are believed to have greater aging potential. Most oloroso is sweetened to some degree.

CREAM SHERRIES are olorosos mellowed by Pedro Ximénez grapes and tend to be even sweeter. As a rule, sweetened sherries begin with more heavily fortified base wines, and carry alcohol in the 18%–23% range

MONTILLA, a wine very similar to sherry, is produced around the town of Montilla. It comes in the full range of sherry styles.

MANZANILLA $12–$20

★ ★ ★ **HIDALGO PASADA:** Subtly spicy nose. Extremely concentrated flavors hint at nuts and spices; gutsy yet uncommonly smooth—a sherry that demands your attention.

★ ★ ★ **HEREDEROS DE ARGÜESO SAN LÉON:** Vibrant, complex, expressive aromas of apples and yeast. Quite dry yet rich, with a smoky nuance in the flavor. A manzanilla with an impressive palate presence and a subtle, lingering aftertaste.

FINO UNDER $12

★ ★ ★ **LUSTAU PUERTO FINO:** Multifaceted aromas of citrus rind, minerals, spice and honeysuckle; calls to mind a complex white Burgundy. A strong impression of acidity gives the wine a slightly harsh, very powerful, and yet thoroughly refreshing finish. This fino comes into its own when served with food.

★ ★ ★ **ALVEAR FINO:** Toasty, yeasty nose shows distinctly fruity aromas of apples and pears, plus a whiff of almond. Pungent, racy and stylish; has a manzanilla-like delicacy and rather low alcohol. Finishes long and fresh, with a suggestion of olive.

★ ★ ★ **LUSTAU LIGHT JARANA:** Brisk, precise mineral, lemon and lime aromas; offers chalky, minerally evidence of the famous white *albariza* soil of the region. Firm, classy and penetrating; impeccably balanced. The mineral tang repeats in the mouthwatering aftertaste.

FINO $12–$20

★ ★ ★ **VALDESPINO INNOCENTE:** Very subtle, mineral-tinged nose. Uncommonly full-bodied but very dry mouth feel; a huge, serious, perfectly balanced single-vineyard fino with a brooding aftertaste.

AMONTILLADO UNDER $12

★ ★ ★ **HIDALGO NAPOLEÓN:** Nose combines walnut, maple sugar and vanilla. This is quite dry and pungent in the mouth, with a rich, round feel. Has a penetrating, saline quality. Powerful, long, fresh, walnut-flavored finish.

★ ★ ★ **ALVEAR MONTILLA:** Fresh salty, nutty nose. Modestly sweet, smooth and intensely flavored; stylish and delicious. Finishes quite firm and dry, with notes of figs and nuts.

AMONTILLADO $12–$20

★ ★ ★ **ALVEAR SOLERA ABUELO DIEGO 27:** Deep, complex aromas of hazelnuts and toast. Dry, penetrating and intensely flavored; shows a slight Calvados-like apple quality in the mouth. A very classy wine with terrific bite and a long, fresh, slightly austere finish.

PALO CORTADO UNDER $12

★ ★ **LUSTAU PENINSULA:** Deeply pitched, nutty nose shows a tangy, sea-salt quality. Smooth, tasty and very easy to drink; enticing dried fruit and citrus skin flavors carry through to the firm finish. Quite dry and nicely balanced.

PALO CORTADO $12–$20

★ ★ ★ **HIDALGO JEREZ CORTADO:** Pungent, high-toned, nutty aroma. Very rich and velvety but totally dry. A tangy, slightly salty aspect keeps it lively on the palate. The finish starts slow and subtle, then builds and lingers. This would be almost austere were it not so rich.

OLOROSO UNDER $12

★ ★ ★ **HIDALGO:** Enticing aromas of nuts and butterscotch. Smooth, supple and user-friendly; not particularly rich or deep but very nicely balanced, with a fresh citrus quality.

OLOROSO $12–$20

★ ★ ★ **ALVEAR SOLERA ABUELO DIEGO 27:** The aroma features notes of walnut and a hint of orange peel. Silky and stylish, but serious and dry, even austere. Still, this rich oloroso has plenty of nutty flavor interest. Excellent length.

CREAM SHERRY UNDER $12

★ ★ ★ ★ **HIDALGO NAPOLEÓN:** Deep amber-mahogany color. Rich, deeply pitched nose combines nuts, raisins, honey and chocolate. Moderately sweet, lush, very concentrated and powerful; thick and serious. A rather uncompromising cream sherry. Nutty, fresh aftertaste.

★ ★ **ALVEAR MONTILLA:** Fruity aroma mixes apricot and nuts, along with hints of maple syrup and herbs. Soft and smooth, yet fresh and precise; not particularly sweet. Concentrated and rather easygoing, with plenty of personality. Finishes with a hint of walnut.

★ ★ **LUSTAU DELUXE CAPATAZ ANDRÉS:** Stewed fruit, figs and raisins on the nose. Quite sweet and rich; complex flavors feature dates and walnuts. Finishes with a faint dry edge.

Your Personal Tasting Journal

PORTUGAL

PORTUGAL IS THE HOME OF TWO OF THE WORLD'S GREAT fortified wines, port and Madeira, and also a major supplier of good, inexpensive table wines. Though Cabernet Sauvignon and Merlot are becoming more common, most of Portugal's best reds are still blends of indigenous grapes such as Periquita and Baga. Portugal's whites, including the bracing Vinho Verde, have benefited from the proliferation of modern winemaking techniques.

RED WINES

ONLY A DECADE AGO, PORTUGAL'S RED WINES TENDED TO BE TOO rustic for American tastes—excessively tannic or just plain rough. But producers with a new orientation toward quality are destemming their grapes to reduce tannins, fermenting in temperature-controlled tanks, aging in smaller, newer barrels and bottling earlier. The result is cleaner wines with more fruit and sweeter tannins.

NOTE: A wine labeled *garrafeira* (wine cellar) is one that a producer feels is of exceptional quality; *garrafeiras* usually get extra aging in both cask and bottle prior to being released.

AT THE TABLE: Most Portuguese red wines are medium- to medium-full bodied, with very ripe, robust flavors that are well suited to red meat.

THE BOTTOM LINE: While a handful of reds have streaked past the $20 barrier, most are still less than $12. The best offer plenty of flavor and personality for such modest prices.

Tasting Notes

UNDER $10

★ ★ CAVES ALIANÇA 1994 DÃO PARTICULAR: Smoky black cherry, spiced apple and a suggestion of exotic sweetness on the nose. Lush and deep; plum and currant flavors coat the mouth. Generous and solidly built.

★ ★ **P.V.Q. 1993 QUINTA DE PARROTES, ALENQUER:** Roasted plum and tobacco aromas. Sweet red currant and tobacco fruit is at once dense and brisk, thanks to juicy acidity. Finishes with fine-grained tannins.

★ ★ **QUINTA DO CASAL BRANCO 1994 FALCOARIA, ALMEIRIM:** Very deep ruby-red color. Inviting aromas of currants, smoke, tobacco and mocha. Dense and lush in the mouth, with strong spicy fruit. Has a lovely sweetness as well as a firm shape. Finishes with soft tannins and a youthful, grapey character.

★ ★ **RAMOS-PINTO 1994 DUAS QUINTAS VINHO TINTO, DOURO:** Slightly earthy aromas of black raspberry, licorice, and chocolate. Silky yet bright in the mouth, with good stuffing and firm framing acidity. Finishes fresh and persistent, with a note of white pepper.

★ ★ **CASA DE SANTAR 1994 RESERVA, DÃO:** Spicy plum and mocha nose; faint hint of roasted meat. Intensely flavored, vibrant and very ripe; manages the neat trick of simultaneously showing very good flavor definition and a seamless texture. Distinct note of pepper on the lingering finish. Tannins are light and nicely integrated.

★ ★ **J.P. VINHOS 1993 HERDADE DE SANTA MARTA, ALENTEJO:** Roasted plum, cherry, cassis and nutty oak notes on the nose. Creamy-sweet and smooth on the palate; fresh and quite fruity, with a pronounced cassis flavor. Finishes with ripe tannins and strong, youthful fruit.

★ ★ **J.P. VINHOS 1991 TINTO DA ANFORA, ALENTEJO:** Deep, mellow aromas of spiced plum, currants, smoke and tobacco; has a faint roasted component. Supple, rich and suave, with complex flavors of currants, tobacco and minerals. Nice balancing acidity gives the wine a firm edge.

★ **CAVES DE SÃO JOÃO 1994 PORTA DOS CAVALEIROS, DÃO:** Cassis, spice and an exotic grapefruit note on the nose. Currant and licorice flavor is given shape and intensity by rather strong acidity. Juicy, firmly tannic and structured to age, but has the freshness and balance to be enjoyed now with food.

★ **JOSÉ MARIA DA FONSECA 1994 PERIQUITA, TERRAS DO SADO:** Bright, fruity cherry and raspberry aromas. Sweet, soft and freshly fruity; easy-going and attractive. Has an almost Burgundian tang and just enough acidity and tannin to give it shape. Drink this graceful wine over the near-term for its youthful fruit.

$10–$15

★ ★ ★ **JOSÉ MARIA DA FONSECA 1991 PASMADOS, TERRAS DO SADO:** Lively berry, licorice and mint aromas. Very concentrated and firmly structured; intense, dry and flavorful, with the texture and shape of a Bordeaux. Brisk acidity gives it lovely clarity of flavor. The fruit hides the firm tannins on the long finish.

★ ★ ★ **GONÇALVES FARIA 1992 RESERVA, BAIRRADA:** Saturated deep red. Exotic, slightly high-toned dark berry, spice and pepper aromas. Impressively concentrated and powerfully built, with penetrating acidity; boasts a terrific core of sweet, peppery fruit. Very distinctive and very long on the palate.

★ ★ ★ **J.P. Vinhos 1995 Quinta da Bacalhôa, Terras do Sado:** Impressive ruby-red color. Pungent, superripe, multifaceted nose combines currant, mineral, oak, chocolate and coffee elements. Very rich and supple, with an almost portlike ripeness. Finishes with dusty, mouth-coating tannins. Mostly Cabernet Sauvignon.

★ ★ **Quinta do Carvalhinho 1991 Reserva, Bairrada:** Nuanced aromas of currant, plum, coffee and mint, plus a hint of grapefruit. Concentrated, spicy and medium-bodied, with the grapefruit character following through. Has the fruit intensity and texture to stand up to its strong acidity. Tannins are dusty but ripe.

★ ★ **Sogrape 1992 Reserva, Douro:** Complex, fresh aromas of plum, cassis, chocolate, herbs and subtle oak. Intense, sharply defined cassis flavor. Strong acidity gives the wine a juicy quality. Finishes rather long, with slightly dry but light tannins and a hint of woodsmoke.

Splurgeworthy:

★ ★ ★ **Jose de Sousa 1991 Garrafeira, Reguengos:** Very ripe, complex aromas of roasted plums, tobacco and minerals; sweet, lush and mouth-filling, with pungent mineral and oak notes providing definition. Just short of overripe but long on personality.

WHITE WINES

VINHO VERDE (VEEN-yo VAIR-day) IS PORTUGAL'S MOST FAMOUS white, called "green wine" because it's meant to be consumed young, before its fruit fades. Classic Vinho Verde, with its high acidity, low alcohol (generally around 9%) and slight fizz, is bone-dry and vibrant, with notes of lemon, lime, minerals and earth. (There is also red Vinho Verde, most of it well worth avoiding.) Other whites from Portugal are fresher than ever before, and generally very inexpensive.

AT THE TABLE: Vinho Verde is the perfect lunch or picnic wine, served with shellfish and other seafood dishes.

THE BOTTOM LINE: Generally under $8, Vinho Verde is an extraordinary bargain. Portugal's other white wines are also notably well-priced.

Tasting Notes

UNDER $8

★ ★ ★ **Quinta da Aveleda 1996 Quinta da Aveleda Vinho Verde:** Deep, complex aroma features a musky suggestion of truffle. Rather full in the mouth, but dry, juicy and intensely flavored. Quite fizzy. The finish is minerally and firm. A Vinho Verde of noteworthy complexity and class.

★ ★ **Adega Cooperativa de Redondo 1996 Porta da Ravessa, Redondo:** Expressive apple, lemon, spice and mint aromas. Vibrant lemon and spice flavors in the mouth; smooth and textured, with good weight. Lingering, firm, fresh aftertaste.

★ ★ **ALCÂNTARA AGRÍCOLA 1995 PROVA RÉGIA, BUCELAS:** Extravagant aromas of orange peel, lime skin, mint, spice and truffle. Medium-bodied, dry and spicy in the mouth; gutsy and textured. The orange peel quality recurs. Finishes ripe but crisp. At once bright and substantial.

★ ★ **QUINTA DA AVELEDA 1996 AVELEDA VINHO VERDE:** Musky, saline aromas of lemon skin and peach; has a slightly candied quality. Gently off-dry, but not at all cloying thanks to penetrating lemony acidity. Spicy, persistent finish.

★ ★ **QUINTA DA AVELEDA 1996 CASAL GARCIA VINHO VERDE:** Tart, gingery nose. Rather full and spicy in the mouth; ripe and gentle. Clean lemon and spice flavors carry into a soft but fresh finish. Quite smooth for Vinho Verde.

★ ★ **QUINTA DA AVELEDA 1996 LOUREIRO DA AVELEDA VINHO VERDE:** Penetrating aromas of flower blossom, grass and lime. Medium-bodied and quite dry, with lovely restrained fruitiness. Has moderate nuance but very good intensity. Lingering, firm and dry.

★ ★ **QUINTA DO MINHO 1995 VINHO VERDE:** High-toned, piney aromas of quinine and apples. On the lean side, but fresh, fairly intensely flavored and spicy. Slight sweetness is nicely balanced by ripe acidity.

★ ★ **REAL COMPANHIA VELHA 1996 EVEL, DOURO:** Fresh spiced apple and herb aromas. Supple, ripe, slightly floral flavors offer lovely clarity and intensity. Quite dry on the palate. Lingering finishing flavors of apple and mint.

$8–$12

★ ★ **FINAGRA 1995 ESPORÃO, REGUENGOS:** Lemon and herb nose, plus oak-induced spice, toast and smoke nuances. Supple, juicy, fresh and delineated; a modern, new-oak style of Portuguese white wine. Has noteworthy flavor intensity and enough material to stand up to the wood. Finish is brisk and spicy.

★ ★ **MONTÊZ CHAMPALIMAUD 1995 PAÇO DO TEIXEIRÓ VINHO VERDE:** Highly nuanced nose combines pine, spice, apple and floral notes, plus a smoky component. Supple, floral and dry; the harmonious acidity gives the flavors very good delineation. Lingering, subtle aftertaste. No fizz.

★ ★ **P.V.Q 1995 QUINTA DE PANCAS CHARDONNAY, ESTREMADURA:** Extravagant clove, truffle and game nose, with peach and mango notes. Supple and bright, with very good texture and enough flavor to support the oak treatment. Juicy, firm and shapely. Finishes long and spicy. A standout for its flavor intensity.

★ ★ **VIMOMPOR 1996 QUINTA DA PEDRA ALVARINHO VINHO VERDE:** Brisk, stony, lemon-lime and herbal aromas. Quite dry but mouth-filling; offers noteworthy intensity of flavor. Lingering, minerally finish shows a refreshing bitter edge.

PORT

PORT IS A FORTIFIED WINE MADE BY ADDING GRAPE SPIRITS TO fermenting wine, a step that halts the fermentation. The result is a wine that retains significant residual sweetness (typically between 9% and 10%) and high alcohol (normally in the 19%–20% range). Although port-style wines are produced around the world, the real article—always labeled Porto—is made from a blend of grape varieties planted on terraced vine-yards in Portugal's spectacularly rugged Douro Valley. Port's name comes from Oporto, the Portuguese coastal town from which the wine has been shipped since the 17th century.

AT THE TABLE: Basic tawny port, or age-designated tawnies up to 20 years old, are ideal for those who want to enjoy a bottle tonight, especially with a slice of Stilton or a dish of nuts. Mature vintage ports, or older tawnies, are the perfect way to extend a meal, savored on their own following dessert or with a good cigar. White port, which is harder to find in the U.S., is a delicious warm-weather aperitif served over the rocks and alongside salty snacks.

THE BOTTOM LINE: Classic vintage port is one of the world's most collectible wines, and it's priced accordingly. With the release of the outstanding 1994s, vintage port prices surged to record levels: $25–$50 for most bottles, with some even higher. Today, many of the best values in port are offered by nonvintage or age-designated tawnies and rubies, which deliver immediate drinkability and can be found for as little as $10.

Tasting Notes

Wood Ports (Nonvintage, unless otherwise noted)

RUBY PORT UNDER $15

★★**SMITH WOODHOUSE LODGE RESERVE VINTAGE CHARACTER:** Dark ruby color. Fresh, fruit-dominated aromas of cassis, black cherry and dried herbs. Sweet, thick and very rich, with noteworthy depth of flavor and a hint of raisin. Finishes somewhat less sweet and quite firm, with notes of spices, raisins and nuts.

★**CÁLEM LBV:** High-toned floral and raisin aromas. Rich, raisiny wine, with toffee and caramel notes. Sweet and smooth. Toffee and maple syrup notes in the mouth. Best suited for fans of mellower, older ports.

★**RAMOS-PINTO FINE RUBY:** Raisins, nuts, smoke and damp earth on the nose. Fat and creamy in the mouth; has lovely raspberry flavor intensity. Gives a slight impression of brandy but is ultimately a rather smooth, mellow ruby.

★ **TAYLOR SPECIAL RUBY:** Black cherry, dark berry and licorice aromas. Sweet but quite firm; there's plenty of strong raspberry fruit to buffer the mild impression of brandy. Slight earth note. Lingering finish.

RUBY PORT $15–$25

★ ★ ★ **GRAHAM 1991 LBV:** Brooding aromas of black currant, licorice, herbs and dark chocolate. Fat, sweet and layered; almost thick with fruit. A larger-than-life, very sweet port with a bit of alcohol showing.

★ ★ ★ **GRAHAM SIX GRAPES:** Youthful aromas of cassis, chocolate, licorice, herbs and damp earth call to mind a topnotch vintage port. Very intensely flavored and fresh, with strong, sharply defined cassis and chocolate flavors. Robust yet smooth. Less obviously sweet than some ports from this outstanding house thanks to firm tannins and acids.

STYLES OF PORT

Port comes in a bewildering variety of styles and types, which fall into two major groups: wood ports and bottle ports. Wood ports are, at least in theory, aged in wooden casks, though in some cases cement tanks are used. Wood ports can be divided into white, ruby and tawny ports. Rubies are more purple in color, and usually quite sweet, with an aggressive, almost peppery fruitiness. Tawnies, confusingly, can be inexpensive, non-age-designated wines made by adding white port to red, or complex, mellow, age-designated wines kept long enough in wood (10-, 20- and 30-year-old tawnies are widely available) to actually acquire a tawny color naturally. Aged tawnies are silkier, generally less fruity and more aromatically complex, with mellow notes of nuts, dried fruits, vanilla and flowers. A Colheita (kohl-YAY-tah) is a tawny from a single vintage. Like all wood ports, tawnies are ready to drink upon their release.

Bottle ports, in contrast, spend a relatively short time in barrel prior to bottling and can require two decades or more of bottle aging to harmonize, soften and express themselves fully. The apotheosis of bottle port is vintage port—wine from a single harvest that has been bottled after spending between two and three years in wood. Classic vintage port is made from superior grapes grown in the finest vineyards owned by the producer, and is released only in years when the wines have the exceptional depth and structure to become vintage ports. Late Bottled Vintage (LBV) ports, which share some characteristics of both bottle and wood ports, are relatively affordable wines from a single vintage—usually an unexceptional one—bottled four to six years after harvest.

★ ★ ★ **TAYLOR 1991 LBV:** Saturated red-ruby color. Black cherry, mocha and toffee aromas, with a pungent minerality. Big and sweet, with intense dark berry flavor and sound acidity. Quite lush but has a firm shape and really grips the palate. Strong, long finish.

★ ★ **FONSECA BIN 27:** Tar, smoked meat, spice and red fruit on the nose. Lush and sweet, with flavors of black cherry, chocolate and earth. A bit fiery but stuffed with fruit.

★ ★ **FONSECA 1990 LBV:** Grapey, curranty nose; hint of walnut when aerated. Fruity and young, with notes of herbs and menthol; very much like a young vintage port. Sweet, spicy, concentrated and quite long.

TAWNY PORT UNDER $15

★ ★ **GRAHAM FINE TAWNY:** Subdued aromas of dried cherry. Full-bodied and silky on the palate, with a fat, rather soft style. Slightly medicinal black cherry flavor. A very easygoing tawny.

★ ★ **FERREIRA DONA ANTONIA PERSONAL RESERVE:** Expressive aromas of walnuts, smoke, raisin, minerals and exotic fruit. Extremely sweet, lush and thick; flavors of currants, orange peel and maple syrup. Very sweet finish features hazelnut and walnut nuances.

★ **CALEM OLD FRIENDS TAWNY:** High-toned raisin and maple syrup nose. Smooth and sweet; has rather youthful fruit character for a tawny. Not at all fiery. Drying hint of walnut on the aftertaste.

TAWNY PORT $15–$25

★ ★ ★ **TAYLOR 10-YEAR-OLD TAWNY:** Spicy cherry and mineral nose; still showing fresh fruit. Intensely flavored, solidly structured and rather powerful; a drier-styled tawny with noteworthy backbone. Long, full finish.

Splurgeworthy:

★ ★ ★ **WARRE'S NIMROD FINEST RARE TAWNY:** Spicy aromas of walnuts, figs and maple syrup; meaty and thick with extract; very long, subtle, walnut-and-raisin finish.

CLASSIC VINTAGE PORT UNDER $30

★ ★ **OSBORNE 1994:** Black-ruby color. Very distinctive aromas of peat, loam, smoke, mint and Islay scotch. Extremely sweet, bordering on syrupy, in the mouth; a bit monolithic. Spice and mint notes dominate. Very long, youthful aftertaste. For fans of the supersweet style.

★ ★ **1991 RAMOS-PINTO:** Black cherry and herbs on the nose. Rich, ripe and slightly soft; a modestly structured, rather stylish port that can be enjoyed now even if it has the backbone to age. Subtle finishing flavor. No shortage of personality.

$30–$50

★ ★ ★ **TAYLOR 1992:** Very deep black-ruby color. High-pitched, very unevolved nose of mint, camphor, violets and cassis; the fruit is currently dormant. Very dense and unforthcoming in the mouth; penetrating and powerfully structured. Finishes with firm tannins and palate-staining fruit. Needs another decade of aging, but will be superb.

★ ★ ★ ★ **TAYLOR 1991 QUINTA DA VARGELLAS:** Opaque black-ruby color. Reticent, subtle, very pure aromas of minerals, licorice, ripe dark berries and grilled nuts. Outstanding intensity and depth of flavor; a slight meaty quality adds to its complexity. Great balance of middle-palate fruit and ripe tannins. Explosive, harmonious finish.

★ ★ ★ **CHURCHILL 1994:** Highly aromatic nose of black fruits, spices and inviting wood scents; suggestions of superripeness. Nicely delineated, intense cassis flavor; a juicy, classy, moderately sweet port. The impressive finish starts slowly, then builds.

★ ★ ★ **COCKBURN 1994:** Saturated black-ruby color. Spice, cassis, blackberry and shoe polish aromas. Very sweet and very intensely flavored cassis and black cherry fruit; smooth and rich. A succulent port that already shows considerable complexity on the palate. Generous, sweet finish tastes of maple syrup and toffee.

★ ★ ★ **CROFT 1994:** Cassis, kirsch and spice on the nose, plus a hint of spearmint. Supple, even creamy, in the mouth, but with a spicy firmness. Quite sweet and fleshy; has personality. Finishes long, with smooth tannins and notes of espresso and chocolate.

★ ★ ★ **QUINTA DO NOVAL 1991:** Complex, very ripe aromas of black fruit and licorice, with notes of tar and resin. Very concentrated and beautifully delineated; quite unevolved but already revealing personality and class. Fresh acids give the wine vibrancy and mask some of its underlying richness. Firm, very long, subtle aftertaste.

★ ★ ★ **SMITH WOODHOUSE 1994:** Black ruby to the rim. Classic young port aromas of cassis, black cherry, herbs, and chocolate, with some perfumed, floral-spicy high tones. Black cherry and chocolate flavor in the mouth. Finishes sweet, long and pure.

★ ★ ★ **WARRE 1994:** Restrained, brooding, licorice and dark berry nose. Very sweet and intensely flavored, but painfully unevolved. Still, the fruit is already quite penetrating. More muscle than fat here; a serious style of port, for extended aging. Concentrated and very long.

═══════════ MADEIRA ═══════════

MADEIRA, A PORTUGUESE-OWNED, VOLCANIC ISLAND FAR OUT IN the Atlantic Ocean off the coast of Morocco, produced the favorite wines of the American colonists. The twin plagues of oidium (powdery mildew) in the 1850s and phylloxera (a vine louse that kills vines by attacking the roots) in the 1870s, followed by replanting with substandard grape varieties, have left the Madeira wine industry a shadow of what it was in its glory days 150 years ago.

But Madeira's steeply terraced mountainside vineyards still produce some astonishingly complex and distinctive wines. Portugal's entry into the European Economic Community—

bringing with it new regulations and new export potential—has triggered a quality revolution there that may ultimately return Madeira's wine industry to its former status, in quality if not in importance.

GRAPES AND STYLES: The four basic styles of Madeira sold today are named after their traditional grape varieties. From lightest and driest to sweetest and richest, these are Sercial, Verdelho, Bual (or Boal) and Malmsey (or Malvasia). Even the sweetest Buals and Malmseys finish fairly dry and are rarely cloying due to their high natural acidity. Rainwater is a lighter, fairly dry style of Madeira. Generic Madeira, usually simply labeled as dry, medium, sweet or rich, is probably best suited to sauce-making.

AT THE TABLE: The especially tangy Sercial makes a perfect aperitif served with nuts or olives, while richer Buals and Malmseys are best consumed after dinner.

THE BOTTOM LINE: Vintage Madeira is rare and extremely expensive. From time to time tiny quantities of wines from the 19th century become available on the U.S. market, for prices generally in the $200–$500 per bottle range. Be aware that vintage dates on these wines, except those from the most reliable producers, may be impressionistic. The five-year-old reserve bottlings (generally $18–$20) or, better yet, the more harmonious ten-year-old special reserves ($30–$35) are better value for most consumers.

THE MADEIRA METHOD

In the 18th century, it was discovered that Madeira wines shipped to the United States actually improved from the heat and constant movement of a long sea voyage. Madeira's vintners developed a way to simulate these conditions: The wine is literally cooked, at temperatures up to 132 degrees, inside *estufas*, or hot houses, giving rise to Madeira's characteristic high-toned smoky, caramel-like aromas and its notes of raisins and nuts. Alcohol is added either before or after the heating process to stabilize the wine. Bottled vintage Madeira is virtually indestructible. This is the only wine in the world that can be left for months on the sideboard after it has been uncorked without oxidizing—basically because it's already oxidized.

Tasting Notes

$15–$20

★★**BLANDY FIVE-YEAR-OLD VERDELHO:** Orange-amber color. Smoky, bright nose features orange peel. Moderately rich and intensely flavored, with lively acidity. Finish is subtle and long, with a persistent fruity quality.

★★**COSSART GORDON FIVE-YEAR-OLD BUAL:** Pale green-edged bronze. Nose combines sharp fruitiness and complex vegetal and butter nuances. Fruity, young and rather dry for Bual; quite fresh and penetrating. Really light on its feet. Racy acidity is not yet completely integrated. Seems as dry as a typical Verdelho. Finish is quite brisk.

★★**LEACOCK FIVE-YEAR-OLD MALMSEY:** Complex, smoky nose has a pungency that suggests sound acidity. Big, round and smooth in the mouth, with healthy acidity; a note of citrus zest leaves the palate quite fresh. Harmonious, youthful aftertaste.

★★**LEACOCK FIVE-YEAR-OLD SERCIAL:** Green-edged light amber. Subtle, complex nose. Rich and lively, with very nicely integrated acidity. Slightly sweet and layered in the mouth. Lightly sweet finishing flavor really clings to the palate.

$30–$40

★★★**BLANDY TEN-YEAR-OLD MALMSEY:** High-toned nose of smoke and raisins, plus a hint of tangy fruit. Very sweet and concentrated, but not especially complex on the palate. Still, this relatively fresh Malmsey finishes long and fruity and wears its alcohol gracefully.

★★★**COSSART GORDON TEN-YEAR-OLD BUAL:** Complex, harmonious aromas of prune, tar and bonfire. Very rich, intensely flavored and quite sweet, but bright acids give the wine a juicy quality. Finishes subtle and long. This is delicious.

★★★**HENRIQUES & HENRIQUES TEN-YEAR-OLD BUAL:** High-toned, expressive nose. Leaner-styled Bual, but with lovely raciness and delineation. In a dryer style, but intensely flavored, bright and long.*

GERMANY

AMERICAN DRINKERS, WITH UNHAPPY MEMORIES OF sugary, cheap German blends, are all too likely to ignore Germany's great Rieslings—some of the world's most captivating white wines. Germany's top Rieslings, even when they have moderate sweetness, are blazingly fresh, remarkably complex and loaded with character; the best winemakers manage to find an exhilarating balance of sweetness and acidity.

GRAPES AND STYLES: German wines get their sweetness in one of two ways: either the fermentation is stopped before all the grape sugar has been fermented to alcohol, or the winemaker allows the wine to finish its fermentation and then adds back some *süssreserve*, or unfermented grape juice.

The winemaker's goal is to find the right level of sweetness for the wine's typically strong natural acidity. And that combination of sugar and bracing acidity is what gives the best Rieslings their impressive longevity: these wines are as capable of gaining complexity with bottle aging as the best white Burgundies.

AT THE TABLE: The trend for the past two decades has been toward drier wines—the response of winemakers to a shift in the domestic market toward lighter cuisines. As a result, many of today's German wines are more food-friendly than ever. Drier German Rieslings work well with freshwater fish, chicken and white meats. With

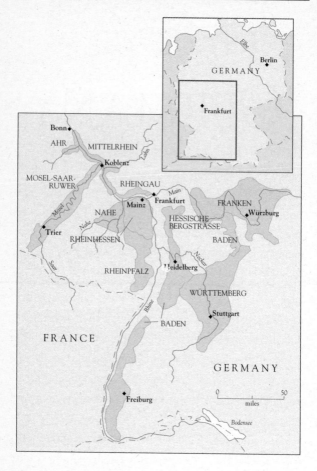

their brisk acidity, they can also take on pastas heavy on garlic or olive oil. Dry *trocken* (TRAW-kin) wines go well with fried foods like calamari and eggplant. Off-dry (*halbtrocken*) versions are perfect with cold shellfish salads or smoked trout; or try them with grilled pork tenderloin served with an apple or apricot glaze.

THE BOTTOM LINE: The white grape Riesling accounts for the majority of Germany's best wines. These wines range in price from outrageous bargains at around $8–$12, to scarce late-harvest releases that can easily exceed $100 for a 375-milliliter bottle! For fine wines at moderate prices, look for *kabinett* (kah-BEE-net) and *spätlese* (SHPAIT-lay-zuh) bottlings (see Decoding the German Wine Label, pg. 133), which typically retail for $12–$25.

MOSEL-SAAR-RUWER

Until a decade ago, most of the estate-bottled German wine exported to America was from a series of dizzyingly steep vineyards alongside the Mosel River and its tributaries, the Saar and Ruwer. This is Riesling country par excellence, producing wines that are delicate, crisp, floral and appley, with a steely, mineral undertone that comes from the slate soils. The wines are generally high in acidity and low in alcohol. The especially cool Saar and Ruwer areas require warm autumn weather to produce wine with natural sugars that will rank them above the *kabinett* level.

Wines from the Mosel-Saar-Ruwer come in green bottles, while those from other regions of Germany come in brown bottles.

Vintage Rating 1994/A– 1995/B– 1996/C+

Tasting Notes
Recommended Producers and Wines

★ ★ ★ ★ **FRITZ HAAG:** Very rich, minerally Rieslings with impeccable balance of grape sugars and acidity. Aromas and flavors run to apple, pear and honeysuckle. Expensive and scarce. **Look for:** Anything from the great Brauneberger Juffer-Sonnenuhr vineyard.

★ ★ ★ ★ **J. J. PRÜM:** Consistently outstanding, vibrant Mosel Rieslings that can be difficult to taste early due to substantial CO_2 and residual sugar; typical aromas of lemon, apple and pear, with passion fruit in the ripest years. Capable of aging for decades. **Look for:** Wines from the Wehlener Sonnenuhr vineyard.

★ ★ ★ ★ **VON SCHÜBERT:** High-acid, minerally wines of extraordinarily high quality, even at the basic QbA level; an estate with a track record for longevity. Among the most expensive wines of Germany. **Look for:** Bottlings from the Abtsberg and Herrenberg vineyards.

★★★**THEO HAART:** Consistently excellent, large-scaled wines (in texture and alcoholic weight) whose opulence often hides very high acidity. *Look for:* Tropical-fruity wines from the Piesporter Goldtröpfchen.

★★★**KARLSMÜHLE:** Slender, snappy wines, with cinnamon-scented cassis and apple blossom tones and generally bracing acidity. *Look for:* Lorenzhöfer Mauerchen Riesling Kabinett, Kaseler Kehrnagel or Kaseler Nieschen Spätlese or Auslese (especially '95s).

★★★**KARTHÄUSERHOF:** Vibrant, almost electric wines with lean, penetrating textures and great intensity. From iron- and mineral-rich soils in the cool Ruwer region. These are wines for connoisseurs. *Look for:* Anything you can find.

★★★**DR. LOOSEN:** Almost painfully concentrated wines from very low yields, with higher than normal residual sugar for each ripeness category; their density gives them an almost grainy, tactile quality. *Look for:* The house specialty Erdener Prälat Auslese; also Erdener Treppchen Kabinett and Ürziger Würzgarten Spätlese.

★★★**SCHLOSS LIESER:** Beautifully balanced wines with the strong acid structure and concentration for long aging. Particularly good value. *Look for:* Estate *qualitätswein* (the most basic level of QmP wine), Kabinett and Spätlese; also Schloss Lieser Kabinett and Spätlese.

★★★**SELBACH-OSTER:** Wines with velourlike texture and emphatic soil tones (flint and cherry in Berncastel, spiced apple and butter in Wehlen, lime and quince in Zeltingen); relatively dry for their category of ripeness. *Look for:* Zeltinger Sonnenuhr ('95s and '96s).

OTHER TOP-NOTCH ESTATES AND WINES TO LOOK FOR: J. J. Christoffel (Ürziger Würzgarten or Erdener Treppchen), Heribert Kerpen (Wehlener Sonnenuhr '96s and '95s), Merkelbach (Erdener Treppchen or Ürziger Würzgarten; '94s and '96s are better than '95s; prices are quite reasonable), Willi Schaefer (Graacher Domprobst and Himmelreich), Zilliken (Saarburger Rausch).

OTHER REGIONS

The somewhat warmer and dryer Rheingau region, less than 50 miles to the east, yields wines with a bit more body than the Mosel's and is its chief rival for international fame. In recent years, energetic U.S. importers have brought back offerings from top producers in other regions, such as the Rheinhessen (whose wines offer citric, floral and smoky aromas and flavors and are a bit more overtly fruity than those of the Rheingau), and the Nahe (with notes of red and black fruits and a balance much like that of the Mosel). The warm Rheinpfalz, once a byword for mediocrity, is now a hotbed of talented producers. Pfalz wines tend to be full-bodied, earthy and pungently spicy.

Vintage Rating 1994/A– 1995/B 1996/B–

Tasting Notes
Recommended Producers and Wines

★ ★ ★ ★ **HERMANN DÖNNHOFF, NAHE:** Refined, ultraclear wines from some of Germany's—and the world's—greatest Riesling vineyards. Intricate and elegant rather than particularly full-bodied. *Look for*: Anything you can find.

★ ★ ★ ★ **GUNDERLOCH, RHEINHESSEN:** Extremely fresh and reserved but rich and concentrated wines that take time to show their best. Typically display smoky, peachy aromas, with a marzipan nuttiness. *Look for*: Nackenheimer Rotenberg ('96 is especially strong).

DECODING THE GERMAN WINE LABEL

Daunting at first sight, a German wine label is actually designed to provide a wealth of information. Besides showing the name of the producer and the vintage, German labels indicate the grape type, the origin of the grapes (region, district, vineyard site) and the degree of ripeness at which they were harvested.

QmP (quality wine with distinction) is the top category of German wine, comprising six levels, in ascending order of ripeness of the harvested grapes, as opposed to the finished wine. For reasonably dry wines, stick to bottles designated *kabinett*; these are delicate, elegant wines, made from grapes of sound but not extreme ripeness, typically featuring a benign 8%-9% alcohol. *Spätlese* wines are made from riper grapes and *auslese* (OUSE-lay-zuh) wines from riper grapes still. These larger-scaled wines generally carry a bit more alcohol as well as higher residual sugar. *Beerenauslese* (beer-en-OUSE-lay-zuh), *eiswein* (ICE-VINE) and *trockenbeerenauslese* are from superripe grapes, often affected by the noble rot, botrytis cinerea. Made only in exceptional years and frequently among the world's most extraordinary sweet wines, they are often priced more for their rarity than for their quality.

If the label reads *trocken* the wine will taste very dry indeed. A wine labeled *halbtrocken* (or "half-dry") is technically slightly sweet, but due to its fresh acidity will likely taste quite dry to many drinkers, especially those accustomed to New World whites.

★ ★ ★ **MÜLLER-CATOIR, RHEINPFALZ:** Superconcentrated, vivid wines from several grape varieties: Riesling, Rieslaner, Scheurebe and Muscat. Made from late-picked, minimally handled grapes. One of the great producers of Germany; prices tend to be high. *Look for*: Anything you can find.

★ ★ ★ **JOSEF BIFFAR, RHEINPFALZ:** Big, dense, mouth-filling wines that combine weight with brilliant flavor definition. More reliable than most German estates for *trocken* and *halbtrocken* wines. *Look for*: Anything from the '95 or '96 vintage.

★ ★ ★ **FREIHERR HEYL, RHEINHESSEN:** Best known for dry and off-dry wines from the finest vineyards of Nierstein; Brudersberg tends to be opulent, tropical fruity and floral—among the most flamboyant wines from the Rheinhessen. *Look for*: Pettenthal Spätlese (normally bottled as *halbtrocken*), Ölberg Spätlese and Auslese.

★ ★ ★ **JOHANNISHOF (H. H. ESER), RHEINGAU:** Restrained, minerally, full-bodied wines, sometimes austere in their youth. *Look for*: Johannisberger Goldatzel and Hölle and Winkeler Jesuitengarten, especially when the vintage produces *spätlese* level or higher. The best price/quality ratio is normally provided by *kabinett* and *spätlese* wines.

★ ★ ★ **TONI JOST, MITTELRHEIN:** Fruit-driven but complex wines with glossy texture; never tooth-rattingly acidic. Aromas and flavors tend toward white nectarine, apples, vineyard peach, tangerine. Rather elegantly styled. *Look for*: Rieslings from the Bacharacher Hahn vineyard, especially the 1996 Kabinett.

★ ★ ★ **KOEHLER-RUPRECHT, RHEINPFALZ:** Burly, powerful but never rustic wines, showing typical Pfalz aromas of ginger, cinnamon and pineapple. *Look for*: Kallstadter Saumagen.

★ ★ ★ **KUNSTLER, RHEINGAU:** One of the great producers of dry (*trocken*) Rieslings of noteworthy purity; also makes fruitier-styled estate *kabinett* and *spätlese* with moderate residual sugar balanced by strong acid. *Look for*: Estate Riesling (from the Reichestal vineyard); also Hochheimer Stielweg Spätlese Trocken.

★ ★ ★ **JOSEF LEITZ, RHEINGAU:** Extremely aromatic wines, aged in barrel and thus more vinous as opposed to simply fruity; thick, powerful, muscular. From very low yields. *Look for*: Rüdesheimer Berg Roseneck or Berg Rottland ('96 has the edge over '95).

OTHER TOP-NOTCH ESTATES AND WINES TO LOOK FOR: Clüsserath-Weiler (Trittenheim Apotheke Spätlese and Auslese), Emrich-Schönleber (Monzinger Frühlingsplätzchen and Halenberg Spätlese and Auslese, often bottled as *trocken* or *halbtrocken*), Lingenfelder (Rieslings and Scheurebes, but avoid 1995), Egon Müller (look for *auslese* level and above, but prices can be very high), Walter Strub (Niersteiner Hipping and Ölberg are best and generally very good value; also look for Niersteiner Paterberg), Robert Weil (rare, pricey noble sweet wines are best), Werlé (Forster Jesuitengarten—usually dry *kabinett* or *spätlese*—Forster Pechstein, and Forster Kirchenstück—normally off-dry *spätlese*).

CALIFORNIA

CALIFORNIA PRODUCES MORE THAN 90% OF THE WINE made in the United States and two-thirds of the bottles Americans drink. The state had a flourishing wine industry by the end of the 19th century, but the twin catastrophes of vine pests and Prohibition ended the early era of prosperity. Although several notable wineries were operating prior to World War II, California's history as a leading producer of world-class wine really dates back little more than 30 years.

The modern age of California wine is widely considered to have begun with the opening of the highly influential Robert Mondavi Winery in 1966. As new, quality-conscious wineries sprang up—seemingly every week—through the late 1970s and 1980s, California's image as a producer of generic "jug" wines faded away. Today, the state's premium wines, the products of a warm and generally benign climate, have never been better, more popular or more expensive.

GRAPES & STYLES: California's finest offerings rank with the best from anywhere. Highlights include ripe, layered, complex Chardonnays from cooler vineyards in Sonoma and Santa Barbara counties; big, boldly flavored (and oaked) Cabernet Sauvignons from Napa Valley; and sappy, berry-scented Zinfandels from pockets of old vines all over the state. Among the most exciting recent developments are the increasingly interesting wines being produced from Rhône Valley varieties like Syrah, Mourvèdre and Viognier.

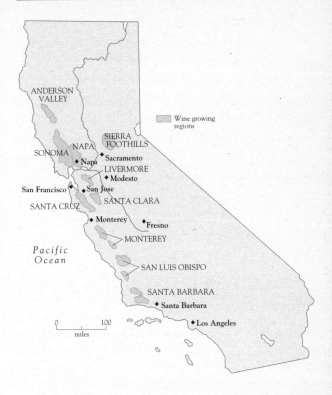

ON THE LABEL: Most of California's wines are labeled by grape variety (for example, Sauvignon Blanc). By law, these varietal wines must contain at least 75% of the named grape, and some contain up to 100%.

Some wineries have sought to escape the rigid confines of the 75% varietal rule by giving their wines fanciful proprietary names (like Opus One) instead of showing the variety on the label. The term Meritage was invented by an association of wineries that produce blended wines, both red and white, in a Bordeaux style.

Though their popularity is waning, there is a still a big market for generic wines with names like burgundy, chablis and rhine. But these wines typically bear little or no relation to their European namesakes.

THE BOTTOM LINE: Pricing of California wines has always been cyclical, and today numerous forces are conspiring to push prices higher, including a string of fine but not especially large harvests, massive replanting of vineyards due to an epidemic of phylloxera (a vine-killing root louse) and strong demand. The result is that grape prices have reached record levels, and wineries that depend on purchased fruit are finding it harder than ever to offer good inexpensive wines.

CHARDONNAY

A t the top quality levels, California provides the world's finest Chardonnays outside of the grape's Burgundian homeland. A broad range of Chardonnay styles can be found within the state's borders, from penetrating, crisp and bone-dry to plump, oaky, palate caressing and exotically fruity.

Unfortunately, however, America's bottomless thirst for Chardonnay has so driven up grape prices in California that it has become difficult to find inexpensive bottles with real personality. All too often, budget-priced bottlings verge on the generic, providing a drinkable white wine but one with little hint of the seductive pleasures of a fine Chardonnay.

WINE GEOGRAPHY: The top California Chardonnays are most likely to come from three relatively cool growing regions: the Russian River Valley in Sonoma County; the Carneros district, which stretches across the southern tips of both Napa and Sonoma counties; and Santa Barbara County. The best wines from each of these areas have in common a lovely fruit-acid balance and purity of flavor.

AT THE TABLE: Chardonnays are well suited to a wide range of fish and shellfish preparations, pastas and white meats. Versions with high acidity can cut through cream sauces or accompany grilled fish. More opulent, oakier Chardonnays can overwhelm delicate fare; such wines normally go better with richer fish, scallops and lobsters or sweetbreads.

THE BOTTOM LINE: California's Chardonnays have stiff competition at the lower end: These wines don't always compare favorably to Australian Chardonnays in the $12-and-under category, or to Chilean wines in the $8 price bracket. Still, many concentrated, character-filled Chardonnays can be found in the $15–$20 range. The state's very best Chardonnays (typically $25 or more) are world-class wines that compare favorably to white Burgundies at two to three times the price.

Vintage Rating 1993/B **1994**/A **1995**/A- **1996**/B+

Tasting Notes

UNDER $15

★★**GALLO SONOMA 1995 STEFANI VINEYARD, DRY CREEK:** Pear, apple, papaya and oak on the nose. Dusty, tactile, palate-coating texture and good inner-mouth flavor. Notes of smoky oak and exotic fruit. Finishes spicy and chewy.

★★**HANDLEY 1995, ANDERSON VALLEY:** Lemon, vanilla and oak; slight high-toned quality. Big and spicy, with strong lemon and grapefruit acidity. Has intensity of flavor and good density. Tart-edged and refreshing.

★★**SEVEN OAKS 1996, CALIFORNIA:** Charred oakiness, creamed corn, peach and nuts on the nose. Bright and spicy in the mouth; the

STYLES OF CHARDONNAY

Chardonnay can vary so dramatically in aromas and flavors, texture and weight and in degree of oakiness that a request for a glass of Chardonnay at a bar or restaurant might as well be simply a request for a glass of white wine. In Chablis, where Chardonnay grapes are planted on chalky soil, the variety yields a steely, austere wine prized by connoisseurs but often difficult for neophytes to appreciate. In Australia and California, the same variety makes a host of fat, buttery-rich, tropical-fruit-flavored wines, including some that seem downright sweet and others whose aromas of vanillin oakiness completely overwhelm any varietal character. The fact that Chardonnay can be (nearly) all things to all people helps explain its runaway popularity. But it is worth tasting around to see which style suits you best.

wine's rich mouth feel is nicely leavened by fresh acidity. Very firm on the aftertaste.

★**BERINGER 1995, NAPA VALLEY:** Pineapple, butter and honey on the nose. Soft, supple, rich, buttery fruit. Finishes quite spicy, with a bit of youthful acidity showing.

★**FETZER 1996 SUNDIAL, CALIFORNIA:** Delicate spiced apple and lemon aromas. Fresh, lively flavors of apple, pear and cinnamon, with a subtle oak component. A lighter style of Chardonnay, showing an attractive juicy quality and a bright, appley finish.

★**MONDAVI 1995 COASTAL, CALIFORNIA:** Melon and spice aromas, plus a brisk, highly aromatic suggestion of lemon oil. Not thick or especially concentrated; the wine is ripe and fresh, with sound acidity. The finish is firm and persistent.

★**NAPA RIDGE 1996 COASTAL VINES, CENTRAL COAST:** Butter, apricot and a faint truffle note on the nose. Ripe, oaky and smooth, with sweet oak balanced by ripe, buttery fruit. Simple and direct Chardonnay, but with intensity and weight.

$15–$30

★★★**BERINGER 1995 PRIVATE RESERVE, NAPA VALLEY:** Complex aromas of lime, charred oak, game and spices. Rich, smooth and intensely flavored. This spicy, truffley Chardonnay maintains its shape through to the firm, long aftertaste. Strong wine.

★★★**BYRON VINEYARD 1995 RESERVE, SANTA BARBARA COUNTY:** Pale yellow-gold color. Flamboyant aromas of grilled nuts and butterscotch; has a yeasty quality reminiscent of Champagne. Intensely flavored and vibrant, but currently a bit disjointed due to its brisk appley acidity; hints of nutmeg and nut oil. Spicy and very long, but youthfully tart.

★★★**MATANZAS CREEK 1995, SONOMA VALLEY:** Spiced apple and pear nose, with an herbal aspect and a hint of game. Supple and fairly rich, but not yet expressive. Quite firm on the finish. Should improve with some additional bottle aging.

★★★**MERRYVALE 1995 RESERVE, NAPA VALLEY:** Smoky, flinty, lemon custard aromas. Juicy and bright in the mouth; intensely flavored. Supple for a Chardonnay that did not undergo malolactic fermentation. Finishes quite firm but ripe and satisfying.

★★★**TALLEY VINEYARDS 1995 ROSEMARY'S VINEYARD, ARROYO GRANDE VALLEY:** Pale gold color. Subtle, pure aromas of lime, clove and spicy oak. Big and rich in the mouth, with strong extract; conveys a sense of brooding power. Juicy lemon oil and orange rind notes give the fruit brilliant definition. Very concentrated and unevolved.

★★**AU BON CLIMAT 1996, SANTA BARBARA COUNTY:** Clove, pineapple and a suggestion of exotic fruits on the nose. The wine's strong, youthful flavor is currently dominated by acidity, but rich underlying fruit and very ripe notes of mango and pineapple suggest that this wine will unfold nicely with time in the bottle.

★★**MERRYVALE 1995 STARMONT, NAPA VALLEY:** Aromas of lemon custard, grapefruit and pineapple. Smooth, fairly rich and nicely focused; notes of citric and exotic fruits, plus suggestions of honey and earth. Slightly hard-edged finish.

★★**ROBERT MONDAVI 1995, NAPA VALLEY:** Pale, green-tinged color. Lime and toast aromas, with an earthy note that calls to mind Chassagne-Montrachet. Good density and extract; has a freshness and a restrained sweetness. Ultimately round and supple despite an initial impression of tart acidity.

★★**QUPÉ 1996 BIEN NACIDO VINEYARD, SANTA BARBARA COUNTY:** Spicy, aromatic nose of lemon, fresh herbs and mustard seed. Stylish and bright, with crisp lemony acidity and a smoky nuance. Lovely clarity and intensity of flavor. Brisk, persistent aftertaste.

★★**RABBIT RIDGE 1996 ESTATE RESERVE, RUSSIAN RIVER VALLEY:** Oak char, peach and lemon aromas. Dense and thick, but with very good freshness; a lime oil aspect gives the wine a perfumed quality in the mouth. Finish is quite crisp, with a strong peachy flavor.

★★**SWANSON 1995, NAPA VALLEY:** Lemon custard and grilled nuts on the nose. Intensely flavored and supple in the mouth; brisk acidity is in harmony with the fruit. Finishes bright, subtle, fresh and long.

OTHER CONSISTENTLY OUTSTANDING SOURCES FOR EXPENSIVE, SMALL PRODUCTION CHARDONNAY: Kalin Cellars, Kistler Vineyards, Marcassin, Mount Eden Vineyards, Peter Michael Winery.

SAUVIGNON BLANC

Sauvignon Blancs range widely in style—and nowhere more so than in California, where you'll find everything from crisp, bracing Loire-like wines, to creamy-rich, barrel-aged examples reminiscent of white Bordeaux, to wines that downplay varietal character altogether in search of a "junior Chardonnay" style.

The best Sauvignon Blancs are food-friendly wines that deliver intense fruit flavor without undue weight, thanks to mouthwatering acidity and restrained oak treatment. Chardonnay wannabes can miss the point of this classic hot weather wine, which is to be refreshing rather than overbearing. Sauvignon Blanc (also called Fumé Blanc) is generally best suited for drinking within a year or two following its release, though the finest examples will reward aging.

AT THE TABLE: California Sauvignon Blanc pairs beautifully with freshwater fish, unadorned chicken dishes and fresh goat cheeses.

THE BOTTOM LINE: Many very good Sauvignon Blancs still retail for $12 or less, and relatively few are priced higher than $16. As a category, these bottles offer good value.

Vintage Rating 1994/A+ 1995/B+ 1996/B

Tasting Notes

Sauvignon Blanc, unless otherwise noted

UNDER $12

★★★**GEYSER PEAK 1996, SONOMA COUNTY:** Gooseberry, melon and fresh herb aromas. Penetrating and a bit aggressive in the mouth, but juicy, bright and focused, and not at all austere. This has intensity of flavor and solid structure, and tastes of fruit, not oak.

★★**BRANDER VINEYARD 1996, SANTA YNEZ VALLEY:** Loire-like musky, spearminty nose, with a faint oak char nuance. Juicy and intensely flavored; medium-bodied but firm-edged. Finishes with noticeable acidity.

★★**FERRARI-CARANO 1996 FUMÉ BLANC, SONOMA COAST:** Perfumed, tangy aromas of orange peel, fennel and oak spice. Supple and ripe, with a silky texture supported by crisp underlying acidity. Has good thickness for Sauvignon Blanc and a spicy, vibrant aftertaste.

★★**SANFORD 1996, CENTRAL COAST:** Fig, honey and charred oak aromas. Minerally, dense and intensely flavored; ripe lemony acidity gives the wine a bitter-edged, penetrating quality.

★**BERINGER 1995, NAPA VALLEY:** Pungent fig and dried fruit aromas. Supple, expansive and soft; a creamy style of Sauvignon with lovely middle-palate sweetness. Slightly harsh on the back end.

★**ROBERT MONDAVI, 1996 COASTAL:** Flinty, resiny nose of melon, pear and herbs. Soft and fairly rich in the mouth, with citrus and floral notes. Has an inviting sweetness and firm, spicy finishing flavor.

★**RABBIT RIDGE 1996, RUSSIAN RIVER VALLEY:** Fresh, slightly grassy orange peel and spice aromas. Spicy and creamy in the mouth; not a big-bodied Sauvignon Blanc but one that offers fresh citric flavor, good texture and concentration.

$12–$20

★★★**MATANZAS CREEK 1995, SONOMA COUNTY:** Bright floral aroma with a figgy undertone. Supple and quite textured for Sauvignon Blanc; complex inner-mouth flavors of gooseberry, flowers and herbs.

★ ★ **J. ROCHIOLI 1996, RUSSIAN RIVER VALLEY:** Pungent aromas of gooseberry, grapefruit, herbs and minerals; Loire-like in style. Spicy and supple in the mouth, with a tart herbal quality contributing freshness. Note of spearmint. Quite mouth-filling, considering its brightness. Slightly aggressive on the finish.

★ ★ ★ **SPOTTSWOODE 1996, NAPA VALLEY:** Perfumed, spicy aromas of grapefruit, mint and honeysuckle. Intensely spicy and quite dry in the mouth; has excellent density. Bright, penetrating and firm.

CABERNET SAUVIGNON

California's Cabernet Sauvignons have benefited from a string of superb vintages in the 1990s. Mother Nature has provided wineries with excellent raw material at a time when many producers have been adapting their methods to create more supple, less tannic, earlier-drinking Cabernets. Many wineries are harvesting later to get thoroughly ripe grapes, racking the wines more often to encourage the tannins to mellow and avoiding harsh filtration prior to bottling. The result has been richly textured Cabernet Sauvignons that are softer and more fruit driven than Cabernet-based Bordeaux reds. Yet these wines also appear to have the balance to develop with bottle age—like the finest Bordeaux, and in sharp contrast to the muscle-bound California bruisers of the not-too-distant past.

Because the better California Cabernets are usually aged in a high percentage of new oak barrels, they often feature aromas of vanilla, spices, cedar and tobacco to go along with the typical Cabernet notes of black currants, black cherries and licorice

AT THE TABLE: California Cabernet is a classic partner for T-bone steak or leg of lamb. These wines typically have a freshness of fruit and ripe tannins that provide a foil for assertive meat flavors (smoke, pepper, pungent spice) that might clash with more austere Cab-based Bordeaux.

THE BOTTOM LINE: It is possible to find California Cabernets that offer good intensity and sound varietal character for $12–$15; these wines represent excellent value. Unfortunately, it's easier to find charmless, tart, unyielding Cabernets for $25 or much more. Tightly allocated "cult" items tend to retail for $30–$60, and a number have gone even higher. The best of these are among the world's greatest examples of the variety.

Vintage Rating 1993/B 1994/A+ 1995/B+ 1996/A-

Tasting Notes

UNDER $15

★ ★ **ESTANCIA LOS ALTOS 1994, CALIFORNIA:** Superripe aromas of red currant and coffee. Supple, spicy fruit shows an intensity on entry, then is flavorful, firm and very focused in the middle palate. The bright fruit has unusual thickness and length for an inexpensive Cabernet.

★ ★ **ST. FRANCIS 1995, SONOMA COUNTY:** High-pitched raspberry and spicy oak aromas. Smooth, sweet, fruit-driven flavors of red currant and boysenberry; an exotic oak component contributes to the wine's appeal. Lovely lingering fruit outlasts soft, ripe tannins. Terrific value.

★ ★ **TERRA ROSA 1995, NORTH COAST:** Very complex but restrained aromas of blackberry, tar and leather, plus a briary, leafy nuance. Juicy, intense dark berry flavor of lovely purity. Offers good weight in the mouth without being at all heavy.

★ **HAYWOOD 1995 VINTNER'S SELECT, CALIFORNIA:** Cassis, tobacco and spice on the nose. Supple and easy in the mouth; a lightly tannic wine of modest nuance and flavor clarity but one that offers good flesh and holds its shape nicely.

★ **VILLA MT. EDEN 1994, CALIFORNIA:** Smoky oak, coffee, currant and black cherry. Juicy cassis and licorice flavor, with an overlay of spicy oak. Not as sweet or fleshy as the nose suggests, but offers good flavor intensity and firmness. A bit lean on the finish.

$15–$30

★ ★ ★ **CHALK HILL 1994, SONOMA COUNTY:** Deep, brooding aromas of black fruits and licorice. Rich, sweet and layered, but quite bright on the palate thanks to nicely integrated acidity. At once subtle and strong on the long finish, which features rich, chewy tannins.

★ ★ ★ **FERRARI-CARANO 1993, SONOMA COUNTY:** Dark berry and truffle nose. Silky-smooth, sweet and stuffed with plum, red currant and cassis fruit. Seamless and gentle. Finishes with sweet, soft tannins and notes of toffee and minerals. Not overly oaky.

★ ★ ★ **FISHER VINEYARDS 1994 COACH INSIGNIA, NAPA VALLEY:** Currants and smoky oak on the nose. Bright, intensely flavored, pure currant fruit in the mouth. Attractive silky texture will encourage early drinking, but this wine has the balance to age.

★★★**MOUNT EDEN 1994, SANTA CRUZ MOUNTAINS:** Sappy, ripe aromas of dark chocolate, cassis, black cherry and resiny oak. Juicy and youthful; the sweet, spicy cassis character is complemented by notes of tar and leather. Lovely acids give this impeccably balanced wine superb delineation.

★★★**PARADIGM 1994 OAKVILLE, NAPA VALLEY:** Nose dominated by notes of cedar, tar, coffee and caramel. Sweet, pure, blackberry and licorice flavor in the mouth. Has a slightly leafy Cabernet Franc component. Firm and long on the finish, with good lingering flavor.

★★**BERINGER VINEYARDS 1994 ALLUVIUM RED TABLE WINE, KNIGHTS VALLEY:** Spicy dark berries and strong oak notes of bourbon, vanilla and clove. Sweet, juicy blackberry fruit offers subtle intensity. Lingering, subtle berry flavor stands up to the wood tones on the finish.

★★**LA JOTA VINEYARD 1994, HOWELL MOUNTAIN SELECTION:** High-toned black currant and leather nose; at once fresh and slightly roasted, with hints of raisin and chocolate. Silky entry, then sweet, fat and expansive; slightly briary flavors of red currant, licorice and tobacco.

★★**ROBERT MONDAVI 1994, OAKVILLE DISTRICT:** Black currant, herbs and mint on the nose. Flavors of black and red currants. A drier-styled but nonetheless suavely textured wine of moderate concentration.

★★**JOSEPH PHELPS 1994, NAPA VALLEY:** Aromas of crushed dark berries, chocolate and mint. Sweet, lush and nicely balanced, with very good concentration. Notes of black currant and mint in the mouth.

★★**SWANSON 1994, NAPA VALLEY:** Tangy raspberry and exotic sandalwood aromas. Supple, sweet and very oaky in the mouth. Not a fat wine but one with nice shape and intensity. Finishes with slightly dry but fine tannins.

Splurgeworthy:

★★★★**BERINGER VINEYARDS 1994 PRIVATE RESERVE, NAPA VALLEY:** Impressive black-ruby color. Brooding cassis, blackberry and mineral aromas. Large-scaled and dense; sweet, spicy dark berry flavor offers outstanding intensity and depth. A major mouthful of wine with the fruit to support the new oak.

★★★★**DALLA VALLE VINEYARDS 1994, NAPA VALLEY:** Deep ruby to the rim. Intensely fruity, floral, cassis-dominated aroma. Dense, supple, and silky, but with lovely brightness and delineation. Elegant, harmonious and long on personality.

★★★★**DUNN VINEYARDS 1994, NAPA VALLEY:** Black-ruby colored. Cassis, licorice, minerals and spicy oak on the nose. Juicy, youthfully unevolved, highly concentrated raspberry and cassis flavor. Ripe and extremely persistent on the palate.

★★★★**LAUREL GLEN 1994, SONOMA MOUNTAIN:** Highly expressive, superripe aromas of cassis, black raspberry and loganberry, with notes of pepper and minerals. Sweet and impressively concentrated. The finish features thoroughly ripe, fine tannins.

EVEN MORE EXPENSIVE BUT CONSISTENTLY OUTSTANDING CABERNET SAUVIGNONS: Araujo Estate Eisele Vineyard, Bryant Family Vineyard, Colgin Vineyard, Dominus Estate, Harlan Estate, La Jota Vineyard Anniversary Release, Robert Mondavi Reserve, Opus One, Phelps Insignia, Ridge Monte Bello, Philip Togni Vineyard.

MERLOT

American restaurant-goers woke up a few years ago and realized that they wanted a red wine less forbiddingly tannic than Cabernet Sauvignon, something rounder, lusher, something like...Merlot! Suddenly, Merlot became America's hottest wine. The price of Merlot grapes soared, and vineyard owners from Petaluma to Perth rushed to plant Merlot vines. The result: For every satisfying bottle of Merlot today you'll find three or four thin, weedy examples from young vines that are not yet ready for prime time. On the other hand, the very best examples—usually produced in limited quantities—number among California's richest, most succulent wines. California's top Merlots offer supple, velvety textures; aromas of cherry, plum, dark berries and chocolate; and smooth, well-integrated tannins.

AT THE TABLE: Merlot goes well with grilled steak and lamb or with soft, creamy cheeses like Brie and Reblochon.

THE BOTTOM LINE: Even the inferior bottles are likely to set you back $15 or more. California Merlot is generally not the place to look for wine value.

Vintage Rating 1993/B- 1994/A+ 1995/B+ 1996/A-

Tasting Notes

UNDER $15

★★ **FETZER VINEYARDS 1995 EAGLE PEAK, CALIFORNIA:** Dark berries and toasty oak on the nose; shows a framboise note with aeration. Juicy red currant and tobacco flavors; medium-bodied and light on its feet. In a drier style, with good complexity, a firm finish and surprising length.

★ **HAYWOOD 1995 VINTNER'S SELECT, CALIFORNIA:** Warm, smoky aroma of cherry, plum and berries. Supple and slightly roasted in the mouth; flavors of loam, tobacco and milk chocolate. Decent intensity and length. Tannins are quite soft.

★ **MEADOW GLEN 1995, CALIFORNIA:** Cherry/berry nose complicated by notes of tar and tobacco. Nicely delineated spicy berry flavor offers good Merlot character and immediate drinkability. Finishes with light tannins and reasonable length.

★ **TAFT STREET 1995, SONOMA COUNTY:** Intriguing aromas of raspberry, milk chocolate and spicy oak. Lush and generous, with plenty of spicy oak framing the red berry flavors. The wood tones give the finish a faint hard edge, but there's also soft, lingering fruit flavor.

★ **TALUS 1995, CALIFORNIA:** Chocolate and dark berry nose, plus a whiff of spearmint. Supple and textured in the mouth, with attractive sweetness; gently fruity blackberry flavor dominates. Light tannins will not stand in the way of immediate gratification. The spicy berry flavor carries through on the aftertaste.

$15–$30

★★★ **HAVENS 1995, NAPA VALLEY:** Cherry/berry and smoke on the nose. Bright, juicy, and intensely flavored; rather closed in on itself. Shapely, firm and long. Includes some Cabernet Franc.

★★ **MERRYVALE VINEYARDS 1994, NAPA VALLEY:** Lively dark berry, clove and tar aromas, plus a hint of dill. Smooth, supple and sweet, with attractive red berry flavor of moderate depth and nuance. Finishes with smooth, tongue-coating tannins.

★★ **PARADIGM WINERY 1994 OAKVILLE, NAPA VALLEY:** Black fruit, spice and smoky oak on the nose. Creamy and sweet in the mouth, with a lovely supple texture. Has balance and personality. The tannins are in the background.

★★ **JOSEPH PHELPS 1994, NAPA VALLEY:** Saturated ruby red, with purple highlights. Inky, smoky, blackberry nose, with nuances of game and menthol. Sweet and silky in the mouth; shows exotic truffle notes and an almost portlike ripeness.

★★ **RAVENSWOOD 1995 SANGIACOMO VINEYARD CARNEROS, SONOMA VALLEY:** Subdued but fresh aromas of red currant, raspberry and flowers. Enticing, sweet cherry flavor in the mouth, with a firm acidity that makes for a solid structure. A wine of moderate flesh, but gentle and sweet on the finish.

★★ **CHATEAU SOUVERAIN 1995, ALEXANDER VALLEY:** Dark berry aromas with notes of meat, oak and mint. Supple in the mouth; dark berry fruit has a creaminess and good flavor depth. Finish is ripe and persistent.

★★ **STONESTREET 1994, ALEXANDER VALLEY:** Smoke, black fruit and roasted nuts on the nose. Supple and quite ripe, bordering on thick; a chocolatey note complicates the dark berry flavors. Finishes well, with sweet fruit and even tannins.

★ ★ **TRUCHARD VINEYARDS 1994, CARNEROS:** Sweetly spicy, aromatic, black cherry nose shows some high tones. Pleasing smoke and pencil lead-like flavor in the mouth; somewhat austere but has good structure and cut. Finishes fresh, with light tannins.

Splurgeworthy

★ ★ ★ **BERINGER 1994 BANCROFT RANCH, HOWELL MOUNTAIN:** Deep red ruby. Alluring aromas of blackberry, spicy oak, coffee and mocha. Superb intensity of flavor; sappy, young and dense, with solid acidity and notes of coffee and bitter chocolate. Palate-staining finish, with a late hint of mint. One of California's elite Merlots.

★ ★ ★ **ARROWOOD WINERY 1994, SONOMA COUNTY:** Blackberry, red currant, licorice and smoke on the nose. Juicy and fairly intensely flavored; bright and delineated. Very good depth of flavor. Finishes with fine, tongue-dusting tannins.

ZINFANDEL

Zinfandel is an American original. While the roots of the variety are European, virtually all the greatest examples of this spicy, mouth-filling red come from the vineyards of California.

Zinfandel is a red grape with a long and checkered past. It was first planted in California in the 19th century, and some century-old vineyards still produce profound, deeply concentrated wine today. But when the popularity of red wines plummeted in the U.S. during the 1970s and early 1980s, Zin's heritage was ignored in favor of what would sell: insipid, sweet, "white Zinfandel," a blush wine made by siphoning the clear juice away from the color-bearing skins. Since the early Eighties, though, true (red and dry) Zinfandel has staged a mighty comeback. Indeed, the finest wines have become pricey and highly sought after.

Today's Zinfandels generally fall into two categories: midweight, Bordeaux-like wines, and outrageously rich, exotically ripe high-alcohol (typically 14%+) heavyweights. Well-made examples of both types offer the classic Zin characteristics: spicy aromas and flavors of citrus zest, black raspberry and blackberry, black pepper and chocolate.

AT THE TABLE: The full-throttle, lavishly fruity Zins can overwhelm most foods (the old joke is that they go best with live game), but try them with barbecued red meats, particularly those grilled over exotic woods. The medium-weight style can play the same role at the table as Cabernet Sauvignon.

THE BOTTOM LINE: For sheer flavor per dollar, the better Zinfandels still offer extremely good value.

Vintage Rating **1994/A 1995/A- 1996/B+**

Tasting Notes

UNDER $15

★ ★ ★ **ROSENBLUM CELLARS 1995, CONTRA COSTA COUNTY:** High-toned raspberry, cassis, tarragon and black pepper aromas. Harmonious, round and fresh on the palate, with good flavor intensity and subtle sweetness. Fresh herbal notes and sound acidity contribute freshness. A solidly structured, serious style of Zinfandel, with strong finishing flavor.

★ ★ ★ **SEGHESIO 1995, SONOMA COUNTY:** Sweet berries, pepper and mint on the nose. Silky-sweet and nicely balanced; has juicy, intense raspberry, cherry and red currant flavor and moderate density. The fruitier side of Zin, with little new oak to get in the way of the nicely focused flavors. Finishes spicy and long.

★ **BERINGER 1994, NORTH COAST:** Spicy blackberry and plum nose. Smooth berry flavor with subtle oak treatment. Has good intensity but only modest delineation. Slightly dry on the finish.

★ **KARLY 1995, AMADOR COUNTY:** Spice and dark berries on the nose. Similar flavors in the mouth. Combines an enticing sweetness with

TWO THINGS TO KNOW ABOUT ZINFANDEL

UNEVEN RIPENING: Zinfandel grape clusters often produce ripe and unripe berries side by side. To get adequate levels of alcohol in the finished wines, growers generally begin with raw materials that include shriveled, overripened raisins as well as pinker, underripe grapes. This mix helps explain how the same Zinfandel can display raisin and prune notes and cooler, greener components. Attempts to harvest completely ripe bunches can lead to wines with unwieldy alcohol content (16% or even higher) and/or substantial residual sugar.

OLD VINES: Old Zinfandel vineyards—50, even 100 years old—are California's greatest wine heirlooms (no Cabernet vineyards come close). The low yields produced by very old vines go a long way toward explaining the extraordinarily creamy texture, density and profound depth of flavor of the top Zinfandels.

firm underlying acidity. Not especially concentrated, but offers good medium body and nice balance for early drinking.

★ **VILLA MT. EDEN 1995, CALIFORNIA:** Brambly raspberry and plum aromas. Smooth, ripe and expansive, with good flavor intensity and an attractive restrained sweetness. Good Zinfandel character at a modest price, and ready to drink now.

$15–$25

★ ★ ★ ★ **RAVENSWOOD 1995 MONTE ROSSO RANCH, SONOMA VALLEY:** Plum, red currant and spice on the nose. Very sweet and supple; broad and generous texture. Offers a juicy, penetrating Zin sweetness that verges on confectionery. Finishes with solid tannins and sweet, lingering berry flavor.

★ ★ ★ ★ **RIDGE 1995 GEYSERVILLE, CALIFORNIA:** From a vineyard with a block of 117-year-old vines. Brambly black cherry, leather, smoke and coffee on the nose. Huge yet silky and stylish, with great intensity. Amazingly suave for such a big wine. Superripe but not a bit pruney. Explosive, palate-staining finish.

★ ★ ★ ★ **RIDGE 1995 LYTTON SPRINGS, CALIFORNIA:** Smoky, black raspberry nose. Big, thick and chewy; a huge, classic Zinfandel that fills the mouth yet possesses a lovely brightness. Outstanding purity and intensity of dark berry flavor.

★ ★ ★ **NALLE 1995 DRY CREEK VALLEY, SONOMA COUNTY:** Exuberant raspberry, orange rind and pepper aromas. Tangy red berry flavor is fresh and delineated. Has a silky texture reminiscent of red Burgundy. Really creamy and concentrated. Quintessential Zinfandel in its sheer berry intensity.

★ ★ ★ **PEZZI KING 1995 OLD VINES, DRY CREEK VALLEY:** Flamboyant aromas of black raspberry, black pepper and mocha. Huge, lush and superripe: a headspinning fruit bomb, with creamy, palate-saturating flavor, near-15% alcohol and just enough acidity to maintain its shape. Finishes with dusty, even tannins that are not tough or dry.

★ ★ ★ **RAVENSWOOD 1995 OLD VINES, SONOMA COUNTY:** Dark berries, smoke and coffee on the nose. Thick, deep and creamy in the mouth, with superb, jammy sweetness of fruit supported by serious structure. Explosive, spicy fruit expands on the finish.

★ ★ ★ **RAVENSWOOD 1995 WOOD ROAD/BELLONI, RUSSIAN RIVER VALLEY:** Bright floral and boysenberry nose, with notes of pepper and oak spice. Strong and powerfully structured on the palate; really lovely fruit is given focus by very good acidity. Fairly tannic finish is supported by sweet, fresh fruit.

★ ★ ★ **ROSENBLUM CELLARS 1995 RICHARD SAURET VINEYARD, PASO ROBLES:** Multidimensional nose combines berries, exotic herbs, smoke, licorice, eucalyptus and roast meat. Large-scaled and very rich, but vinous and spicy, with strong acidity. A big, flamboyant, ambitious wine that's almost painfully spicy today. Finishes with a mouthful of coarse tannins.

RHÔNE-STYLE WINES

Lovers of the rich, spicy, flavor-packed reds and whites of France's Rhône Valley and Mediterranean rim have welcomed a mini-explosion in California plantings of varieties like berry-scented Syrah and flowery Viognier over the past decade. America's Rhône revolution has also encouraged a rediscovery of vineyards already in the ground, often in out-of-the-way locations: old-vine plantings of Mourvèdre, Carignan and Grenache. In a market increasingly dominated by Chardonnay, Cabernet and Merlot, Rhône-style wines offer a range of fascinating and food-flexible alternatives.

AT THE TABLE: Befitting their origin, Mourvèdre and Grenache are extremely useful wines to pair with California's heavily Mediterranean-influenced cuisine. Syrah complements boldly flavored red meat dishes, winter stews and wilder fare such as venison, goose and duck.

THE BOTTOM LINE: Red Rhône-style wines, particularly blends from old vines, are among the best values in California wine. Viognier prices, however, tend to be high, reflecting the strong cult following for this variety.

Tasting Notes

RED WINES UNDER $12

★★**EDMUNDS ST. JOHN 1995 L'ENFANT TERRIBLE MOURVÈDRE, CALIFORNIA:** Blueberry, blackberry, leather, licorice and herbs on the nose. Sweet entry, then rather tight and youthfully harsh in the mouth. Still needs some time to harmonize and open.

★**LAUREL GLEN 1995 REDS, CALIFORNIA:** Cherry, leather, herbs and pepper, plus a candied nuance. Supple and juicy, with a restrained sweetness and modest depth. Good everyday drinking wine; finishes with light tannins and notes of leather and cherry. Includes a dollop of Zinfandel.

RED WINES $12–$25

★★★**CLINE CELLARS 1995 MOURVÈDRE ANCIENT VINES, CONTRA COSTA COUNTY:** Complex, fruity aromas of dark berries, black olive, leather, herbs and earth. Firm and sweet in the mouth; suggests very good levels of extract. Finishes with firm tannins.

★ ★ ★ **EDMUNDS ST. JOHN 1995 SYRAH, CALIFORNIA:** Perfumed violet, tar and smoke nose, with a hint of talc. Very concentrated and tightly structured; currently shows more acidity than tannins. Hints at an incipient smoky-meaty quality. Again, very tightly wrapped, but offers strong potential.

★ ★ ★ **HAVENS 1995 SYRAH, CARNEROS:** Highly nuanced aromas of black fruits, smoke and meat. Fabulous silky texture and fleshy mouth feel. Flavors of licorice and dark berries, with just the slightest hint of game. Finishes with supple tannins. The solid structure is buried in fat fruit.

★ ★ ★ **JOSEPH PHELPS 1994 VIN DU MISTRAL SYRAH, NAPA VALLEY:** Bright, dark red ruby. Aromas of black cherry, black raspberry, tar and dill; sweetly spicy oak is currently in the foreground. Dense and supple in the mouth, with very good depth and sweetness of fruit. Quite youthful and unevolved. The finish is very long, coating the tongue with dusty, even tannins.

★ ★ ★ **RIDGE VINEYARDS 1995 BRIDGEHEAD MÁTARO, CALIFORNIA:** Varietally accurate aromas of berries and spice. Lush, sweet and concentrated; has really terrific middle-palate fruit and plenty of nuance. Quite long on the finish. Superb Mourvèdre.

★ ★ ★ **TRUCHARD 1995 SYRAH, CARNEROS:** Lovely, accurate aromas of black cherry, dark berries, smoke, meat and white pepper. Juicy and bright, with very good depth of flavor and harmonious acidity. Finishes with sweet cherry-berry flavor and fine tannins.

★ ★ **CLINE CELLARS 1995 ANCIENT VINES CARIGNAN, CONTRA COSTA COUNTY:** Black cherry, chocolate and a sappy, resiny quality; suggestions of roasted ripeness. Similar flavors in the mouth, along with a licorice nuance.

★ ★ **EDMUNDS ST. JOHN 1995 LES CÔTES SAUVAGES, CALIFORNIA:** Aromas of black cherry, tar and smoke. Concentrated and delineated, but a bit wrapped up in its own structure today. Firm, peppery finish. Currently slightly rigid for this wine: the Syrah and Mourvèdre need time to harmonize.

★ ★ **QUIVIRA VINEYARDS 1995 DRY CREEK CUVÉE, DRY CREEK VALLEY:** A blend based on Grenache and Mourvèdre. Bright dark cherry color. Black cherry, licorice and a slight bittersweet leafy quality. Sweet and supple, with refreshing juiciness and modest complexity.

WHITE WINES $12–$20

★ ★ ★ **CALLAWAY 1996 VIOGNIER, TEMECULA:** Vibrant, lightly oak-spicy, lime, peach and mint nose. Offers silky, palate-caressing texture yet manages to hold its shape; has both brightness of flavor and good weight. Notes of grapefruit, spice and lichee. Dry, very persistent finish.

★ ★ **CLINE CELLARS 1996 VIOGNIER, CARNEROS:** Spicy grapefruit and smoke aromas. Boasts very good flavor intensity and an impression of density in the mouth. A citrus-skin quality gives the wine good cut and shape. Strong juice.

SPARKLING WINE

Calfornia's sparkling wines cannot match the best Champagnes for subtlety of flavor or persistence on the palate, but the California versions are vastly better today than they were just a decade ago. A number of Champagne houses have made major investments in land and wineries in the cooler growing areas of California, evidence in itself of the state's exceptional potential.

AT THE TABLE: Serve these wines with fried fish and shellfish or stir-fried chicken.

THE BOTTOM LINE: California's better sparkling wines are rarely bargain-priced, especially when wine lovers in many urban centers can find excellent nonvintage brut Champagne for $25 or less during the winter holiday season.

Tasting Notes

UNDER $20

★★★ **ROEDERER ESTATE NV BRUT, ANDERSON VALLEY:** Fresh, lemony nose, with a subtle toasty quality and an exotic peach hint; has the nuance of Champagne. Creamy, toasty, dry and smooth; rich but not at all heavy. Lovely balance of elements. Finishes suave, firm and long.

★ **GLORIA FERRER NV BRUT, SONOMA COUNTY:** Apple, lime and a floral note on the yeasty nose. Easygoing and gentle, with a hint of licorice. Creamy and rather sweet for a brut. Shows decent length.

$20–$25

★★ **DOMAINE CARNEROS (TAITTINGER) 1992 BRUT:** Vaguely stony aromas of apple, lemon and orange peel. Frothy and rich but quite dry; has good weight and texture. Slight toasty quality. Fairly persistent if slightly harsh on the finish.

★★ **IRON HORSE 1990 BLANC DE BLANCS LD, SONOMA COUNTY:** Lemon, vanilla and orange peel aromas, with floral and toasty components. Good intensity and thrust on the palate; not overly fruity or sweet, but possesses good underlying richness. Fresh and polished.

★★ **IRON HORSE 1994 WEDDING CUVÉE, SONOMA COUNTY:** Pale rosé color. Soft strawberry and raspberry nose, with a hint of earth. Fresh, fruity and quite dry, with good precision of flavor and snap. Very Pinot Noir-like. Finishes dry, with a slightly bitter edge.

OTHER WINES

Tangy white wines based on grapes like Muscat, Riesling and Sémillon can be very affordable and remarkably flexible with a range of spicy cuisines such as Southwestern, Thai and Indian. The Mediterranean variety Malvasia Bianca makes a perfumed, minty wine that can play a similar role at the table.

California produces a number of excellent Pinot Noirs, but the best usually run $25 or more and are made in very limited quantities. Among the other red wines frequently seen on store shelves are Bordeaux-style blends like the Meritage wines (which may combine Cabernet Sauvignon, Merlot, Cabernet Franc, Petit Verdot and even Malbec), and varietal Cabernet Franc bottlings.

Tasting Notes

WHITE WINES UNDER $12

★★**HANDLEY 1996 GEWÜRZTRAMINER, ANDERSON VALLEY:** Spearmint, lime blossom, orange zest and earth tones on the nose. Supple and fairly rich, but has a floral tang and fresh acidity. A shapely, dry style of Gewürztraminer, finishing with lemony notes.

★★**MONDAVI 1995 MALVASIA BIANCA, CALIFORNIA:** Honey, earth, lime and nutmeg aromas. Full, nicely concentrated and intensely flavored, with solid underlying structure. Brisk, gingery finishing flavor. The flavors and refreshing bitter edge would pair well with Asian dishes.

★**BONNY DOON 1996 CA' DEL SOLO BIG HOUSE WHITE, CALIFORNIA:** Perfumed lemon and mint nose. Slightly floral, lemony fruit has good intensity and acidity. Finishes dry, crisp and firm. A very flexible food wine, from a hodgepodge of varieties.

WHITE WINES $12–$20

★★★**BRANDER 1996 CUVÉE NATALIE, SANTA YNEZ VALLEY:** Stony, minerally, lime-scented nose has a deep oily quality and terrific freshness. A very dry, compelling, food-friendly wine of impressive subtlety. Mostly Sauvignon Blanc and Riesling.

★★★**MARTINELLI 1996 GEWÜRZTRAMINER MARTINELLI VINEYARD, RUSSIAN RIVER VALLEY:** Juicyfruit and mint aromas. Rich and supple. Floral, spicy flavors give the wine enticing freshness. Finishes slightly sweet, with a smoky nuance. Easy to drink for a wine with 14.3% alcohol.

★ ★ **BERINGER VINEYARDS 1995 ALLUVIUM BLANC, KNIGHTS VALLEY:** A blend of Viognier, Chardonnay, Sémillon, and Sauvignon Blanc. Exotic, fresh fig, oak spice and lemon peel aromas. Supple, gentle and generous; strong fruit flavors of pineapple and pear, plus a figgy nuance. Persistent, clove-flavored aftertaste.

★ ★ **STERLING VINEYARDS 1995 MALVASIA BIANCA, CALIFORNIA:** Complex floral, lemony, spearminty, spicy nose complicated by fresh herbs. Quite dry on the palate but has decent intensity and unusual delicacy, as well as a waxy, honeyed quality. Perked up by lemony acidity.

★ ★ **WILD HORSE 1996 MALVASIA BIANCA, MONTEREY:** Vibrant nose combines pineapple, orange peel, tangerine, lime and oak spice. Dry and refreshing in the mouth, but the subtly intense spice and ripe citrus flavors convey an impression of sweetness. Finishes spicy, dry and firm.

RED WINES $12–$20

★ ★ **AU BON CLIMAT 1996 PINOT NOIR, SANTA MARIA COUNTY:** Red fruit (cherry, red currant, raspberry), mocha, dill and cinnamon on the nose. Initially dominated by firm, juicy acidity but becomes sweeter and silkier as it opens in the glass; flavors of red fruits and underbrush. Finishes quite fresh, with notes of vanilla and smoke.

★ ★ **STEELE WINES 1995 PINOT NOIR, SANGIACOMO VINEYARD, CARNEROS:** Fruity nose of strawberry, raspberry, cherry and smoked meat. Sweet, juicy and easygoing; has lovely lush texture, with enough acidity to maintain its balance. A fat, tasty Pinot for early consumption.

★ ★ **TRUCHARD VINEYARDS 1995 PINOT NOIR, CARNEROS:** Cherry, herbs and cinnamon on the nose. Bright and oaky on the palate; offers good intensity of red fruit flavor but only modest texture. Finishes slightly tart, with more acidity than tannins.

★ **HANDLEY CELLARS 1995 PINOT NOIR, ANDERSON VALLEY:** Tart cherry and cranberry aromas, plus an herbal nuance. Refreshing bitter cherry flavor; not a fleshy style of Pinot but juicy and delicate. Slight green streak carries through the wine.

★ **SHOOTING STAR 1995 CABERNET FRANC, CLEAR LAKE:** Berries and a tarry note on the nose. Supple cherry/berry and herb flavor; a fruity wine with a restrained sweetness and little obvious oak influence. Finishes with fairly light, dusty tannins and fresh, lingering fruit.

OREGON & WASHINGTON

OREGON

Pinot Noir, the grape that makes winedom's most seductive reds, puts Oregon on the world's wine map. Oregon's finest Pinot Noirs offer fruit-driven, solidly built alternatives to red Burgundy—perhaps the finest examples of the grape made outside France. The state's hottest white variety, Pinot Gris, is actually a centuries-old white mutation of Pinot Noir. Oregon Pinot Gris produces one of the most satisfying American white wines in the under-$15 price range.

WINE GEOGRAPHY:
Most of Oregon's vineyards lie between the Pacific Ocean and the Cascade Range. In these ocean-influenced microclimates temperatures are less extreme, fruit ripens gently and rain at harvest time is always a possibility. The Willamette Valley just south of Portland

is the heart of Pinot Noir country and by far the state's most important viticultural region. The Umpqua Valley, farther to the south, and the Rogue Valley, near the California border, are warmer and drier; a number of wineries in these regions grow Merlot and Cabernet.

BEHIND THE SCENES: With a very few exceptions, wineries in Oregon tend to be small and winemaking rather idiosyncratic.

Fortunately, this scale and approach perfectly suit the hands-on demands of producing Burgundian-style wine.

AT THE TABLE: Pinot Noir with grilled salmon is a classic Northwest pairing, but this food-friendly variety also complements beef, coq au vin, squab and other game birds. Oregon's Pinot Gris is well suited to a wide range of dishes, including richer shellfish preparations, finfish and pork. It generally has the texture and fresh acidity to work well with fish or chicken in cream sauces.

PINOT NOIR

OREGON'S PINOTS TYPICALLY FEATURE BLACK CHERRY AND raspberry aromas and flavors (which can come across as jammy in hot vintages), varying degrees of spicy oak and medium body. They are rarely austere or tough when young, but the best wines are worth aging and will grow in complexity with three to five years additional time in the bottle. Note that wines from very ripe, low-acid years like 1994 are generally best consumed early for their youthful fruit.

THE BOTTOM LINE: Oregon still offers a number of Pinots for less than $20, but prices for many of the state's most popular labels have broken the $30 barrier, and several have reached $40. The priciest wines, especially those from the mostly weak 1995 vintage, generally offer questionable value. Oregon's less expensive Pinots don't provide the nuance of great red Burgundy, but they can suggest the texture, freshness and spicy red fruit character of these wines at a fraction of their price.

Vintage Rating 1993/B+ 1994/B+ 1995/C- 1996/B-

Tasting Notes

UNDER $20

★★**BRIDGEVIEW VINEYARDS 1996, OREGON:** Enticingly sweet aromas of toasty oak, cinnamon and cherry. Cherry/raspberry fruit offers good texture, intensity and sweetness, if limited complexity. Finishes with light tannins. Superb value for a Pinot Noir at around $10.

★★**CRISTOM 1995 MT. JEFFERSON CUVÉE, WILLAMETTE VALLEY:** Raspberry, wild strawberry, mocha and underbrush on the nose, plus spicy oak notes of nutmeg and sandalwood. Supple, smooth and easygoing; a nicely balanced Pinot of moderate flesh and ripeness.

★ ★ **FIRESTEED 1996, OREGON:** Aromatic notes of cinnamon, cola, light spices and a subtle perfume. Supple and rather stylish; shows a lovely restrained sweetess, very little evidence of oak and a tangy cherry quality that carries through to the lightly tannic finish. A terrific value at $10.

★ **BROADLEY VINEYARDS 1995 RESERVE, OREGON:** Slightly candied aromas of cherry, raspberry, spice and orange zest; shows an exotic sandalwood quality as it opens in the glass. Suggestion of old wood on entry, then spicy, refreshing cherry and cranberry flavor. Finishes firm, with slightly dry tannins.

★ **REX HILL VINEYARDS 1995, WILLAMETTE VALLEY:** Complex aromas of cassis, raspberry, clove, tar and earth. Spicy dark berry flavor in the mouth. Fresh and firm but slightly pinched on the lightly tannic finish.

$20–$40

★ ★ ★ **BEAUX-FRÈRES 1995, WILLAMETTE VALLEY:** Cherry, red berries, coffee and toast on the nose. Good tangy spice and red berry flavor of noteworthy depth and freshness. Nicely focused. Vibrant hints of cranberry and pomegranate give the wine a lively finish.

★ ★ ★ **DOMAINE DROUHIN 1995, OREGON:** Complex floral, minty, spicy nose hints at red fruit, clove and caramel. Delicious strawberry and spice flavor in the mouth; fresh, tangy and firm. Subtle floral and spicy aftertaste. The light tannins are perfectly suited to the delicate fruit.

★ ★ ★ **KING ESTATE 1994 RESERVE, OREGON:** Very good dark-red color. Deep aromas of black fruits, cola and damp earth. Juicy and intensely flavored, with a cool, blackberry flavor that's quite bright for this super-ripe vintage. The fruit offers mouthwatering freshness.

★ ★ ★ **REX HILL 1994 RESERVE, OREGON:** Aromas of cranberry, black cherry, licorice and coffee. Supple, sweet and generously textured, with nicely integrated acidity. Ripe and chocolatey in the style of the vintage, but some youthfully tart cherry flavor gives the wine grip and shape.

★ ★ **OAK KNOLL 1994 VINTAGE RESERVE, WILLAMETTE VALLEY:** Rather brawny aromas of woodsmoke, coffee and green and black pepper; little sign of primary fruit. Silky and smooth in the mouth, with deep wood tones. A rich middle palate, but not at all a fruity style of Pinot.

PINOT GRIS

PINOT GRIS ATTAINS ITS HEIGHTS IN ALSACE, BUT OREGON IS coming up fast. Here the grape yields flavorful dry wine in a range of styles, from lean and refined to lush and exotic. Thanks to its enticing aromas and flavors of spiced apple, peach and citrus fruits, its crisp acidity and a level of richness approaching that of Chardonnay without the oakiness, many insiders consider Pinot Gris Oregon's most successful white wine.

THE BOTTOM LINE: With prices generally $12 to $16, Oregon Pinot Gris offers an economical alternative to Chardonnay.

Vintage Rating 1995/C+   1996/B-

Tasting Notes

UNDER $12

★★DUCK POND CELLARS 1996, WILLAMETTE VALLEY: Charred oak, nuts and cantaloupe on the nose. Bright, nicely textured and fairly intensely flavored, with medium body and moderate complexity. A fresh lime flavor gives the finish a brisk quality.

★★OAK KNOLL WINERY 1995, WILLAMETTE VALLEY: Deep, rather exotic aromas of smoke, honey, spices and dried fruits. Big, rich, ripe and layered; has a Chardonnay-like texture, plenty of flavor intensity and good backbone. Spicy and stuffed with fruit. The bold side of Pinot Gris.

$12–$16

★★★EYRIE VINEYARDS 1995, WILLAMETTE VALLEY: Rose-tinged straw color. Pungent aromas of lees, smoke and peach. Spicy, tactile and mouth-filling; a large-scaled, practically thick wine whose fruit is nicely framed by a solid structure. Acidity is strong but harmonious. Finishes spicy and impressively persistent. Very rich Pinot Gris.

★★★WILLAMETTE VALLEY VINEYARDS 1996, OREGON: The aroma features notes of apple, smoke, melon, peach and a leesy complexity. Impressively rich, layered, ripe and deep: very sweet peach and apple flavors are given delineation by lively acidity. Finishes sweet and ripe, with a touch of tangerine.

★★ERATH VINEYARDS 1996, WILLAMETTE VALLEY: Brisk, delineated aromas of spicy apple cake. Bright and intensely flavored, with ripe citric notes of orange peel and tangerine. Quite light on its feet: offers strong flavor without undue weight. Vibrant, pure finishing fruit.

★★KING ESTATE 1995 RESERVE, OREGON: Honey, licorice and exotic apricot and mango elements on the nose. Very rich and honeyed in the mouth; an opulent, large-scaled Pinot Gris with the creamy texture and weight of Chardonnay. This wine has just enough acidity to keep its shape.

OTHER WINES OF OREGON

OREGON'S CHARDONNAYS ARE RAPIDLY IMPROVING AS GROWERS plant clones more appropriate to their local microclimates. Oregon also offers delicate, often floral Rieslings and stylish, spicy Gewürztraminers. Noteworthy Merlots and Cabernet Sauvignons are a relatively recent phenomenon. In years to come, vineyards in warmer spots in the Umpqua and Rogue valleys should yield better and better examples of these varieties.

THE BOTTOM LINE: Few Oregon Chardonnays priced higher than $15 offer real value, but well-made $10 Chardonnays are a steal. Oregon's Rieslings and Gewürztraminers are reasonably priced.

Tasting Notes

UNDER $10

★★**WILLAMETTE VALLEY VINEYARDS 1996 DRY RIESLING, WILLAMETTE VALLEY:** Floral aromas of melon, peach and mint. Quite dry yet round in the mouth, with the melon quality complemented by a softly citric orange note. Intensely flavored and firm on the finish.

★**AMITY VINEYARDS 1996 DRY RIESLING, OREGON:** Floral pear and lemon nose shows a distinctly petrolly suggestion of German Riesling. Quite dry, but with intensely flavored peach and ripe citrus flavors. The wine's stony underpinning gives it a long, firm finish.

★**ARGYLE 1995 DRY RESERVE RIESLING, OREGON:** Aromatically complex, slightly high-toned but pure aromas of peach, pear and licorice. Round, fruity and ready to drink; a dry wine whose ripe fruit makes it taste slightly sweet. But obviously dry on the finish.

★**BRIDGEVIEW VINEYARDS 1996 CHARDONNAY, OREGON:** Lime and apple nose shows a spicy gingery aspect. Good intensity of lime flavor, but quite youthful and tightly wound. Has the acid/sugar balance of a ripe apple. A leaner style of Chardonnay, slightly skinny on the finish.

★**DUCK POND CELLARS 1996 CHARDONNAY, WILLAMETTE VALLEY:** Aromatic mint, licorice and clove nose. Juicy, high-pitched and penetrating; fairly intense flavors of lime and clove.

$10–$20

★★**CRISTOM 1995 CHARDONNAY, COLUMBIA VALLEY:** Champagne-like yeasty, appley nose. Penetrating and fresh in the mouth, with intense apple-flavored fruit given shape by gentle, ripe acidity. Spicy oak frames, rather than overwhelms, the wine's fruit.

WASHINGTON STATE

The most important wine-producing state after California, Washington excels in providing both inexpensive, crisp white wines and somewhat pricier Cabernet Sauvignons and Merlots—the best of which can compete with the world's finest examples of these varieties.

WINE GEOGRAPHY: Most of Washington's grapes are grown east of the Cascade mountains, in the irrigated desert of the Columbia and Yakima river valleys. The vineyards benefit from long daylight hours during the summer and a lengthier growing season overall than California (grapes are usually picked well into October). Although daytime temperatures can be quite hot, generally cool September nights allow the grapes to retain a healthy acidity, resulting in wines with strong varietal character and flavor intensity.

GRAPES & STYLES: Cabernet Sauvignon and Merlot are Washington's most serious and successful wines. The best examples offer terrific purity of fruit flavor and juicy acidity; they are highly distinctive wines, neither Bordeaux nor California in style. Washington's Sémillons and Rieslings offer excellent varietal character and food compatibility. The best of the state's Sauvignon Blancs and Chenin Blancs can also be delicious and versatile at the table.

BEHIND THE SCENES: Chateau Ste. Michelle and its sister winery, Columbia Crest, dominate Washington's production, accounting for more than half the bottles shipped out of the state.

THE BOTTOM LINE: Although prices are rising, many of Washington's red wines still offer very good quality/price rapport. Sémillons and Rieslings carry notably gentle price tags, but Chardonnay bargains are more elusive.

═══ SÉMILLON AND SAUVIGNON BLANC ═══

A SPECIALTY OF WASHINGTON STATE, SÉMILLON TYPICALLY PRODUCES dry wines that combine enticingly plump texture with striking fresh-fruit character. Aromas and flavors range from bright citric fruits, minerals and spearmint to lower-toned melon, fig and honey. Sauvignon Blanc, which, like Sémillon, pairs well with the shellfish dishes widely enjoyed in the Pacific Northwest, is growing in popularity; this is normally a slightly crisper, lighter, more penetrating wine. A bit of Sémillon may be added to Sauvignon Blanc to give more middle-palate texture, while Sauvignon can be used to perk up Sémillon.

AT THE TABLE: Unoaked Sauvignon Blancs go well with asparagus or goat cheese, while Sémillon is a local favorite with Dungeness crab and salmon.

THE BOTTOM LINE: These wines are among the first places to look for fresh, under-$10 white wines.

Vintage Rating 1994/A+ 1995/C+ 1996/B+

Tasting Notes

UNDER $10

★★**COLUMBIA CREST 1995 SAUVIGNON BLANC, COLUMBIA VALLEY:** Restrained, citric, floral nose, with a yeasty nuance. Shapely, textured and fairly rich, but kept fresh by lemony acidity. Intriguing hint of honeysuckle. Dry but not austere.

★**CATERINA WINERY 1996 SAUVIGNON BLANC, WASHINGTON STATE:** Floral, herbal, minty nose. Lean, fairly intense floral and mint flavors are a bit simple but refreshing. Finish is slightly harsh but persistent.

★**COVEY RUN 1995 FUMÉ BLANC, COLUMBIA VALLEY:** Aromas of oak spice and lemon. Lean and lemony, with modest texture but good flavor intensity. On the skinny side, but juicy and fresh. Firm but not hard.

★**COVEY RUN 1995 FUMÉ BLANC RESERVE, YAKIMA VALLEY:** Smoky, spicy oak and a note of butterscotch on the nose. Fat and supple, with good palate presence but limited real flavor intensity. Broad rather than intense. A bit dry on the finish. Oakier than the Fumé Blanc above.

★**HOGUE CELLARS 1996 FUMÉ BLANC, COLUMBIA VALLEY:** Cool lemon, melon and spearmint nose. Lemony, juicy and firm, with good flavor intensity. The brisk finish offers lingering lemon and herb flavor.

★**HOGUE CELLARS 1996 SÉMILLON, COLUMBIA VALLEY:** Honey, spice and mint on the nose. Supple, dry and substantial; flavors of honey, mint and fig. Acids are ripe and harmonious. Finishes with fresh lemony flavor.

═══════ CHARDONNAY ═══════

WASHINGTON'S CHARDONNAYS ARE ITS MOST AMBITIOUS WHITES, though bargains can be difficult to find. Today's Washington Chardonnays are richer and more textured than ever, as many wineries have switched to Burgundian-style barrel fermentation. Styles range from brisk, fruity and more affordably priced (under $15) to toasty, nutty, creamy-rich and more expensive.

AT THE TABLE: Serve Washington's lighter Chardonnays with less assertive fish dishes. Oakier versions can stand up to grilled fish, including salmon.

THE BOTTOM LINE: There are bargains to be found in the $10–$15 range.

Vintage Rating 1994/A- 1995/C+ 1996/B+

Tasting Notes

UNDER $10

★**COLUMBIA CREST 1995, COLUMBIA VALLEY:** Aromatic nose of tropical fruit, honey and spicy, nutty oak. Soft, lush and mouth-filling.

$10–$20

★ ★ COVEY RUN 1995, COLUMBIA VALLEY: Lime, mint and flowers on the nose. Supple and very ripe, with good texture, excellent depth of flavor and a limey lift. Juicy, lingering finish shows minerals and spice.

★ ★ COVEY RUN 1994 CELILO VINEYARD, WASHINGTON STATE: Clove oil on the nose. Fat, sweet and generous. The fresh peach and apricot fruit has a tangy quality that stands up to the wood treatment. Finishes ripe and reasonably long.

★ ★ McCREA CELLARS 1995, COLUMBIA VALLEY: Fairly complex lime, apricot and buttery scents. Supple, spicy and fairly rich, but quite firm. More nuanced than most Washington Chardonnays. Persistent, slightly hard finish.

★ HOGUE CELLARS 1995, COLUMBIA VALLEY: Aromas of ripe peach, creamed corn and spice. Rich and lush; soft around the edges. The peach flavor repeats in the mouth. Just short of heavy, but has good texture, and shows a light hand with the oak.

OTHER WHITE WINES

RIESLING HAS TRADITIONALLY BEEN A WASHINGTON STAPLE, A FAIRLY ripe but crisp and fruity wine with flavors of peach, apricot and apple. Washington's Rieslings are among the most satisfying examples of this variety made outside Europe, and versions bottled with residual sugar generally have enough piquant acidity to balance their sweetness. Their low prices make these Rieslings some of the state's best values. Chenin Blanc and Muscat are, like Riesling, often slightly sweet but kept fresh by sound natural acidity. These can be perfumed, delicious, inexpensive wines ideal for warm-weather drinking.

AT THE TABLE: Rieslings and Chenin Blancs make good partners for lighter sushi and sashimi. Slightly sweet versions work well with richer fish like sea bass and salmon served with cream sauces.

THE BOTTOM LINE: These wines usually sell for single-digit prices and offer superb value.

Vintage Rating 1994/A- 1995/C+ 1996/B+

Tasting Notes

UNDER $10

★ ★ COLUMBIA WINERY 1996 CELLARMASTER'S RESERVE RIESLING, COLUMBIA VALLEY: Perfumed, lime-scented nose. Medium sweet, juicy and floral, with enough limey acidity for balance. Flavors of apple cider, honeysuckle and apricot. A nicely balanced wine with wide appeal.

★★**HOGUE CELLARS 1996 LATE HARVEST WHITE RIESLING, COLUMBIA VALLEY:** Vibrant aromas of citrus skin and white flowers. Medium sweet, fresh and intensely flavored; has a subtle floral quality in the mouth. Sound acidity gives the wine very good delineation.

★ **BOOKWALTER 1996 WINERY RIESLING VINTNER'S SELECT, WASHINGTON STATE:** Delicate aromas of lemon, orange peel and flowers. Round and moderately sweet, with just enough acidity to maintain its balance. Has a floral, honeyed sweetness and very good flavor intensity.

★**COLUMBIA WINERY 1996 GEWÜRZTRAMINER, YAKIMA VALLEY:** Spice, quinine, honey, lemon and smoke on the nose. Medium sweet, with floral and honey notes. A bit thick, even verging on cloying, but has just enough acidity to maintain its balance.

★**HOGUE CELLARS 1996 CHENIN BLANC, COLUMBIA VALLEY:** Lemon, lime, spearmint, herbs and a mineral note on the nose. Silky and slightly sweet, but nicely balanced thanks to sound acidity. The slight residual sugar makes for a pleasing drink.

★ **HOGUE CELLARS 1996 DRY JOHANNISBERG RIESLING, COLUMBIA VALLEY:** Aromas of tangerine and orange blossom. Supple, spicy and easygoing, with good flavor intensity. Not at all lean; in fact, the wine's softness makes it seem slightly sweet. Dusty finish coats the palate.

★ **HOGUE CELLARS 1996 JOHANNISBERG RIESLING, COLUMBIA VALLEY:** Floral, minty nose offers a suggestion of tangy orange peel. Medium sweet, but with good buffering acidity. No shortage of flavor intensity. Has a slightly perfumed aftershave character in the mouth.

★**WASHINGTON HILLS 1996 GEWÜRZTRAMINER, COLUMBIA VALLEY:** Delicate grassy nose. Fairly dry and intense, with decent texture and rather soft acids. Has texture and shape, but lacks real nuance. Ripe back end is gentle but firm. A Gewürztraminer with rather understated varietal character.

★**WASHINGTON HILLS 1996 LATE HARVEST WHITE RIESLING, COLUMBIA VALLEY:** Delicate, reticent nose shows high-pitched citric and mineral notes. Medium sweet, with firm acidity, fresh peachy flavor and modest complexity. The fruit carries through to the lingering finish.

★**YAKIMA RIVER WINERY 1995 JOHANNISBERG RIESLING, YAKIMA VALLEY:** Stony/floral nose, with notes of charred oak. Slightly sweet, but comes across as fairly dry thanks to some CO_2 and firm acidity. Note of rose petal. Nicely balanced, if a bit simple, with sound varietal character.

═══ CABERNET SAUVIGNON & MERLOT ═══

WASHINGTON'S TOP CABERNETS AND MERLOTS COMBINE THE intense, dark berry flavors of California Cabernet with the more generous and fleshy textures of Bordeaux. While capable of many years of positive development in bottle, they generally offer considerable appeal when young. Some of Washington's finest reds are expensive cult items from boutique-size wineries, and are snapped up by collectors almost before they hit the store shelves. But a handful of larger producers with wide distribution also offer excellent, moderately priced reds.

AT THE TABLE: Serve these wines with lamb dishes. Pricier wines made with substantial new oak generally have a sweet quality that also complements beef.

THE BOTTOM LINE: The high prices of many of these wines is largely a function of limited production and stiff demand in the local Northwest market. As a general rule, Cabs and Merlots from larger wineries offer better value.

Vintage Rating 1993/B- 1994/B+ 1995/B+ 1996/B+

Tasting Notes

$10–$20

★★★ **CANOE RIDGE 1995 MERLOT, COLUMBIA VALLEY:** Currants and cranberry on the nose, along with a restrained oakiness. Silky, concentrated, curranty fruit is fresh, delineated and pliable, if somewhat unforthcoming at this stage. Finishes crisp, fresh and focused. A serious Merlot with lovely balance and backbone.

★★ **COLUMBIA WINERY 1993 CABERNET SAUVIGNON, COLUMBIA VALLEY:** Sweet, smoky, dark berry nose, with a note of tobacco. Fat, layered and sweet in the mouth; flavors of black raspberry, black currant and minerals. Finishes with soft, ripe tannins and very good length.

★★ **PORTTEUS 1994 WINERY CABERNET SAUVIGNON, YAKIMA VALLEY:** Black-ruby color. Smoke, coffee, grilled nuts, sandalwood and tarragon on the nose. Sweet and easy, but nicely focused; berry and oak flavors are framed by juicy acidity. A bit grapey.

★★ **PRESTON 1994 CABERNET SAUVIGNON RESERVE, COLUMBIA VALLEY:** Ruby red. Burgundian aromas of coffee, charred oak, sandalwood, grilled nuts and cherry cola. Fat, smooth and sweet; broad more than especially intense. Tannins begin slightly dry but light, then become a bit gritty with aeration.

★★ **PRESTON 1994 MERLOT RESERVE, COLUMBIA VALLEY:** Good dark red, with ruby tones. Woodsmoke, oak char, mocha and coffee on the nose. Fat, sweet and silky; lush fruit has a smooth, Burgundian texture. Slightly edgy finish, with the tannins hitting the palate late. Will be most appreciated by fans of new oak.

★★ **WASHINGTON HILLS 1995 W.B. BRIDGMAN MERLOT, COLUMBIA VALLEY:** Dark red. Smoky, nutty aromas of roasted oak and currants. Sweet, supple and smooth, with flavors of smoke, coffee, currant and chocolate. Not particularly fleshy but suave.

★ **COLUMBIA CREST 1994 CABERNET SAUVIGNON, COLUMBIA VALLEY:** Currants, oak spice and herbal notes on the nose. Supple and fresh, with currant and cherry flavor, along with a suggestion of caramel. Has an attractive pliant texture. Finishes with dusty tannins and a bit of acidity.

★**COLUMBIA CREST 1993 MERLOT, COLUMBIA VALLEY:** Black raspberry fruitiness along with smoky, toffeed oak tones. Juicy, reasonably intense black raspberry flavor and good density on the palate; solid acidity gives the wine a firm shape and a slightly edgy finish.

★**COLUMBIA WINERY 1994 MERLOT, COLUMBIA VALLEY:** Reticent black currant and roasted nut aromas. Restrained berry sweetness on the palate; bright and fresh but a wine of only modest complexity. Finishes with dusty, slightly dry tannins.

★**HOGUE CELLARS 1994 MERLOT, COLUMBIA VALLEY:** Red currant, smoke and truffle aromas. Sweet and truffley in the mouth, with moderate body and intensity and good varietal character. Has a pleasing shape. Finishes with light, dusty tannins and good lingering fruit.

★**PRESTON 1994 CABERNET SAUVIGNON, COLUMBIA VALLEY:** Aromas of toasty, charred oak, mocha and earth. Supple and generous, with very good depth of fruit; a mouth-filling Cabernet in a rather straightforward style. More acid than tannins on the finish.

★**WASHINGTON HILLS 1995 W.B. BRIDGMAN CABERNET SAUVIGNON, COLUMBIA VALLEY:** Gingerbread, currants and oak on the nose. Sweet cherry/berry fruit in the mouth; a medium-bodied, nicely made wine showing plenty of oak spice and just enough supporting fruit flavor. Finishes crisp, with a slightly tart edge.

$20–$30

★★★**COLUMBIA WINERY 1994 MILESTONE RED WILLOW VINEYARD MERLOT, YAKIMA VALLEY:** Rather unforthcoming nose. Initially rather mute on the palate, but with aeration shows intensely flavored, sharply focused flavors of pomegranate and cranberry, a solid spine and excellent persistence. An uncompromising, unevolved Merlot that should be quite long-lived.

★★★**COLUMBIA WINERY 1993 RED WILLOW CABERNET SAUVIGNON, YAKIMA VALLEY:** Subdued aromas of crystallized dark berries, sassafras and cedar. Flavors of violet, dark berries and black cherry, along with a faint green streak. Bright and penetrating, with a powerful spine and fresh acidity. Finishes firmly tannic, brisk and long. Will require extended bottle aging but should be worth the wait.

★★★**COLUMBIA WINERY 1993 OTIS VINEYARD CABERNET SAUVIGNON, YAKIMA VALLEY:** Expressive aromas of red and black currant, black cherry, loamy earth and underbrush. Silky-rich, fat and pliant, but with excellent flavor definition. Intriguing notes of bitter chocolate. Really lovely fruit sweetness. Finishes long and firmly tannic.

★★★**DELILLE CELLARS 1994 D2:** Ruby-red color. Sappy, sweet aromas of raspberry, roasted nuts, chocolate and vanillin oak. Thick, lush, black raspberry fruit is creamy and deep, with a texture like liquid velvet. Finishes with a burst of sweet raspberry flavor and soft tannins. Perfect for early drinking. A blend of Cabernet and Merlot.

★ ★ ★ **L'ECOLE NO. 41 1994 PEPPER BRIDGE VINEYARD APOGEE:** Deep ruby red. Exotic cassis and bourbon nose. Cassis and oak spice on the palate; shows lovely sweetness and excellent concentration. Brisk acidity and firm tannins give it backbone and grip. Long, ripe back end. A Merlot-Cabernet blend.

★ ★ ★ **L'ECOLE NO. 41 1994 CABERNET SAUVIGNON, COLUMBIA VALLEY:** Subtle aromas of cassis, mint, violet, game, roasted nuts and creosote. Smooth and extremely unevolved on the palate; not at all fat or thick, but juicy and intensely flavored. Bright and stylish. Finishes with persistent cassis and violet flavor and lightish tannins.

★ ★ ★ **L'ECOLE NO. 41 1994 SEVEN HILLS VINEYARD MERLOT, WALLA WALLA:** Knockout nose of black raspberry, coffee, sandalwood and smoky oak. Juicy, spicy, and intensely flavored, with strong, sweet black cherry fruit. Finishes firm and very long, with succulent fruit to support the sweet oak. Wonderfully vibrant Merlot.

★ ★ ★ **PRESTON NV PLATINUM RED:** Crushed boysenberries and a hint of meatiness on the nose. Boasts terrific fruit intensity and clarity of flavor, plus some smoky oak around the edges. Sweet, fresh and layered. Finishes with sound acidity, moderate tannins and strong fruit.

★ ★ ★ **CHATEAU STE. MICHELLE 1994 COLD CREEK VINEYARD MERLOT, COLUMBIA VALLEY:** Inviting aromas of spicy red currant, raspberry, coffee, and sandalwood. Dense, fat and sweet, yet shows excellent clarity of flavor. Notes of cocoa butter and chocolate in the mouth. Long, oaky aftertaste hints at cassis, chocolate and espresso.

OTHER RED WINES

AN INCREASING NUMBER OF WASHINGTON'S WINERIES ARE EXPERImenting with red Rhône varieties, especially Syrah. Lemberger is an obscure Washington State grape whose exuberant berry aromas remind many tasters of Zinfandel.

AT THE TABLE: Washington's Syrah-based wines are generally fresh and a bit less roasted in character than their counterparts from California, and thus go well with lighter red meats and pork. The fruity Lemberger is a good accompaniment to roast chicken and hamburgers.

THE BOTTOM LINE: These wines are frequently better values than the state's Merlots and Cabernets.

Tasting Notes

UNDER $10

★ ★ **KIONA VINEYARDS 1995 LEMBERGER, WASHINGTON STATE:** Oak spice, raspberry and eucalyptus on the nose. Sweet, supple and spicy in the mouth, with bright red berry flavor and a briary, Zinfandel-like quality. Fat, round and user-friendly. Has the sheer depth of fruit flavor to support the rather forceful oak treatment.

$10–$20

★ ★ **COLUMBIA WINERY 1994 RED WILLOW VINEYARD CABERNET FRANC, YAKIMA VALLEY:** Aromas of cocoa, bitter cherry, cinnamon and nutmeg. Floral, faintly leafy and minerally in the mouth, with the green-edged cherry note repeating. But ripe and reasonably round, not to mention bright and sharply defined. Has loads of personality. Finishes with firm tannins.

★ ★ **McCREA CELLARS 1994 TIERRA DEL SOL, COLUMBIA VALLEY:** Raspberry, red currant and loam on the nose. Sweet, pliant and super-ripe in the mouth, with excellent depth of fruit. Red fruit flavors are complicated by notes of clove spice. Finishes with ripe, smooth tannins. A blend of Syrah and Grenache.

★ **WASHINGTON HILLS 1996 W.B. BRIDGMAN LEMBERGER, YAKIMA VALLEY:** Grapey, candied aromas of cherry, bitter chocolate, and licorice; has briary, herbal notes not unlike Zinfandel. Candied red fruit in the mouth. A soft, quaffable style of Lemberger: a bit lacking in verve, but has plenty of fruit.

$20–$30

★ ★ ★ **COLUMBIA WINERY 1994 SYRAH RED WILLOW VINEYARD, YAKIMA VALLEY:** Reticent nose hints at violets. Spicy and rich; though extremely young, this wine already displays lovely inner-mouth flavors of black fruits and licorice. A terrific combination of weight and precision of flavor. Finishes with soft tannins and juicy berry flavor. Loads of potential.

Your Personal Tasting Journal

AUSTRALIA

AUSTRALIA CONTINUES TO PROVIDE AMERICAN WINE drinkers with a wide range of generously fruity red and white wines that rank among the world's great values. As a rule of thumb, Australian wines tend to be softer and more immediately accessible than those from Old World vineyards. They are also generally less oaky and tannic—and lower in alcohol—than wines from California.

WINE GEOGRAPHY: Virtually all Australian wine comes from the warm southeastern portion of the country—from the states of South Australia, New South Wales and Victoria. The catchall South Eastern Australia appellation, which appears on many bargain bottles, covers all the major wine regions except for Western Australia. More specific, high-quality regional appellations include such areas as Barossa Valley, Coonawarra, Hunter Valley and Margaret River.

ON THE BOTTLE: Like most New World wines, Australian bottles are usually varietally labeled (e.g., Chardonnay).

THE BOTTOM LINE: Superb values at the lower end of the price range with world-class high-end offerings as well.

===== CHARDONNAY =====

CHARDONNAY IS THE REIGNING CHAMP AMONG AUSTRALIA'S WHITE varieties. The stereotypical Australian Chardonnay is a buttery, oaky wine with bold tropical-fruit flavors and low acidity, but the trend today is toward less oaky, crisper, more refined wines. In fact, a number of small wineries located in cooler growing areas are crafting more nuanced, ageworthy wines in the style

NEW SOUTH WALES
MARGARET RIVER
TASMANIA
MUDGEE
HUNTER VALLEY
Lachlan
CLARE VALLEY
RIVERLAND
MILDURA
Murrumbidgee
Sydney
BAROSSA VALLEY
Adelaide ADELAIDE
Murray
McLAREN VALE
RUTHERGLEN/COROWA
PADTHAWAY
VICTORIA
MILAWA/GLENROWAN
SOUTH AUSTRALIA
GREAT WESTERN
GOULBURN VALLEY
COONAWARRA
Melbourne
YARRA VALLEY
GEELONG
Wine growing regions
Indian Ocean
Tasman Sea

of Chardonnay from Burgundy. Such pricier versions are still the exception, however. Most Australian Chardonnay is made for maximum up-front flavor and charm and should be consumed within two or three years of the vintage.

AT THE TABLE: Many popular Australian Chardonnays can overwhelm subtle dishes; serve them instead with Asian preparations and with Southwestern-influenced or grilled foods. They are also ideal with fish like tuna, swordfish and salmon.

THE BOTTOM LINE: At the top levels, Australia's Chardonnays rarely equal the best from California, but they are also considerably less expensive. Australian Chardonnay in the $8–$12 range far surpasses in sheer drinkability our own inexpensive examples.

Vintage Rating 1995/B+ 1996/B+

Tasting Notes

UNDER $10

★ ★ **ROTHBURY ESTATE 1996, HUNTER VALLEY:** Peach, clove and curry spice on the nose. Intensely flavored, spicy and dry; has a chewy texture. Pineapple, melon and peach flavors are nicely delineated. Shows the balance, subtlety and tactile quality of a more expensive wine.

★ **DEAKIN ESTATE 1996, VICTORIA:** Pineapple, herbal and floral aromas, plus hints of Indian spices. Supple, bordering on thick, yet quite dry.

★ **LINDEMANS 1996 BIN 65, SOUTH EASTERN AUSTRALIA:** Aromas of vanillin oak, melon, clove and green apple, plus a mintiness that contributes to its impression of freshness. Flavors of apple, pear and spice are given shape by healthy acidity. Firm-edged, slightly dry finish.

★ **PENFOLDS 1996 KOONUNGA HILL, SOUTH AUSTRALIA:** Lively aromas of lemon, spicy oak, resin and butterscotch. Big, sweet and fat, with flavors of dried peach and apricot. Loads of fruit for the price.

★ **SEAVIEW 1996, MCLAREN VALE:** Grilled nuts, apricot, and melon on the nose. Spicy, medium-bodied Chardonnay with flavor intensity and brisk balancing acidity. Finishes with lingering fruit.

$10–$20

★ ★ **D'ARENBERG 1995 THE OLIVE GROVE, MCLAREN VALE:** Smoke, herbs, roasted nuts and marzipan on the nose. Fat and soft in the mouth; perked up by a bit of CO_2. Shows a yeasty Champagne quality, along with deeper cashew and spice notes.

★ ★ **MITCHELTON PREECE 1996, VICTORIA:** Subdued aromas of toasty oak, lemon and grass, plus a stony note. Intensely flavored fruit offers lemon and spicy oak nuances and mouthwatering acidity. Finish is persistent and ripe, with a touch of oak spice.

★ ★ **ROSEMOUNT ESTATE 1995 SHOW RESERVE, HUNTER VALLEY:** Fruit cocktail and complex oak spices on the nose. Sweet, smooth, concentrated and strongly oaky; sound framing acidity gives this stylish wine clarity and freshness. Pronounced oak spice on the aftertaste.

★ ★ **YALUMBA 1995 RESERVE, EDEN VALLEY/YARRA VALLEY:** Exotic peach and butterscotch aromas, plus a smoky nuance. Lively and fresh in the mouth, with a subtle spiciness and notes of lemon and honey. Nicely balanced wine. Dry lemon and spice finish.

★ **HARDYS 1995, PADTHAWAY:** Perfumed, oily, oak-dominated aromas of clove and spice; slight floral nuance. Sweet, supple and spicy. Rather simple, but possesses good texture. Oak-spicy finish.

$20–$30

★ ★ ★ **VASSE FELIX 1996, WESTERN AUSTRALIA:** Perfumed, leesy nose of peach, butterscotch and spicy oak. Thick, ripe and very concentrated, with an oily, mouth-filling, layered texture and perfectly integrated acidity. Very long and spicy on the ripe, lush finish.

OTHER DRY WHITE WINES

BEFORE AUSTRALIA EMBARKED ON ITS LOVE AFFAIR WITH Chardonnay, Sémillon and Riesling were its two most important white table wines. Even today, oak-aged Sémillon from the Hunter Valley makes one of Australia's most distinctive and longest-lived white wines. Sémillon blended with Chardonnay makes an easygoing wine that is one of Australia's most popular whites, and the combination is now cropping up in California and Washington. Riesling (usually called Rhine Riesling in Australia) is generally a dry to just off-dry wine with a brisk lemon-limey fruitiness.

AT THE TABLE: Australia's dry Rieslings are excellent accompaniments to smoked salmon and other oily fish, while the Sémillons work well with fish terrines and crab.

THE BOTTOM LINE: Australia's non-Chardonnay whites rarely carry steep price tags and offer excellent value.

Tasting Notes

UNDER $10

★ ★ **MITCHELTON 1996 THOMAS MITCHELL MARSANNE:** Spice, honey and lemon on the nose. Good intensity and texture; has enough fruit to support the oak spice. Brisk lemony acidity keeps the wine fresh.

★ ★ **ROSEMOUNT ESTATE 1996 SÉMILLON, HUNTER VALLEY:** Saline, toasty, lemony nose. Supple, easygoing fruit offers a lemon-cream flavor and noteworthy intensity. Light oak tones contribute to the wine's appeal. Vibrant, strongly fruity aftertaste.

★ **LINDEMANS 1995 BIN 95 SAUVIGNON BLANC, SOUTH EASTERN AUSTRALIA:** Spicy, flinty, herbaceous aromas; faint candied note. Round and textured, with accurate varietal flavors unsullied by oak. Quite dry but not austere; has just enough flavor intensity. Dry, crisp finish.

★ **PENFOLDS 1996 KOONUNGA HILL SÉMILLON-CHARDONNAY, SOUTH AUSTRALIA:** Aromas of smoke, spice, honey, peach and resiny oak. Fresh and reasonably intense, with lemon-lime acidity and some CO_2 contributing to its vibrancy. A bit hard-edged on the finish.

★ **SALISBURY 1996 SAUVIGNON BLANC, VICTORIA:** Pineapple, mint, spice and a faint menthol nuance on the nose. Soft, supple and fruity; in a gentle, low-acid style.

$10–$20

★ ★ ★ **TIM ADAMS 1996 SÉMILLON, CLARE VALLEY:** Delicate flinty, spicy, lemony nose. Penetrating, sharply etched pear and lemon flavor in the mouth; offers outstanding flavor intensity and superb cut thanks to bracing acidity.

★ ★ ★ **GROSSET 1996 RIESLING POLISH HILL, CLARE VALLEY:** Highly aromatic nose of pine, citrus rind and spice. Rich, textured, and fleshy, but juicy and firm, with terrific precision of flavor. A dry Riesling with lovely ripeness and a suggestion of oak. Very long, pure aftertaste.

★ ★ ★ **HENSCHKE 1996 JULIUS RIESLING, EDEN VALLEY:** Nuanced, stony nose combines red currant, minerals, quinine, lime skin and peach syrup. Dry, brisk and focused on the palate, with bright, juicy, citrus skin flavors. Distinctive soil tones. Brisk, firm and long on the finish.

★ ★ ★ **LEEUWIN ESTATE 1996 RIESLING, MARGARET RIVER:** Restrained, musky aromas of green herbs, citrus skin and pine. Supple, broad and packed with fruit; intensely flavored and nicely focused. Lovely ripe acidity gives the wine excellent grip. Finishes with palate-staining fruit.

SHIRAZ

STYLISTICALLY, SHIRAZ RUNS THE GAMUT FROM EASYGOING, berry-flavored quaffers to superripe, ultraconcentrated wines to be sipped and savored. While Australia's versions of Syrah generally lack the structure and ageworthiness of the best Syrahs of the Rhône Valley, they offer easier drinking in their youth. Think of Shiraz as Australia's Merlot: a wine with forthright fruit flavors, broad appeal and softer acidity and tannins than the local Cabernet Sauvignon.

AT THE TABLE: Shiraz complements the heartiest full-flavored cuisines, such as game or meats grilled over wood (its sweet fruit pairs perfectly with roast lamb). The sweetly spicy character of Shiraz also plays nicely off the chile-pepper heat of Southwestern cooking.

THE BOTTOM LINE: Australia's best examples of Shiraz, particularly those from very old vines, command high prices (the great Penfolds Grange costs more than $150), but the overwhelming majority of these wines are priced in the $8 to $20 range, where they offer excellent value.

Vintage Rating 1993/B- 1994/A- 1995/B+ 1996/B+

Tasting Notes

UNDER $10

★★ **MITCHELTON 1995 THOMAS MITCHELL:** Expressive aromas of red currant, chocolate and oak spice. Rich, sweet and chewy, with violet and pepper notes. The tart-edged finish features ripe fruit.

★ **LINDEMANS 1995 BIN 50, SOUTH AUSTRALIA:** Pepper, cherry and leather aromas. Fat, peppery and fruity on the palate, but could use more flavor definition. Finishes with easy tannins. Very good value.

$10–$20

★★★ **ROSEMOUNT ESTATE 1994 RESERVE, MCLAREN VALE:** Impressive dark ruby color to the rim. Flamboyant aromas of crushed blackberry, chocolate, mint and iodine. Fresh, juicy and dense, with a stony, floral pungency. Tart fruit acidity gives the flavor excellent delineation. Pure Syrah fruit unobscured by oak.

★★ **D'ARENBERG 1994 THE OLD VINE, MCLAREN VALE:** Expressive raspberry, chocolate, pepper and tar nose; has a mineral pungency. Creamy and concentrated, with a penetrating freshness. Packed with fruit but not especially complex. Nicely balanced, shapely wine.

★★ **CORIOLE 1995, MCLAREN VALE:** Very dark ruby to the rim. Expressive aromas of dark berries, chocolate, cola, woodsmoke and eucalyptus. Concentrated black currant and black raspberry fruit is creamy and sweet. Finishes with smoky oak and moderate ripe tannins.

★ ★ **GEOFF MERRILL 1994 OWEN'S ESTATE, SOUTH EASTERN AUSTRALIA:** Medium-dark red. Cassis, currant, pepper and mint overlaid by pungent oak scents. Silky and fairly intensely flavored; lovely sweetness is balanced by harmonious acidity. Lots of spicy oak tones.

★ ★ **ROSEMOUNT ESTATE 1996, SOUTH EASTERN AUSTRALIA:** Black cherry and pepper aromas, plus a gingerbread component. Sweet and lush, with very good weight and intensity. Has a grapey fruitiness and lovely sweetness. Finishes with strong, lingering fruit.

$20–$30

★ ★ ★ **HENSCHKE 1994 KEYNETON ESTATE, BAROSSA VALLEY:** Wild aromas of black raspberry, plum and smoky, spicy oak. Sweet, concentrated and deep but rather unforthcoming. Strong acidity gives the wine a penetrating quality. Has a powerful backbone for aging.

★ ★ ★ **PENFOLDS 1992 ST. HENRI, SOUTH AUSTRALIA:** Expressive aromas of black and red currant, blueberry, cherry, chocolate and tobacco. The authoritative dark fruit flavor practically makes the spicy oak disappear. Has the structure to age.

══════ CABERNET SAUVIGNON ══════

AUSTRALIA'S BETTER CABERNETS DISPLAY RICH, VIBRANT CASSIS AND berry fruit, medium body and varying degrees of sweet, toasty oak. As a rule, they are far less expensive than California Cabernets of similar quality. They also have more personality and richness, not to mention fruit, than most South American Cabernets or inexpensive bottlings from southern France.

AT THE TABLE: Serve Australia's Cabernets as you would Cabs from California: alongside hearty red meat and lamb dishes, grilled game birds or aged, hard cheeses. Keep in mind that Australian Cabernets are often pungently oaky and can overwhelm more subtle foods.

THE BOTTOM LINE: A host of exceptional values can be found in the $10–$15 price range. As with Shiraz, some of Australia's higher-priced examples of Cabernet are truly world-class.

Vintage Rating 1993/B- **1994**/A- **1995**/B **1996**/B+

Tasting Notes

UNDER $10

★ **SEAVIEW 1994, SOUTH AUSTRALIA:** Black currant, clove and vanillin oak on the nose. Supple and forthcoming on the palate, with enough ripeness and fruit intensity to stand up to the oak treatment.

$10–$20

★ ★ ★ **PENFOLDS 1994 BIN 407, SOUTH AUSTRALIA:** Saturated dark ruby to the rim. Multifaceted nose combines blackberry, roasted coffee, licorice, smoked meat and lead pencil. Lush on entry, then rather closed in the middle. Long, dark berry-flavored finish, with some slightly dry tannins. Needs bottle aging.

★ ★ ★ **CHATEAU TAHBILK 1993, GOULBURN VALLEY:** Highly nuanced nose combines pungent crushed berries, bitter cherry, tar, leather and tobacco. Fat, sweet and rich on the palate, with the crushed fruit and iron components repeating. Broad yet juicy, and structured to age.

★ ★ **CHATEAU REYNELLA 1994 BASKET PRESSED, MCLAREN VALE:** Pungent oak and game nose, with notes of smoked duck. Dense, with an attractive balance of fat fruit and acidity. Very good concentration. Finishes long and spicy.

★ **PETER LEHMANN 1995, BAROSSA VALLEY:** Aromas of crushed blackberry, mint and spicy, vanillin oak. Silky, oaky and moderately concentrated; broad and inviting.

$20–$30

★ ★ ★ **VASSE FELIX 1995, MARGARET RIVER:** Nuanced nose of black currants, cedar, coconut and soft fresh herbs. Sweet and silky in the mouth; packed with dark berry fruit. In an essentially gentle style, but delineated and stylish. The Bordeaux side of Australian Cabernet.

Splurgeworthy:

★ ★ ★ **LEEUWIN ESTATE 1993, MARGARET RIVER:** Saturated red-ruby color; aromas of cassis, plum and beefsteak tomato. Very dense and concentrated; stuffed with spicy black currant fruit. Finishes with ripe tannins and explosive flavors.

═══OTHER AUSTRALIAN RED WINES═══

MANY OF THE MOST SATISFYING AUSTRALIAN RED WINES ARE blends of Cabernet Sauvignon and Shiraz. (The dominant variety is listed first on the label.) This combination can offer the best of both worlds: the rich, spicy fruit of Shiraz and the elegance and structure of Cabernet. Other Rhône-style varieties like Grenache and Mourvèdre are increasingly turning up in lush, ripe red wines ideal for early drinking.

AT THE TABLE: Cabernet-Shiraz blends possess a juicy but firm sweetness that complements steak and hamburgers. Wines based on Grenache or Mourvèdre can be paired with barbecued ribs, mixed grills or lighter game preparations.

THE BOTTOM LINE: These wines vary widely in price, but there are terrific bargains to be found in the $8–$12 range.

Tasting Notes

UNDER $10

★ **LINDEMANS 1995 BIN 40 MERLOT, SOUTH AUSTRALIA:** Faintly high-toned aromas of cherry, plum, leather and tobacco. Fresh but somewhat lean, with juicy acidity but only modest flesh.

★ **LINDEMANS 1996 BIN 99 PINOT NOIR, SOUTH AUSTRALIA:** Clean cherry and raspberry aromas. Supple, ripe and soft, with broad cherry and spice flavors. A wine of modest delineation and nuance, but it's hard to complain about tasty Pinot under $10.

★ **PENFOLDS 1995 BIN 2 SHIRAZ-MOURVÈDRE, SOUTH EASTERN AUSTRALIA:** Slightly candied nose of black cherry, cassis and mocha. Supple, ripe currant and mocha flavor in the mouth; becomes lusher and sweeter as it opens in the glass. Finishes with even, slightly dry tannins.

★ **ROSEMOUNT ESTATE 1996 GRENACHE-SHIRAZ, SOUTH EASTERN AUSTRALIA:** Modestly saturated bright red. Black cherry, chocolate, tar and pepper nose has a slightly sweaty quality. Supple and sweet; an easy-drinking, very soft wine. Light tannins and acids.

★ **ROSEMOUNT ESTATE 1996 SHIRAZ-CABERNET SAUVIGNON, AUSTRALIA:** Jammy, candied, cherry-scented nose. Bright, firm and fairly intense; in a fruity style. Not fleshy or fat, but the dark berry flavor is brisk and penetrating. Finishes with notes of raspberry and black pepper.

$10–$20

★★★ **PENFOLDS 1994 BIN 389 CABERNET-SHIRAZ, SOUTH AUSTRALIA:** Opaque ruby. Brooding, superripe aromas of dark berries and mocha. Lush, but a firm spine of acidity gives the wine good flavor definition. Finishes firm and rather long, with harmonious tannins.

★★ **ROSEMOUNT ESTATE 1994 G-S-M, McLAREN VALE:** A blend of Grenache, Shiraz and Mourvèdre. Its bright, aromatic nose combines spicy, charred oak, black raspberry, mocha and pepper. Peppery and exotically oaky in the mouth, but with plenty of sappy supporting fruit. Tart currant and pomegranate flavors contribute to the wine's freshness.

★★ **YALUMBA 1994 BUSH VINE GRENACHE, BAROSSA:** Intriguing aromas of smoked meat, tobacco and earth. Sweet and silky, with an edge of acidity that gives shape to the mellow, maturing flavors. A smooth, interesting wine that puts on weight as it opens in the glass.

$20–$30

★★★ **LINDEMANS 1993 PYRUS, COONAWARRA:** A blend based on Cabernet. Pungent dark berry, orange rind, bitter chocolate, clove and eucalyptus aromas, plus hints of minerals and cedary oak. Sweet and powerfully fruity. Tangy acids brighten the plum, cassis and blackberry flavors.

★★★ **PENLEY ESTATE 1994 SHIRAZ-CABERNET, SOUTH AUSTRALIA:** Sappy black cherry, cassis, raspberry, cedar and chocolate aromas. Supple, thick and concentrated; mineral and spice notes give an impression of firmness and freshness.

SWEET AND FORTIFIED WINES

LONG BEFORE AUSTRALIA BECAME A RELIABLE SOURCE FOR DRY table wines, the country was renowned for its sweet and fortified wines, generally referred to as "stickies" in the home market. With few exceptions, Australia's port-style fortified wines are blends of grape varieties and vintages, ready to be consumed upon their release. Its fruit-driven dessert wines are often based on the same grapes—Sémillon and Sauvignon Blanc—as France's Sauternes.

AT THE TABLE: The port-style wines are best served at the end of a meal, with richer desserts or on their own. Serve the Sauternes-style wines with rich first courses such as foie gras, with blue cheeses toward the end of the meal or with a fruit-based dessert such as apricot tart.

THE BOTTOM LINE: Wines in each of the above categories range widely in price, but at the lower end of the spectrum the better examples offer stunning value.

Tasting Notes

$10–$20

★ ★ ★ CHAMBERS ROSEWOOD VINEYARDS NV LIQUEUR MUSCAT: Orange-bronze color. Fresh aromas of quince, orange skin and flower blossoms. Fairly viscous yet fresh. An exotic citrus quality gives delineation to the concentrated flavors. A long and stylish wine, and a terrific value.

★ ★ ★ CHATEAU REYNELLA 1981 VINTAGE PORT MUSEUM RELEASE, MCLAREN VALE: Initially high-toned, with aeration the truffley nose shows a complex mélange of black fruits, herbs, mocha, raisin and resin nuances. Strikingly fresh, very concentrated kirsch and cassis flavors complicated by raisin and tobacco notes. Really uncanny retention of youthful fruit given the age of the wine.

$20–$40

★ ★ ★ YALUMBA 1996 BOTRYTIS SÉMILLON-SAUVIGNON, FAMILY RESERVE: Knockout nose offers lively, botrytis-rich aromas of tropical fruits, peach, honey, licorice and spice. Viscous, buttery and extremely rich, with a note of apricot jam. Has just enough acidity to buffer the residual sugar. Nectarlike and amazingly fruity. Finishes with a refreshing bitter edge.

★ ★ ★ YALUMBA MUSEUM SHOW RESERVE NV RUTHERGLEN MUSCAT: Pale, green-edged tawny color. Aromas of toffee, coffee and raisin, plus a burnt, smoky aspect. Viscous in the mouth, with flavors of smoke and grilled nuts. A slight raisiny component is brightened by orange zest. A harmonious, silky wine that finishes with a firm edge.

NEW ZEALAND

NEW ZEALAND'S OCEAN-INFLUENCED CLIMATE YIELDS
wines with admirable fruit intensity and crisp acidity. In
general, New Zealand is markedly cooler than its neigh-
bor Australia, and its growing conditions are best suited
to white grape varieties. In recent years, the workhorse
grape Müller-Thurgau, an early-ripening, largely undistinguished German variety, has been supplanted by the
nobler Chardonnay and Sauvignon Blanc.

New Zealand's Cabernet Sauvignons and Merlots can
be lean, green and mean in cooler vintages, and virtually
undrinkable for those weaned on superripe California
reds. Increasingly, however, red wine grapes are being
planted in drier, warmer spots and today's reds show riper
flavors and more flesh on their bones. Pinot Noir in particular holds out considerable promise. At present,
though, the country's red wines are vastly overpriced for
the competitive American marketplace.

BEHIND THE SCENES: New Zealand's wine industry is
dominated by three major firms: Montana (which alone
accounts for nearly 50% of wine bottled), Corbans/
Cooks and the Villa Maria/Vidal/Esk Valley group,
which specializes in red wines mostly from the warmer
North Island.

THE BOTTOM LINE: The country's best limited-production
wines are fully priced for their quality. Happily, though,
better values come from larger wineries, whose wines are
also more likely to be found in export markets.

SAUVIGNON BLANC

NEW ZEALAND'S MOST ACCLAIMED VARIETY, SAUVIGNON BLANC here is generally a sharply focused, unoaked wine, with bracing acidity, excellent fruit intensity and a pungent citric-grassy-herbal character not unlike Sauvignon Blanc from France's Loire Valley.

AT THE TABLE: Sauvignon Blancs from ripe vintages make refreshing accompaniments to vegetable antipasti, light pastas, river fish and smoked salmon or trout.

THE BOTTOM LINE: The better New Zealand Sauvignon Blancs compare favorably with the finest Sauvignons anywhere in the world. Their prices are generally in the $10–$16 range, making them reasonable values in light of their quality, but there are few bargains.

Vintage Rating 1995/C 1996/A-

Tasting Notes

$10–$20

★★★★ **CLOUDY BAY 1996, MARLBOROUGH:** Pungent grassy-herbal nose, with tropical fruit notes of pineapple and papaya. Very ripe, fruity, and superconcentrated; has an almost three-dimensional texture. Perfectly integrated acidity gives the wine great backbone and grip. Explosive, palate-staining finish goes on and on. An extraordinary Sauvignon Blanc.

★★ **DE REDCLIFFE 1996, MARLBOROUGH:** Gooseberry nose shows game and floral nuances. Ripe and spicy in the mouth; rather thick and full-bodied. Has plenty of fruit to support the strong strain of acidity. Persistent aftertaste.

★★ **DE REDCLIFFE 1996 RESERVE, MARLBOROUGH:** Exotic aromas of passion fruit, orange peel, lichee and licorice. Sweet, fat and full in the mouth; has a slightly truffley character. Then surprisingly brisk and firm in the finish. A rich, easygoing Sauvignon Blanc with the palate presence of Chardonnay.

★★ **GROVE MILL 1996, MARLBOROUGH:** Tangy aromas of lime, orange peel and honey, plus faint candied and minty nuances. Quite supple and fairly dense, but fresh and delineated. Vibrant flavors similar to the aromas. Has a bit more ripeness and texture than most New Zealand Sauvignons. Lingering, sweet aftertaste.

★★ **NAUTILUS 1996, MARLBOROUGH:** Creamed corn and truffle aromas, along with exotic hints of tangerine and mango. Lemony, brisk and packed with fruit; rich and thick for Sauvignon. Strong acidity gives the wine firmness and shape.

★★ **PALLISER ESTATE 1996, MARLBOROUGH:** Aromas of spice and grass. Fat and full, with very sweet, somewhat atypical Chardonnay-like peach and pear flavors. But generous, mouth-filling, completely ripe and very long.

★★ **VILLA MARIA 1996 CELLAR SELECTION, MARLBOROUGH:** Loire-like gooseberry, mint and herbal scents. Silky and concentrated, with ripe acidity and a grassy note. Has noteworthy density of texture, like so many New Zealand Sauvignon Blancs. Persistent on the finish.

★ **MORTON ESTATE 1996, HAWKES BAY:** Pretty, reticent aromas of ripe citrus fruits and grass. Fresh fruit perked up by lively acidity. Has good depth and intensity of flavor. The strong finish is vibrant and persistent. Ripe and satisfying.

★ **STONELEIGH 1996, MARLBOROUGH:** Notes of pine and fresh herbs on the nose. Bright and penetrating in the mouth, with flavors of mint and tarragon. On the lean side, but doesn't lack for flavor intensity. A very brisk style of Sauvignon that should be served with food.

CHARDONNAY

NEW ZEALAND'S CHARDONNAYS RANGE FROM LEAN, REFRESHING, unoaked and fairly inexpensive to riper, richer, more textured, barrel-fermented wines that are comparable to premium California Chardonnays in price.

AT THE TABLE: Thanks to their brisk acidity and freshness of fruit, unoaked New Zealand Chardonnays can be used almost like Sauvignon Blancs, but oakier versions overwhelm delicately flavored dishes. Pair these latter wines with chicken and fish in cream sauces and pork or veal.

THE BOTTOM LINE: As a general rule, the larger, more export-minded producers are most likely to offer wines at palatable prices, and a number of succulent, food-friendly Chardonnays can be found in the $10–$18 range.

Vintage Rating 1995/C+ 1996/A-

Tasting Notes

$10–$20

★★ **MORTON ESTATE 1996, HAWKES BAY:** Herbs, butter and pineapple scents, along with a floral component. Lush and pineappley in the mouth; on the soft side. There is spicy oak on the ripe, lingering finish.

★★ **ST. CLAIR 1996, MARLBOROUGH:** Aromas of peach and pineapple. Focused and expressive in the mouth, with strong fruit. Notes of herbs, mint and licorice give the wine attractive freshness. Quite persistent aftertaste.

★ ★ **VILLA MARIA 1995 BARRIQUE FERMENTED RESERVE:** Butterscotch and pineapple on the nose. Rich, intensely flavored and well-balanced; pineapple flavor combines nicely with subtle oak. Has a suave texture and impressive ripeness.

★ ★ **VILLA MARIA 1995 CELLAR SELECTION, MARLBOROUGH/GISBORNE:** Highly aromatic pear, peach and tangerine nose. Dense and ripe, with bright acidity framing the fruit. Nicely balanced.

Splurgeworthy:

★ ★ ★ **CLOUDY BAY 1994, MARLBOROUGH:** Penetrating spiced peach and herbal aromas. Deep, very concentrated and intensely flavored; peach and apricot flavors are complicated by notes of spicy oak and coconut. Very long and firm on the aftertaste.

OTHER WHITE WINES

WHEN VINE YIELDS ARE CAREFULLY CONTROLLED, EVEN MÜLLER-Thurgau can be crisp and refreshing. Other commonly seen New Zealand whites include Riesling and Gewürztraminer, but intensely flavored examples are scarce.

Tasting Notes

$10–$20

★ **DE REDCLIFFE 1996 DRY RIESLING, MARLBOROUGH:** Tangy nose of pine, lime and pineapple. Supple and ripe in the mouth, with good texture for Riesling. Flavors of pineapple and grapefruit. An easygoing rather than austere style of Riesling, with soft acidity.

★ **DE REDCLIFFE 1996 SÉMILLON RESERVE, AUCKLAND:** Lime, honey and herbs on the nose. Fat but reasonably brisk in the mouth, with the honey and herbal character following through. Nicely balanced, distinctly dry Sémillon.

★ **GROVE MILL 1996 RIESLING, MARLBOROUGH:** Somewhat floral aromas of mint and orange peel. Slightly sweet and easygoing in the mouth, with good intensity, sound acids and an intriguing red berry note. The minty nuance carries through on the palate. Distinctly drier on the firm finish.

SOUTH AFRICA

SOUTH AFRICAN WINE RETURNED TO AMERICAN STORES after U.S. trade sanctions on South Africa were lifted in 1991. Several of the first brands to arrive here were simply not ready for prime time, and have already disappeared. But quality has improved rapidly in just the past few years, reflecting the increasingly international outlook of South Africa's winemakers. Today, the best South African wines make for satisfying drinking and generally very good value.

WINE GEOGRAPHY: South Africa's wine-producing areas are located in the extreme southwestern tip of the country, close to Cape Town. Grapes are grown in a generally warm and dry climate, in vineyards that rely on irrigation. In recent years, fresher, more complex wines have come from cooler spots closer to the Atlantic or Indian oceans.

BEHIND THE SCENES: Although the cultivation of grapes here dates back more than 300 years, South Africa only relatively recently began to focus on the production of table wine. Traditionally, many of the country's growers sold their grapes to co-ops, which turned the juice into distilled alcohol, sherry or port. Even today, the Cape wine industry is dominated by giant cooperatives whose wine is generally of middling quality. Most of the more interesting wines shipped to America come from smaller, independent producers.

THE BOTTOM LINE: Some very good values in both red and white dry table wines.

WHITE WINES

WHITE WINES ACCOUNT FOR ABOUT THREE QUARTERS OF SOUTH Africa's exports. The prolific and versatile Chenin Blanc (called Steen in South Africa) is the most widely planted variety, making generally clean, somewhat simple but refreshing wines ranging from dry to very sweet, as well as sparkling wines. Riesling is also popular. Plantings of Chardonnay and Sauvignon Blanc have surged in recent years.

AT THE TABLE: Use these wines as you would the same varieties from California, but keep in mind that because South Africa's whites are generally less concentrated they are likely to be overwhelmed by more assertive flavors.

THE BOTTOM LINE: South Africa is becoming an increasingly interesting source of white wine bargains, as few are priced above $15 and most are less than $10.

Vintage Rating 1995/B- 1996/B+

Tasting Notes

UNDER $10

★★ **GROOT CONSTANTIA 1995 WEISSER RIESLING, CONSTANTIA:** Copper-tinged straw. Pungent resin, spice and earth nose perked up by a hint of orange peel. Supple and slightly sweet in the mouth, with a flavor of fruit salad. Has a tactile mouth feel, bright acidity, and a firm, lingering finish.

★ **BOSCHENDAL 1996 SAUVIGNON BLANC, PAARL:** Musky, complex aromas of fresh herbs, lemon and lime. Penetrating, grassy and lemon-limey on the palate, with nicely integrated acidity. Fresh and firm.

★ **CAPE BAY 1996 CHARDONNAY, WESTERN CAPE:** Green apple, cinnamon and nutmeg on the nose, along with a juicyfruit minty/floral quality. Has good spicy intensity and creamy texture. Spicy oak flavors are complicated by hints of peach and fresh pineapple.

★ **DEWETSHOF 1996 BON VALLON CHARDONNAY, ROBERTSON:** Smoke, lemon cream and melon on the nose. Textured, round and easy; shows a juicy quality and sound varietal character. Lingering, ripe finish.

$10–$15

★★ **NEIL ELLIS 1996 CHARDONNAY, ELGIN:** Butterscotch, peach, pear and curry aromas. Rich, spicy and complex, with a restrained sweetness. Crisp, lingering, very dry finish shows smoke and spice notes.

★★ **MULDERBOSCH 1996 SAUVIGNON BLANC, STELLENBOSCH:** Fresh nose combines grapefruit, lemon sorbet, green herbs and a hint of asparagus. Silky-rich and creamy, but perked up by crisp citric acidity. Spicy and complex, with finishing flavors of lime and fennel.

RED WINES

AMONG RED TYPES, CINSAUT (SPELLED CINSAULT IN FRANCE), Shiraz (Syrah) and a uniquely South African wine called Pinotage (a cross between Pinot Noir and Cinsaut) are the varietal wines most likely to be found in the U.S. market. In recent years, however, producers have increasingly turned to the popular international standbys Cabernet Sauvignon, Merlot and Pinot Noir. Most of South Africa's red wines offer the advantage of early drinkability.

AT THE TABLE: Pinotage goes well with roast chicken and beef stew. Cabernets can be served with lamb chops, while Shiraz is a good match for turkey, hamburger or barbecued ribs.

THE BOTTOM LINE: Even though South Africa's reds are climbing in price, the best bottles from smaller producers generally possess the character to justify their prices.

Vintage Rating 1994/A- 1995/B- 1996/B+

Tasting Notes

UNDER $10

★ ★ **BEYERSKLOOF 1996 PINOTAGE, STELLENBOSCH:** Aromatic cherry, pepper, spice and herb nose. Supple, smooth and sweet in the mouth, with notes of kirsch and dark berries. Fruity and charming.

★ **CAPE INDABA 1996 PINOTAGE, COASTAL REGION:** Bitter cherry, iron and smoke on the nose, plus a slight roasted aspect. Supple and smoky in the mouth; the iron flavor repeats. Finishes slightly dry, but the tannins are light.

★ **SPRINGBOK 1995 CABERNET SAUVIGNON, WESTERN CAPE:** High-toned plum, currant and herbal aromas. Fat and sweet, with currant and tar notes. Finishes with soft tannins.

$10–$20

★ ★ ★ **CLOS MALVERNE 1995 CABERNET SAUVIGNON, STELLENBOSCH:** Saturated ruby-red color. Sweet aromas of red currants, smoke, tobacco and cinnamon. Thick and truffley in the mouth; harmonious and silky. Really loaded with fruit, and complicated by a vegetal nuance.

★ ★ ★ **CLOS MALVERNE 1996 PINOTAGE, STELLENBOSCH:** Fresh ruby-tinged red. Exotic aromas of boysenberrry, banana and woodsmoke. Thick and concentrated; raspberry, strawberry and cinnamon flavors. Finishes with dusty tannins and lingering sweet fruit.

★ ★ ★ **KANONKOP 1995 PINOTAGE, STELLENBOSCH:** Nose features tobacco, smoke and leather. Lush, deep and concentrated; strong red berry flavors along with notes of leather. Multilayered and long on personality. Very persistent on the aftertaste; tannins are ripe and fine.

★★★**SAXENBURG 1995 SHIRAZ, STELLENBOSCH:** Impressive ruby-red color. Cassis, raspberry, kirsch and spearmint on the nose. Sweet, supple, berry flavor fills the mouth; concentrated and deep. Finishes with thoroughly ripe tannins and subtle length. Really lovely sweetness.

★★★**WARWICK 1994 TRILOGY, STELLENBOSCH:** A blend of Cabernet Sauvignon, Cabernet Franc and Merlot. Highly aromatic plum, currant and spice nose; hint of meat. Sweet, palate-staining fruit is supple and harmonious with sound balancing acidity.

★★**BACKSBURG 1993 SHIRAZ, PAARL:** Warm, inviting aromas of raspberry, cassis, cinnamon and loam. Fresh and spicy, with clearly delineated black fruit flavor. Finishes with firm, even tannins.

★★**NEIL ELLIS 1994 CABERNET SAUVIGNON, STELLENBSCH:** Complex nose combines currants, black raspberry, tobacco and spice, plus a woodsy nuance. Juicy, penetrating dark berry flavor; firm of texture and rather stylish. A dryer, serious style of Cabernet: there's more going on here than simply fruit flavor.

★★**LA MOTTE ESTATE 1992, FRANSCHOEK VALLEY:** Mellow aromas of roasted plums, woodsmoke, coffee and tobacco. A suave and understated Cabernet-Merlot blend offering good volume and an elegant shape. Tart cranberry and cherry notes give clarity to the flavors.

★★**RUST EN VREDE 1994 SHIRAZ, STELLENBOSCH:** Woodsmoke and red berry aromas, along with a vegetal complexity. Fresh, nuanced and slightly gamy; has a roasted aspect. The tannins are refined and the finish is complex. Possesses the suave texture and firm structure of a French wine.

★★**WARWICK 1993 SHIRAZ, PAARL:** Warm, inviting aromas of raspberry, cassis, cinnamon and loam. Fresh and spicy in the mouth, with clearly delineated black fruit flavor. Finishes with firm, even tannins.

★**KANONKOP 1995 KADETTE, STELLENBOSCH:** Juicy berry and smoked meat flavor; has the texture and sweetness of Pinot Noir. Crisp acidity gives the wine good snap. Finishes with harmonious tannins and a raspberry note.

YOUR PERSONAL TASTING JOURNAL

CHILE

THE CHILEAN WINE COUNTRY, SPREAD OVER A SERIES of valleys between the Pacific Ocean and the towering Andes, is an almost Edenic zone for grape growing. Blue skies rule during the growing season, and rain is rare. As a result, irrigation—made possible by melting snow from the mountains—is required in nearly all of Chile's vineyards. Easy access to water helps explain the high vine yields and relatively modest concentration of most Chilean wines—and accounts for their low prices.

Today, most exported Chilean wine is soundly made, thanks in part to an infusion of capital and technology from Europe and California. Only the best bottles, however, possess the flavor intensity and personality to capture the affections of American wine lovers with access to a world of vinous bargains. Still, the list of ambitious producers is growing, and Chile must now be viewed as more than simply a source of decent cheap wine.

THE BOTTOM LINE: Chile's cleanly made wines with single-digit prices should be near the top of the list for the budget-minded wine drinker.

WHITE WINES

CHILE'S CHARDONNAYS ARE RIPE AND ACCESSIBLE WINES WITH LITTLE pretense, though recent investments in stainless-steel vats for temperature-controlled fermentation, and in new oak barrels, now enable the better producers to bottle fresher and richer wines. Sauvignon Blancs are typically crisp and fresh.

AT THE TABLE: Chile's Chardonnays are excellent accompaniments to simple chicken dishes and delicate river fish like perch and flounder. The Sauvignon Blancs can be served as aperitifs. You can also use them as the base for shellfish broths or soups.

THE BOTTOM LINE: Chile's better Chardonnays and Sauvignon Blancs are some of the best white wine values on the market.

Vintage Rating 1995/A- 1996/A

Tasting Notes

UNDER $10

★★CONCHA Y TORO 1996 CASILLERO DEL DIABLO CHARDONNAY, CASABLANCA VALLEY: Cool aromas of pineapple, pear, toffee and buttery oak. Rich and nicely concentrated; good spicy character keeps it fresh. Ripe, lingering finish.

★★SANTA RITA 1996 120 SAUVIGNON BLANC, LONTUE VALLEY: Ripe, spicy, pear, herb and melon aromas. Fat, spicy and layered; has the silky palate presence of Chardonnay. Rich, persistent aftertaste.

★BEL ARBOR 1996 CHARDONNAY, VALLE CENTRAL: Spiced apple and canteloupe on the nose. Fat, gentle and easygoing but fresh. Very good fruit and palate presence. Hint of sweetness is countered by firm, slightly hard-edged acidity.

★CASA LAPOSTOLLE 1996 SAUVIGNON BLANC, RAPEL VALLEY: Cool aromas of lemon peel, fresh herbs and spices. Supple, ripe and creamy; thick and mouth-filling.

★SANTA MONICA 1996 CHARDONNAY, RANCAGUA: Sweet scents of peach, licorice and tarragon, plus an intriguing stony nuance. Fresh, spicy and fairly intense; juicy rather than fat. Fresh and persistent on the firm finish.

★SANTA RITA 1996 MEDALLA REAL CHARDONNAY, CASABLANCA: Aromas of lemon cream pie and spicy oak. Fresh lemon and spice flavors; has good intensity and weight. Cleanly made and ripe on the aftertaste.

★WALNUT CREST 1997 CHARDONNAY, RAPEL VALLEY: Fruit cocktail nose, with citric and spice notes and a slightly candied quality. Juicy and fruity in the mouth; a slight spritz of CO_2 gives the wine good vivacity.

$10–$15

★★CASA LAPOSTOLLE 1995 CUVÉE ALEXANDRE CHARDONNAY, CASABLANCA VALLEY: Smoky, spicy oak plus a hint of asparagus on the nose. Rich, very ripe and substantial, with a velvety texture and a suggestion of truffle in the mouth. Lots of spicy, toasty oak on the finish; really grips the palate.

★CONCHA Y TORO 1995 MARQUES DE CASA CONCHA CHARDONNAY, MAIPO VALLEY: Very ripe, buttery aromas of creamed corn, apricot and smoke. Silky but bright in the mouth, with very good flavor intensity and a stony bite. Sweet, lingering aftertaste.

RED WINES

CABERNET SAUVIGNON IS CHILE'S SINGLE MOST IMPORTANT EXPORT variety. These wines tend to be lush, fruity and exuberant, and best suited for drinking within three or four years after the vintage. A number of Chile's wineries have planted Merlot to capitalize on the bottomless worldwide thirst for this variety.

AT THE TABLE: Try these Cabernets with flank steak or lamb chops. Chile's fruit-driven Merlots are perfect with hamburgers.

THE BOTTOM LINE: Chile is one of the world's best sources of competently made red wine under $10. The slightly more expensive versions often justify their price premium by providing greater character and concentration.

Vintage Rating 1994/B 1995/B+ 1996/B+

Tasting Notes

UNDER $10

★★**CALITERRA 1996 MERLOT, VALLE CENTRAL:** Cherry, mocha and smoky oak on the nose. Soft and smooth, but juicy and nicely delineated; flavors of blackberry and black currant. Finishes with cherry flavor and fine tannins. Plush Merlot texture at a remarkably low price.

★★**SANTA RITA 1995 120 CABERNET SAUVIGNON, RAPEL VALLEY:** Lively black cherry nose hints at smoked meat. Rich and expansive yet rather laid-back; flavors of cherry and red currant. In a drier style. Finishes with fine-grained tannins and a grapey note.

★★**UNDURRAGA 1995 CABERNET SAUVIGNON, COLCHAGUA VALLEY:** Ripe aromas of currants, soy sauce and leather. Sweet, shapely and perfumed in the mouth; currant and plum flavors offer very good intensity. Finishes fairly long and ripe, with firm but supple tannins and a toasty nuance.

★**CALITERRA 1995 CABERNET SAUVIGNON, VALLE CENTRAL:** Cherry/berry and eucalyptus aromas. Supple, fresh, cherry and dark berry flavors are enticingly sweet. Finishes with soft tannins.

★**CONCHA Y TORO 1996 CABERNET SAUVIGNON-MERLOT, VALLE CENTRAL:** Tangy cherry, raspberry and herbal aromas. Similar flavors in the mouth. Supple and fresh. Finishes with light tannins and sweet fruit.

★**CONCHA Y TORO 1996 CASILLERO DEL DIABLO MERLOT, RAPEL VALLEY:** Perfumed nose of black raspberry and earth. Black fruit (cassis, blackberry) and licorice flavors offer good intensity. Juicy and firm. Needs aeration before serving.

★**SAINT MORILLON 1995 MERLOT, LONTUE:** Modestly saturated medium red. Inviting aromas of cassis, plum, chocolate, tobacco and mint. Flavors of soft, sweet berries; not particularly concentrated but sappy and easygoing. Finishes with ripe, smooth tannins.

★ SANTA MARVISTA 1995 MERLOT, RAPEL: Good deep red-ruby color. Licorice and black cherry on the nose. Fat, soft and truffley in the mouth, with a jammy cherry flavor and low acidity.

$10–$15

★ ★ ★ CASA LAPOSTOLLE 1995 CUVÉE ALEXANDRE MERLOT, RAPEL VALLEY: Impressive ruby color. Bright aromas of cassis, black cherry, licorice and beefsteak tomato. Smooth, supple, ripe and deep on the palate; enticing, sweet notes of cocoa and woodsmoke. Concentrated and velvety. Long, ripely tannic finish.

★ ★ CALITERRA 1994 CABERNET SAUVIGNON RESERVA, MAIPO VALLEY: Expressive aromas of black plum, tobacco, and eucalyptus. Sweet, smooth and stuffed with fruit; has enough acidity to maintain its shape. Hints of iron and tobacco on the long aftertaste. Loads of personality.

★ ★ CASA LAPOSTOLLE 1995 CUVÉE ALEXANDRE CABERNET SAUVIGNON, RAPEL VALLEY: Expressive nose combines tart cranberry and pomegranate, plus a meaty quality. Fat, rich and chocolatey, with a loamy nuance. Stuffed with fruit. Finishes with dusty, ripe tannins.

★ ★ SANTA CAROLINA 1992 CABERNET SAUVIGNON GRAN RESERVA, MAIPO VALLEY: Roasted black plum and a mellow note of smoky oak on the nose. Slightly gamy, roasted plum flavor complicated by hints of minerals and tobacco. In a drier, leaner style, but has a firm acid and tannin structure.

★ CONCHA Y TORO 1994 MARQUES DE CASA CONCHA CABERNET SAUVIGNON, MAIPO VALLEY: Deep ruby-red color. Slightly medicinal aromas of black cherry, currant, leather and herbs. Black cherry and cassis flavors on the palate; in a tougher, adult style but has good gutsy fruit. Fairly tannic.

★ COUSINO MACUL 1994 MERLOT, MAIPO VALLEY: Light-medium red. Aromas of red currant, tobacco and smoky oak. A Merlot of modest complexity, but has a sappy quality that gives it freshness. Firm, dry, lightly tannic finish.

★ SANTA CAROLINA 1993 MERLOT GRAN RESERVA, MAULE VALLEY: Cherry/berry nose, with nuances of tobacco. Supple and substantial on the palate, with the wine's sweetness balanced by a slight tart edge. Plum and black currant flavor carries through to the lightly tannic finish.

ARGENTINA

ARGENTINA IS ACTUALLY THE FIFTH-LARGEST WINE producer in the world, but until recently its rather rustic and often somewhat oxidized wines were consumed mostly by wine-loving locals and offered little interest to export markets. Today, however, a growing number of Argentina's wineries are producing wines of international quality and appeal.

GRAPES & STYLES: For American consumers, Argentina's red wines—generally moderately priced in the $10–$15 range—are of greatest interest, led by Malbec and Cabernet Sauvignon. Malbec, a grape that was once important in Bordeaux and is still the backbone of the burly "black wine" of Cahors in southwestern France, has traditionally been Argentina's most widely planted red, producing dense, somewhat coarse wines with plenty of aromatic interest and noteworthy depth of fruit.

WINE GEOGRAPHY: Argentina's most important wine region, Mendoza, is considerably hotter than the grape-growing areas of neighboring Chile. The effects of this heat are partly mitigated by planting at high altitudes.

BEHIND THE SCENES: As local consumption of wine has declined in recent years, a number of wineries have looked urgently to export markets. Under the leadership of the massive Peñaflor winery, which also operates Trapiche, Argentina's wine industry is in the process of modernizing. Vines are being planted in somewhat cooler areas, yielding more concentrated fruit flavors. And the country's previously somewhat insular producers have benefited from the experience of visiting enologists from France and California.

THE BOTTOM LINE: Moderately priced, sturdy red wines offer plenty of aromatic interest.

RED WINES

ARGENTINA'S BEST REDS, MOST FROM CABERNET, MALBEC AND blends of the two varieties, offer aromatic, spicy currant and black cherry aromas, good texture and noteworthy depth of flavor. The country's red wines in the $10 price category tend to be more concentrated than similarly priced bottles from Chile.

AT THE TABLE: Argentine Cabernets are excellent with lamb shanks, as are the Malbecs, which can also be served with roast beef or pork chops.

THE BOTTOM LINE: Argentina's reds are generally a bit more expensive than their counterparts from Chile, and there are fewer striking values to be found. A handful of very good wines in the $15 range offer the best quality/price rapport.

Vintage Rating 1994/B 1995/A- 1996/A-

Tasting Notes

UNDER $12

★★**BODEGA NORTON 1995 MALBEC, MENDOZA:** Very dark red-ruby. Sweet cherries, licorice, chocolate and tar on the nose, along with a suggestion of cooked fruit. Rich, supple and concentrated; flavors of black cherry and chocolate. Finish is sweet and persistent.

★ **TRAPICHE 1993 OAK CASK MALBEC, MENDOZA:** Aromas of black plum, oak spice and tar. Supple and soft in the mouth; lush, broad fruit offers good sweetness but only modest delineation. Light tannins will not stand in the way of immediate enjoyment.

★ **TRUMPETER 1996 MERLOT, TUPUNGATO:** Cherry, raspberry, mint and spicy oak aromas. Bright and spicy in the mouth; not fat or fleshy but sweet and appealing. Finishes firm and ripe.

★ **BODEGAS WEINERT 1993 CARRASCAL, MENDOZA:** Dusty aromas of iron and dried rose, a bit like Nebbiolo. Smooth and fairly intense, but on the dry side; not at all plush but offers good balance and flavor intensity. The iron note repeats on the palate. Opens up nicely on the lightly tannic finish. Needs to be served with food.

$12–$20

★★★**BODEGAS WEINERT 1992 MALBEC, MENDOZA:** Extravagant aromas of blueberry, leather, smoke; a raisiny superripeness. Not for the faint-hearted. Big, sweet, rich and generous; a pliant, deep wine with briary, peppery, ironlike flavors and extraordinary sweetness. Dry-edged, slightly peppery finish. A flamboyant example of Argentine Malbec.

★★**CATENA 1994 CABERNET SAUVIGNON AGRELO VINEYARD, MENDOZA:** Aromas of cassis, earth, leather and smoky, vanillin oak. Rich and sweet in the mouth, with tobacco flavors. Firmly structured but not hard. A substantial wine whose solid tannins are balanced by fruit.

★★**TRAPICHE 1994 MEDALLA, MENDOZA:** Plum, dark berry and black pepper on the nose. Spicy and bright in the mouth, with very good intensity and nicely delineated berry flavor; pliant and easy to drink. Ripe, lingering finish. A tangy blend based on Cabernet Sauvignon.

WHITE WINES

UNTIL RECENTLY, ARGENTINA'S WHITE WINES TENDED TO BE OVERLY oxidized or lacking in fruit. The main grape was Pedro Ximénez, a variety used in sherry production in Spain. International varieties like Chardonnay, Sauvignon Blanc and Sémillon are now widely planted.

AT THE TABLE: Argentina's Chardonnays go well with roast chicken, as well as with grilled swordfish and tuna.

THE BOTTOM LINE: There are good values to be found, but careful selection is essential.

Vintage Rating 1995/B- 1996/B+

Tasting Notes

UNDER $12

★★**ALAMOS RIDGE 1995 CHARDONNAY, MENDOZA:** Tangy nose combines quince, pineapple and honey. Thick and concentrated, but nicely focused; flavors of tropical fruit, honey, licorice, grapefruit and watercress. A slightly sweet Chardonnay but one with very good balancing acidity. Finishes firm and long. A lot of wine for the price.

★**TRUMPETER 1996 CHARDONNAY, TUPUNGATO:** Bright aromas of herbs and pear, plus suggestions of smoke and spice. Supple and fresh in the mouth, with medium weight and decent flavor intensity. Not especially complex, but holds its shape and shows some finishing persistence.

$12–$20

★★**CATENA 1995 CHARDONNAY AGRELO VINEYARD, MENDOZA:** Fairly deep gold-tinged straw color. Exotic, tangy aromas of honey, grilled nuts and oak spice. Fat and spicy in the mouth; thick and slightly sweet, but reasonably fresh. Very ripe flavors of honey and apricot.

Starting a Wine Cellar

Why collect wine when more than 95% of the world's wines are meant to be consumed within a year or two after release? I can give you two compelling reasons: first, a small percentage of the greatest wines—mostly reds, but many dry white and sweet wines, too—need anywhere from a few years to several decades to achieve their mellow, multifaceted maturity. By then you won't be able to find them or afford them—unless you already own them. Second, the wines you age yourself will probably be in better condition than most older bottles you'll find withering away on retailers' shelves.

All you need is a place that is dark, humid but not too damp, reasonably cool (preferably below 60 degrees but definitely below 70) and safe from daily temperature fluctuations. That, plus the following suggestions, will help you avoid the most commonly made mistakes in wine collecting.

BEGIN WITH A GAME PLAN: Some wine lovers buy without making a realistic estimate of their future needs and quickly accumulate more bottles than they can possibly drink over a lifetime. Other collectors cellar too many wines that mature quickly and fade or overload on one type of wine.

Do some reading, or take a course on the world's major wine regions, or join a wine club that holds frequent tastings before you embark on collecting. Tastings of older vintages can show you what to expect from the wines you are laying down. If you realize now, for example, that you prefer the youthful, spicy red fruit flavors of Pinot Noir to the earthy notes this variety shows in its golden years, you won't waste time and space aging these wines.

DON'T OVERLOOK WHITE WINE, BUT CHOOSE CAREFULLY: It's a matter of personal taste, of course, but as a rule of thumb you may want to stock your cellar with a rough ratio of three reds to one white. Remember that most white wines don't reward extended cellaring and that it's always possible to find an excellent, ready-to-drink young white wine at your local shop. Moreover, many dry whites—with the notable exception of some top Chardonnays, Rieslings and Loire Valley Chenin Blancs—quickly lose their freshness and begin to oxidize if subjected to less-than-wonderful storage conditions. On the other hand, far too many of the world's greatest, collection-worthy whites are consumed before they have reached their flavor-filled potential. A young Alsatian Riesling might be austere today, offering only a hint of its future richness and personality. How can you know which whites to cellar? Ask around, read up and, best of all, taste for yourself.

DON'T OVERBUY BORDEAUX: Red Bordeaux has traditionally been the foundation of most great cellars—owing not only to the wine's slow development and legendary longevity, but to its track record for price appreciation. (Case lots of classified-growth Bordeaux from the best years remain the safest investments in the notoriously conservative auction market.) If you're cellaring wine to savor rather than resell, keep in mind that a top-notch red Bordeaux may need at least a decade of aging, and may go through a muted stage during which it will disappoint your expectations.

Some non-Bordeaux, world-class reds to look for: Hermitage and Côte Rôtie from the Rhône Valley; Italy's Killer Bs: Barolo, Barbaresco and Brunello; and California's Cabernet Sauvignons. Red Burgundy, though tricky to buy due to high prices and limited production, can be transcendently good, and is infinitely versatile with food. The underappreciated wines of Provence and the Languedoc deliver an exhilarating range of spicy, herbal flavors. Spain's already well-aged Rioja *reservas* and *gran reservas* offer the elegance of claret without the weight—or the wait. Many of the wines above will provide delicious drinking soon after reaching wine store shelves, yet can still improve in bottle for a decade or more.

DON'T LOSE IT ON A SINGLE VINTAGE: Collectors often trample one other in a rush to acquire wines from vintages hyped by the wine press—almost invariably the superripe years. Yet these vintages frequently yield wines that are fiery with alcohol or short on balancing acidity. Drought conditions common in hot years can produce tannic monsters that may require decades to soften. Although the so-called great years may be your best bet for *investing* in wine, they do not always provide the most user-friendly bottles to enjoy with a meal. Good wines from less ripe vintages will

THE WELL-ROUNDED WINE CELLAR

RED WINES (75%), 75 bottles

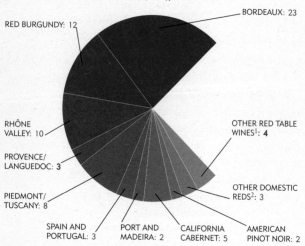

BORDEAUX: 23

RED BURGUNDY: 12

RHÔNE VALLEY: 10

PROVENCE/ LANGUEDOC: 3

PIEDMONT/ TUSCANY: 8

SPAIN AND PORTUGAL: 3

PORT AND MADEIRA: 2

CALIFORNIA CABERNET: 5

AMERICAN PINOT NOIR: 2

OTHER DOMESTIC REDS[2]: 3

OTHER RED TABLE WINES[1]: 4

WHITE WINES (25%), 25 bottles

WHITE BURGUNDY: 8

ALSACE RIESLING: 3

GERMAN RIESLING: 4

CHAMPAGNE: 1

WEST COAST CHARDONNAY: 2

DESSERT WINES[3]: 3

OTHER WHITE TABLE WINES[4]: 4

[1] Other Italian Reds; Cabernet and Shiraz from Australia, Southwest France, the Loire Valley; etc.

[2] California Merlots, "Rhône clones" and Zinfandels; Washington State Cabernets and Merlots.

[3] Sauternes and Late-Harvest Wines from the Loire Valley, Alsace and Germany, etc.

[4] Dry Wines from Bordeaux, the Loire Valley, Alsace, Northeastern Italy, Oregon and Washingon State, Australia and New Zealand, etc.

often prove far more flexible with food because of their thirst-quenching acidity and subtler flavors.

REMEMBER SWEET AND FORTIFIED WINES: Just as no self-respecting food lover would think of leaving the table after the meat course, no wine lover wants to end a great meal on a dry note. The best Sauternes, along with late-harvest wines from Germany, Alsace and the Loire Valley, are ideal candidates for cellaring because they require a decade or two of aging to unleash their volatile esters. But because these lovely "sticky" wines are generally made in small quantities, they tend to disappear early from retail shops and thus deserve space in your cellar. So do vintage ports. These special-occasion fortified wines can take up to 25 years to reach their full, mellow maturity and can last for generations. You may drink only a couple of bottles of vintage port a year, but no serious cellar is complete without them.

THINK BIG, THINK SMALL: At a dinner party for eight, a bottle of wine (750 ml) will give everyone one small glass; a magnum (1.5 liters) will please your guests twice. Magnums also age more slowly due to their greater mass. And a few magnums of nutty, mature Champagne will dazzle your guests on special occasions.

It's also wise to think small. Sometimes a half-bottle is all you want, or a half-bottle of white for starters and a half-bottle of red for the main course. Half-bottles of luxury dessert wines are a perfect size, since such rich wines are best served in small doses. Wines high in sugar, alcohol and acidity are more resistant to oxidation, so you should not have to worry about premature aging in smaller bottles.

TASTE 'EM IF YOU GOT 'EM: How do you know if a wine is ready unless you taste it? Pop a cork from time to time, and judge for yourself. Thanks to later harvesting and modern winemaking techniques, today's wines are often accessible in their youth, even if they are capable of extended aging. Besides, storage conditions vary and your wines may reach maturity a lot faster or slower than the wine pundits suggest.

Where to Buy Wine

Although the American landscape is dotted with many thousands of wine and liquor shops, only a small percentage of these take wine seriously. Buying and stocking the good stuff takes a special effort on the part of the merchant, not to mention good connections with the most quality-conscious importers.

Here is a list of retail merchants who can be relied upon to carry many of the wines recommended in this guide—or to special order wines for you at your request. Retailers are listed alphabetically by city and state.

Top Wine Retailers in America

SPORTSMAN'S FINE
WINES & SPIRITS
Phoenix, AZ
602-955-7730

NORTH BERKELEY
WINE
Berkeley, CA
510-848-8910
800-266-6585

HI-TIME WINE
CELLARS
Costa Mesa, CA
714-650-8463
800-331-3005

WALLY'S FOOD,
WINES AND SPIRITS
Los Angeles, CA
310-475-0606
800-892-5597

THE WINE HOUSE
Los Angeles, CA
310-479-3731
800-626-9463

BELTRAMO'S WINE
& SPIRITS
Menlo Park, CA
650-325-2806

DRAEGER'S
SUPERMARKET
Menlo Park, CA
650-688-0688
800-642-9463

WINE EXCHANGE
Orange, CA
714-974-1454
800-769-4639

ST. HELENA WINE
MERCHANTS
St. Helena, CA
707-963-7888
800-729-9463

PLUMPJACK
WINES
San Francisco, CA
415-346-9870
888-415-9463

THE WINE CLUB
San Francisco, CA
415-512-9086
800-966-7835

THE WINE HOUSE
LIMITED
San Francisco, CA
415-495-8486

WINE CASK
Santa Barbara, CA
805-966-9463

MISSION WINES
South Pasadena, CA
626-403-9463

PRIMA TRATTORIA E
NEGOZIO DI VINI
Walnut Creek, CA
510-935-7780

LIQUOR MART
Boulder, CO
303-449-3374
800-597-4440

APPLEJACK LIQUORS
Wheatridge, CO
303-233-3331
800-879-5225

HORSENECK WINE &
LIQUOR
Greenwich, CT
203-869-8944

FOREMOST SUNSET
CORNERS
Miami, FL
305-271-8492

ABC FINE WINE &
SPIRITS
Tampa, FL
813-876-5330

B-21 FINE WINE &
SPIRITS
Tarpon Springs, FL
813-937-5049

DEXTER'S OF
WINTER PARK
Winter Park, FL
407-629-1150

ANSLEY WINE
MERCHANTS
Atlanta, GA
404-876-6790

BUCKHEAD FINE
WINE
Atlanta, GA
404-231-8566

R. FIELD WINE
COMPANY
Honolulu, HA
808-596-9463
800-524-4275

GOLD STANDARD
Chicago, IL
773-935-9400

SAM'S WINES &
SPIRITS
Chicago, IL
312-664-4394
800-777-9137

FAMOUS LIQUORS
Forest Park, IL
708-366-2500

SCHAEFER'S
Škokie, IL
847-673-5711
800-833-9463

THE PARTY SOURCE
Bellevue, KY
606-291-4007

MARTIN WINE
CELLAR
New Orleans, LA
504-899-7411
800-298-4274

NORTH CHARLES
FINE WINE & SPIRITS
Baltimore, MD
410-377-4655

WELLS DISCOUNT
LIQUORS
Baltimore, MD
410-435-2700

JAYCO LIQUORS
Elkton, MD
410-398-4744
800-528-9463

STATE LINE LIQUORS
Elkton, MD
410-398-3838
800-446-9463

BROOKLINE LIQUOR
MART
Boston, MA
617-731-6644

MARTY'S FINE
WINES GOURMET
FOOD SPIRITS
Newton, MA
617-332-1230

BIG Y WINES &
LIQUORS
Northampton, MA
413-584-7775

YANKEE SPIRITS INC.
Sturbridge, MA
508-347-2231

VILLAGE CORNER
Ann Arbor, MI
313-995-1818

HASKELL'S INC.
Minneapolis, MN
612-333-2434

SURDYK'S LIQUOR
Minneapolis, MN
612-379-3232

GOMER'S MIDTOWN
FINE WINES &
SPIRITS
Kansas City, MO
816-931-4170

THE WINE
MERCHANT LTD.
St. Louis, MO
314-863-6282

BROWN DERBY INT'L
WINE CENTER
Springfield, MO
417-883-4066

CAROLINA WINE
COMPANY
Raleigh, NC
919-852-0236
888-317-4499

CARLO RUSSO'S
WINE & SPIRIT
WORLD
Ho-Ho-Kus, NJ
201-444-2033

POP'S WINES &
SPIRITS
Island Park, NY
516-431-0025

ASTOR WINES AND
SPIRITS
New York, NY
212-674-7500

CORK & BOTTLE
New York, NY
212-838-5300

CROSSROADS WINES
AND LIQUORS
New York, NY
212-924-3060

GARNET WINES &
LIQUORS
New York, NY
212-772-3211

MORRELL & CO.
New York, NY
212-688-9370

PARK AVENUE
LIQUOR SHOP
New York, NY
212-685-2442

SHERRY-LEHMANN
New York, NY
212-838-7500

67 WINE & SPIRITS
New York, NY
212-724-6767

WALDORF WINES &
SPIRITS
New York, NY
212-288-1800

ZACHYS WINE AND
LIQUOR, INC.
Scarsdale, NY
914-723-0241

PARKHILL'S LIQUORS
& WINES
Tulsa, OK
918-742-4187

LINER & ELSEN, LTD.
Portland, OR
503-241-9463

PORTLAND WINE
MERCHANTS
Portland, OR
503-234-4399
888-520-8466

PREMIUM WINE &
SPIRITS SHOPS
Harrisburg, PA
717-783-8089

NASHVILLE WINE &
SPIRITS
Nashville, TN
615-292-2676

TWIN LIQUORS
Austin, TX
512-323-2775

WIGGY'S
Austin, TX
512-474-9463

MARTY'S
MERCHANTS OF FINE
FOODS
Dallas, TX
214-526-7796
800-627-8971

POGO'S BEVERAGES
Dallas, TX
214-350-8989

SIGEL'S BEVERAGES
Dallas, TX
214-350-1271

RICHARD'S LIQUORS
& FINE WINES
Houston, TX
713-783-3344

SPEC'S LIQUOR
STORES
Houston, TX
713-526-8787
888-526-8787

ARROWINE
Arlington, VA
703-525-0990

TOTAL BEVERAGE
Chantilly, VA
703-817-1177

ADDY BASSIN'S
MACARTHUR
BEVERAGES, INC.
Washington, D.C.
202-338-1433

CALVERT-WOODLEY
Washington, D.C.
202-966-4400

DELAURENTI
SPECIALTY FOODS &
WINES
Seattle, WA
206-622-0141

LARRY'S MARKETS
Seattle, WA
206-527-5333

MCCARTHY &
SCHIERING WINE
MERCHANTS
Seattle, WA
206-524-9500

PIKE & WESTERN
WINE SHOP
Seattle, WA
206-441-1307

SEATTLE CELLARS,
LTD., A WINE
MERCHANT
Seattle, WA
206-256-0850

STEVE'S LIQUOR
AND MORE
Madison, WI
608-833-5995

Surviving the
Restaurant Wine List

Diners who ask for a restaurant's wine list tend to fall into two groups: those who know what they're after and will be disappointed if they don't find it, and those who accept the *carte des vins* gingerly, as though it might explode in their hands. If you're in the latter camp, your aim is probably just to find a tasty, affordable bottle to enhance your meal. Here are some basic principles that will increase your odds of achieving your objective without losing your shirt.

AVOID THE CHEAPEST AND THE MOST EXPENSIVE WINES: Most restaurants calculate a minimum price for simply handling a bottle: for storing it, for rooting around in the bin to find it, for opening and serving it—one hopes at the proper temperature and in suitable glassware. In a low-end eatery, this overhead cost may be as little as $5, while in a ritzier spot it may be $15 or $20. Markups tend to be figured on a sliding scale: higher for inexpensive items and lower for pricier wines. A wine listed for $20 may have been purchased wholesale for $4, while one selling for $45 might have cost the restaurant $18. As a general rule, you don't want the $4 bottle, especially if it has been marked up 500%. At the top end, wine-savvy diners can often find relative bargains, although many restaurants apply breathtaking markups to the most widely prized prestige wines and scarce items. If you don't know roughly what these wines should cost, proceed with extreme caution.

LOOK FOR OFF-THE-BEATEN-TRACK AREAS THAT ARE WELL-REPRESENTED: Most wine lists in America are heavy on California, France's snob areas like Bordeaux and Burgundy, and the more famous wines of Italy (Chianti, Barolo and the like). If your *carte des vins* offers multiple selections from a region such as Alsace, the Loire Valley, South Africa or Washington State, chances are that there is someone on the premises who genuinely appreciates these wines and would like you to enjoy them as well. Their prominent position on the wine list is a message that the restaurant managers feel these wines go well with the house cuisine.

DON'T GET HUNG UP ON VINTAGE CHARTS: Most vintage charts give only a rudimentary overview of how a broadly defined region performed in a given year. The producer's name on the label is easily as important an indicator of quality as the vintage or the specific vineyard the wine is from. The most talented growers and winemakers manage to make very good wine in average years, while under-achievers will make mediocre juice even under ideal conditions. On the other hand, if you're in a restaurant that lists its wines without showing their vintage, it's a good bet that the management is heedlessly buying the same uninspiring items year after year. In this case, I'd recommend finding out the year and then consulting your vintage chart—to know which years to avoid.

WHEN IN DOUBT, ASK: My own exhaustive research reveals that at least three out of four sommeliers genuinely enjoy wine. They frequently buy what they like, and they want you to share their enthusiasm. Besides, it's in their financial interest for you to relish the wines they choose for you. If you're at your wit's end decoding the wine list, summon the wine person (sommelier, wine buyer, beverage manager), explain roughly what you're after (for example an inexpensive red wine with fresh fruit flavors and soft tannins) and what dishes you plan to order, and leave it to the pro.

GLOSSARY OF TASTING & WINEMAKING TERMS

TASTING TERMS:

Aftertaste The flavor that lingers in your mouth after you swallow the wine. The length of the aftertaste is perhaps the single most reliable indicator of wine quality (see Finish).

Aroma The primary smell of a young, unevolved wine, consisting of the odors of the grape juice itself, of the fermentation process and, if relevant, of the oak barrels in which the wine was made or aged.

Astringent Having mouth-puckering tannins; such a wine may merely need time to soften.

Austere Tough, dry and unforthcoming, often due to a severe tannic structure or simply to the extreme youth of a wine.

Balance The ratio of a wine's key components, including fruitiness, sweetness, acidity, tannin and alcoholic strength. A balanced wine shows a harmony of components, with no single element dominating.

Body The weight of a wine on the palate, determined by its alcoholic strength and level of extract (see Extract). Wines are typically described as ranging from light-bodied to full-bodied.

Bouquet The richer, more complex fragrances that develop as a wine ages.

Closed Not especially aromatic, most likely due to recent bottling or to the particular stage of the wine's development. *Dumb* is a synonym.

Corked, Corky Contaminated by a tainted cork (affected by a mold known as 2,4,6-trichloroanisole), which gives the wine a musty, wet cardboard smell. Bad corks are a major problem, as they can ruin otherwise sound bottles. By most accounts 2 to 5 bottles out of 100 are affected by bad corks.

Crisp Refreshing, thanks to sound acidity.

Earthy Can be a component of complexity deriving from the wine's distinctive soil character or a pejorative description for a rustic wine.

Extract Essentially the minerals and other trace elements in a wine; sugar-free dry extract is everything in a wine except water, sugar, acids and alcohol. High extract often gives wine a dusty, tactile impression of density. It frequently serves to buffer, or mitigate, high alcohol or strong acidity.

Fat Rich to the point of being unctuous, with modest balancing acidity.

Finish The final taste left by a sip of wine after you swallow. Wines can be said to have long or short finishes (see Aftertaste).

Firm Perceptibly tannic and/or acidic, in a positive way.

Flabby Lacking acidity and therefore lacking shape.

Fruity Aromas and flavors that derive from the grape, as opposed to the winemaking process or the barrels in which the wine was aged.

Green Too acid, raw or herbal; this may be due to underripe grapes or stems but may simply mean the wine needs time to develop.

Grip An emphatically firm, tactile finish.

Hard Too tannic or acidic; often a characteristic of a wine that needs more time in bottle.

Hot Noticeably alcoholic.

Jammy Slightly cooked flavors of jam rather than fresh fruit, often a characteristic of red wines from hot climates.

Lean Lacking flesh and body. Not necessarily pejorative, as some types of wines are lean by nature.

Middle Palate Literally, the part of the tasting experience between the nose of the wine and its finish. The impact of a wine in the mouth.

Mouth Feel The physical impression of a wine in the mouth; its texture.

Nose The aroma or bouquet of a wine.

Oaky Smell or taste of the oak cask in which the wine was vinified and/or aged; oak notes can include such elements as vanilla, clove, cinnamon, cedar, smoke, toast, bourbon and coffee.

Oxidized Possessing a tired or stale taste due to excessive exposure to air. An oxidized white wine may have a darker than normal or even brown color.

Powerful Generally high in alcohol and/or extract.

Sharp Unpleasantly bitter or hard-edged.

Soft Low in tannin and/or acidity.

Spritz The faint prickle on the tongue of carbon dioxide (*pétillance* in French), generally found in young, light white wines.

Steely An almost metallic taste often noted in wines high in acidity and/or made from mineral-rich soil—especially Riesling.

Supple Round and smooth, as opposed to noticeably tannic or acidic.

Sweet A term applied not just to wines with significant residual sugar but also to those that show outstanding richness or ripeness.

Tart Noticeably acidic.

Tough Generally, a red wine that shows excessive tannin.

Vinous Literally wine-like, in terms of liveliness and acidity; but often used to describe the overall impression conveyed by a wine beyond simple fruitiness. This can include subtle flavors that come from the soil that produced the grapes, as well as from the winemaking and aging process.

Volatile Slightly vinegary due to a high level of acetic acid, referred to as volatile acidity (VA). But a minimum level of VA often helps to project a wine's aromas without resulting in an unstable bottle. "High-toned" is jargon for faintly volatile, and is not necessarily pejorative.

WINEMAKING TERMS:

Acidification The addition of acid (usually tartaric) during fermentation, frequently necessary in hot climates where grapes tend to overripen and become deficient in acidity, thereby losing freshness.

Acidity The acids in a wine (principally tartaric, malic, citric and lactic) provide liveliness, longevity and balance: too much leaves a sour or sharp taste on the palate, while too little results in a flabby, shapeless wine. If tannin is the spine of a wine, then acidity is its nervous system.

Barrel or Cask Most of the world's greatest wines are at least partially aged in barrels, usually made from oak. A *barrique* is the standard Bordeaux barrel, holding 225 liters or the equivalent of about 300 bottles of wine. But casks may be as large as 100 hectoliters (i.e., 10,000 liters) or more.

Chaptalization The addition of sugar during fermentation to increase a wine's alcoholic strength.

Fermentation The conversion of grape juice into wine through the action of yeasts present in the juice, which turn sugar into alcohol. This alcoholic fermentation is also known as primary fermentation. (See Malolactic Fermentation.)

Filtration A method of clarifying and stabilizing wine to give it a pleasingly lucid color and to remove yeasts, bacteria or other solid matter that might otherwise spoil the wine after it has been bottled. Excessive filtration, like excessive fining, can strip a wine of aroma, body, texture and length.

Fining A method of clarifying wine by pouring a coagulant (such as egg whites) on top and letting it settle to the bottom. In general, a fining agent is allowed to fall through the wine, while in filtration the wine is passed through a filter.

Lees Solid residue (mostly dead yeast cells and grape pulp, pips and skins) that remains in the cask after the wine has been drawn off. Many white wines and some reds are kept on their lees for a period of time to protect them from oxidation, enrich their textures and add complexity. Wines protected by lees contact can often be made with less sulfur addition, but careful technique is essential to ensure that off aromas don't develop.

Malolactic Fermentation A secondary fermentation in which the more tart malic acid is converted into softer lactic acid and carbon dioxide. Malolactic fermentation, which generally follows the alcoholic fermentation, is nearly always carried out in red wines. Some producers of white wines encourage malolactic fermentation, while others, especially those in hot regions that produce grapes with low levels of acidity, avoid it in order to retain the wine's freshness.

Must Grape juice not yet fermented or in the process of being fermented into wine.

Racking Transferring the wine from one cask to another to separate it from its lees.

Sediment Solid matter deposited in a bottle during the course of the maturation process. Sediment is generally a sign that the wine was not excessively filtered prior to bottling.

Sulfur The most common disinfectant for wine. Most winemakers feel that it is nearly impossible to produce stable wine without judicious use of sulfur products at one or more stages of vinification: just after the harvest to thwart fermentation by the wrong yeasts, in the cellar to prevent microbial spoilage and oxidation and at the time of bottling to protect the wine against exposure to air. But as a general rule, the amount of sulfur used in the production of fine wine has never been lower than it is today.

Tannin A bitter, mouth-drying substance found in the skins, stalks and pips of the grapes—as well as in wood barrels. Tannin acts as a preservative and is thus an important component if the wine is to be aged over a long period. Tannins are frequently harsh in a young wine, but gradually soften or dissipate as the wine ages in the bottle.

Yeast The various microorganisms that cause fermentation. Wild yeasts are naturally present on grape skins, but cultivated yeasts are generally used to control fermentation more carefully.

BEST BUYS BY COUNTRY

ALL RATED TWO STARS OR HIGHER, ALL UNDER $15

FRANCE

★★★ André Neveu 1995 Sancerre Le Manoir Vieilles Vignes, **47**

★★★ Bourillon-Dorléans 1996 Vouvray Demi-Sec, **50**

★★★ Bourillon-Dorléans 1996 Vouvray Sec Vieilles Vignes La Coulée d'Argent, **50**

★★★ Célestin Blondeau 1995 Pouilly-Fumé Les Rabichottes, **47**

★★★ Château Mansenoble 1995 Réserve du Château Corbières, **72**

★★★ Château de la Morinière 1995 Muscadet Domaine de la Morinière, **52**

★★★ Château d'Oupia 1995 Minervois, **71**

★★★ Château de Rochemorin 1994 Blanc, Pessac-Léognan, **22**

★★★ Clos des Allées 1995 Muscadet Vieilles Vignes, **51**

★★★ Domaine d'Aupilhac 1995 Montpeyroux, **69**

★★★ Domaine Déletang 1996 Montlouis Les Batisses, **51**

★★★ Domaine Déletang 1996 Touraine Cépage Sauvignon, **46**

★★★ Domaine de la Fruitière Muscadet 1995, **51**

★★★ Domaine la Garrigue 1995 Côtes du Rhône Cuvée Romaine, **62**

★★★ Domaine de Marcoux 1995 Côtes du Rhône, **63**

★★★ Domaine des Murette 1995 Minervois Clos de l'Olivier, **71**

★★★ Domaine Richeaume 1996 Rosé, Côtes de Provence, **65**

★★★ Jean-Claude Dagueneau 1996 Pouilly-Fumé, **47**

★★★ Lucien Thomas 1995 Sancerre Clos de la Crèle, **47**

★★★ Mas des Bressades 1995 Cabernet-Syrah, VdP du Gard, **73**

★★ Boyer-Domergue 1994 Campagne de Centeilles Minervois, **71**

★★ Chapoutier 1995 Belleruche Côtes du Rhône, **62**

★★ Charles Joguet 1996 Chinon Varennes du Grand Clos, **49**

★★ Château Belle Évèque 1995 Corbières, **72**

★★ Château Bonnet 1995 Blanc, Entre-Deux-Mers, **22**

★★ Château la Caussade 1996 Blanc, Bordeaux, **22**

★★ Château de Cruzeau 1994, Graves, **23**

★★ Château du Donjon 1994 Cuvée Tradition Minervois, **71**

★★ Château de Flaugergues 1995, Coteaux du Languedoc La Méjanelle, **70**

★★ Château Grande Cassagne (**32**) 1996, Costières de Nîmes, **69**

★★ Château de Jau 1995 Côtes du Roussillon-Villages, **71**

★★ Château Mansenoble 1995, VdP des Coteaux de Miramont, **73**

★★ Château Maravenne 1995 Grande Réserve, Côtes de Provence, **65**

★★ Château Maris 1995 Comte Cathare Minervois, **71**

★★ Château Puech-Haut 1995 Cuvée Tradition St-Drézéry, Coteaux du Languedoc, **69**

★★ Château Puech-Haut 1996 Rosé Saint-Drézéry, Coteaux du Languedoc, **69**

★★ Château de la Ragotière 1996 Muscadet, **52**

★★ Château de Targé 1995 Saumur-Champigny, **49**

★★ Château de Valcombe 1995, Costières de Nîmes, **69**

★★ Château de Villespassans 1994, St-Chinian, **69**

★★ Château Viranel 1994, St-Chinian, **69**

★★ Château Viranel 1996 Rosé, St-Chinian, **69**

★★ Choblet Côtes de Grandlieu 1995 Muscadet, **52**

★★ Clos Roche Blanche 1996 Touraine Sauvignon, **46**

★★ Col des Vents 1995 Corbières, **71**

★★ Commanderie de Peyrassol 1996, Côtes de Provence, **66**

★★ Commanderie de Peyrassol 1996 Rosé Cuvée Eperon d'Or, Côtes de Provence, **65**

★★ Les Comtes de Jonqueyres 1995 Blanc Cuvée Alpha, Bordeaux, **23**

★★ Daniel Brusset 1995 Cairanne Côtes du Rhône-Villages, **62**

★★ Domaine des Aires Hautes 1996 Sauvignon, VdP d'Oc, **72**

★★ Domaine d'Andézon 1996 Côtes du Rhône Vieilles Vigne, **62**

★★ Domaine de l'Arjolle 1995 Cuvée del'Arjolle, VdT des Côtes de Thongues, **73**

★★ Domaine Baillat 1996 Rosé Corbières, **71**

★★ Domaine Capion, VdP d'Oc, **73**

★★ Domaine Capion 1996 Marsanne-Roussanne, VdP de l'Herault, **72**

★★ Domaine de Coussergues 1996 Sauvignon Blanc, VdP d'Oc, **72**

★★ Domaine de l'Ecu 1996 Muscadet, **52**

★★ Domaine de Fenouillet 1995 Côtes du Rhônes Villages Beaumes de Venise, **62**

★★ Domaine au Grand Prieur 1996 Côtes du Rhône, **62**

★★ Domaine L'Hortus 1995 Grande Cuvée, Pic-St-Loup, **70**

★★ Domaine Maris 1995 Carte Noir Cuvée Spéciale Minervois, **71**

★★ Domaine de Marotte 1995 Côtes du Ventoux, **63**

★★ Domaine de la Mordorée 1996 Côtes du Rhône, **63**

★★ Domaine du Roncée 1995 Chinon, **48**

★★ Domaine St-Martin de la Garrigue 1995 Cuvée Réservée,

VdP des Coteaux de Bessilles, **73**

★★ Filliatreau 1995 Saumur-Champigny La Grande Vignolle, **48**

★★ Gilbert Alquier 1995 Faugères, **70**

★★ Guigal 1994 Côtes du Rhône, **63**

★★ Maurice Barbou 1996 Touraine Sauvignon, **46**

★★ Les Palais 1994 Randolin Vieilles Vignes Corbières, **72**

★★ Vignerons d'Estezargues 1995 Cuvée du Vent Axe Nord Côtes du Rhône, **63**

ITALY

★★★ Albino Rocca 1996 Dolcetto d'Alba Vignalunga, **82**

★★★ Bucci 1995 Verdicchio dei Castelli di Jesi, **96**

★★★ La Cadalora 1996 Pinot Grigio Vallagarina, **86**

★★★ Le Corti 1995 Chianti Classico, **90**

★★★ Icardi 1996 Dolcetto d'Alba Rousori, **82**

★★★ Pojer e Sandri 1996 Sauvignon Atesino, **87**

★★★ Pojer e Sandri 1996 Traminer di Faedo, **87**

★★ Acinum 1995 Valpolicella Classico Superiore, **87**

★★ Albino Rocca 1995 Barbera d'Alba, **82**

★★ Antinori 1996 Castello della Sala Chardonnay, **97**

★★ Argiolas 1996 Bianco, **99**

★★ Arnaldo Caprai 1995 Montefalco Rosso, **97**

★★ Attilio Ghisolfi 1995 Dolcetto d'Alba, **82**

★★ Boccadigabbia 1996 Garbì Bianco, **97**

★★ Le Bocce 1995 Chianti Classico, **90**

★★ Cantele 1995 Primitivo, **100**

★★ La Carraia 1996 Orvieto Classico Poggio Calvelli, **97**

★★ Castello di Farnetella 1995 Chianti Colli Senesi, **90**

★★Cataldi Madonna 1995 Montepulciano d'Abruzzo, **97**

★★Cataldi Madonna 1996 Trebbiano d'Abruzzo, **97**

★★Cavalchina 1995 Bardolino Superiore Santa Lucia, **88**

★★Coppo 1995 Barbera d'Asti L'Avvocata, **82**

★★Covio 1994 Fantasie del Cardeto VdT dell'Umbria, **97**

★★Falesco 1996 Vitiano, **97**

★★Fattoria La Braccesca 1995 Rosso di Montepulciano, **93**

★★Fattoria di Vetrice 1995 Chianti Rùfina, **90**

★★Feudi di San Gregorio 1996 Albente, **100**

★★Francesco Boschis 1996 Dolcetto di Dogliano, **82**

★★Librandi 1995 Ciró Rosso Classico, **100**

★★Marcarini 1996 Barbera d'Alba Camerano, **82**

★★Moris Farms 1994 Morellino di Scansano Riserva, **93**

★★Palazzone 1996 Orvieto Classico Terre Vineate, **97**

★★Prunotto 1996 Barbera d'Asti Fiulot, **82**

★★Rocca delle Macìe 1995 Chianti Classico, **91**

★★Saracco 1996 Moscato d'Asti, **83**

★★Sartarelli 1996 Verdicchio Classico dei Castelli di Jesi, **97**

★★Suavia 1996 Soave Classico Superiore, **86**

★★Taurino 1994 Salice Salentino, **100**

★★Terra d'Aligi 1995 Trebbiano d'Abruzzo, **97**

★★Tiefenbrunner 1996 Pinot Grigio Alto Adige, **86**

★★Villa Cafaggio 1995 Chianti Classico, **91**

SPAIN
★★★★Hidalgo Amontillado Napoleón, **115**

★★★★Hidalgo Manzanilla Fina La Gitana, **114**

★★★★Hidalgo Napoleón Cream, **116**

★★★★Lustau Puerto Fino, **115**

★★★Alvear Amontillado Montilla, **115**

★★★Alvear Fino, **115**

★★★Bodegas Guelbenzu 1995 Tinto, Navarra, **109**

★★★Bodegas Julian Chivite 1996 Gran Feudo Rosé, Navarra, **110**

★★★Bodegas Montecillo 1989 Rioja Reserva, **106**

★★★Hidalgo Cream, **116**

★★★Hidalgo Oloroso, **116**

★★★Lustau Light Fino Jarana, **115**

★★Alvear Cream Montilla, **116**

★★Bodegas Agapito Rico 1996 Carchelo Monastrell, Jumilla, **109**

★★Bodegas Berberana 1990 Rioja Reserva, **106**

★★Bodegas Bretón 1996 Loriñon Blanco, Rioja, **111**

★★Bodegas Inviosa 1994 Lar de Barros Reserva, Extremadura, **109**

★★Bodegas Martinez Bujanda 1994 Conde de Valdemar Rioja Crianza, **106**

★★Bodegas Muga 1992 Rioja Reserva, **107**

★★Bodegas Muga 1996 Rosado, Rioja, **110**

★★Bodegas Ochoa 1996 Rosado de Lagrima, Navarra, **110**

★★Bodegas Nekeas 1995 Vega Sindoa Cabernet-Tempranillo, Navarra, **109**

★★Bodegas Nekeas 1996 Vega Sindoa Chardonnay Cuvée Allier, Navarra, **112**

★★Bodegas Nekeas 1995 Vega Sindoa Merlot, Navarra, **109**

★★Bodegas Sierra Cantabria 1994 Rioja Crianza, **106**

★★Bodegas de Vilariño-Cambados 1996 Martin Codax, Rias Baixas, **112**

★★Grandes Bodegas 1996 Marqués

de Velilla, Ribera del Duero, **108**

★★Hartley & Gibson Manzanilla "Fine Very Pale Extra Dry Sherry," **114**

★★Lustau Deluxe Cream Capataz Andrés, **116**

★★Lustau Peninsula Palo Cortado, **115**

★★Marqués de Cáceres 1994 Rioja Crianza, **106**

★★Marqués de Cáceres 1995 Rosé, Rioja, **110**

★★Martinsancho 1996 Verdejo, Rueda, **111**

★★Mont-Marçal 1993 Brut **112**

★★Palau NV Brut, **112**

★★Segura Viudas Aria Estate NV Brut, **113**

★★Torres 1993 Gran Sangre de Toro, Penedès, **109**

★★Torres 1995 Las Torres Merlot, Penedès, **110**

PORTUGAL

★★★Gonçalves Faria 1992 Reserva, Bairrada, **119**

★★★José Maria da Fonseca 1991 Pasmados, Terras do Sado, **119**

★★★J. P. Vinhos 1995 Quinta da Bacalhôa, Terras do Sado, **120**

★★★Quinta da Aveleda 1996 Quinta da Aveleda Vinho Verde, **120**

★★Adega Cooperativa de Redondo 1996 Porta da Ravessa, Redondo, **120**

★★Alcântara Agrícola 1995 Prova Régia, Bucelas, **121**

★★Casa de Santar 1994 Reserva, Dão, **119**

★★Ferreira Dona Antonia Personal Reserve, **124**

★★Finagra 1995 Esporão, Reguengos, **121**

★★Graham Fine Tawny, **124**

★★J. P. Vinhos 1993 Herdade de Santa Marta, Alentejo, **119**

★★J. P. Vinhos 1991 Tinto da Anfora, Alentejo, **119**

★★Montêz Champalimaud 1995 Paço do Teixeiró Vinho Verde, **121**

★★P.V.Q 1995 Quinta de Pancas Chardonnay, Estremadura, **121**

★★P.V.Q. 1993 Quinta de Parrotes, Alenquer, **119**

★★Quinta da Aveleda 1996 Aveleda Vinho Verde, **121**

★★Quinta da Aveleda 1996 Casal Garcia Vinho Verde, **121**

★★Quinta da Aveleda 1996 Loureiro da Aveleda Vinho Verde, **121**

★★Quinta do Casal Branco 1994 Falcoaria, Almeirim, **119**

★★Quinta do Carvalhinho 1991 Reserva, Bairrada, **120**

★★Quinta do Minho 1995 Vinho Verde, **121**

★★Ramos-Pinto 1994 Duas Quintas Vinho Tinto, Douro, **119**

★★Real Companhia Velha 1996 Evel, Douro, **121**

★★Smith Woodhouse Lodge Reserve Vintage Character (Ruby Port), **122**

★★Sogrape 1992 Reserva, Douro, **120**

★★Vimompor 1996 Quinta da Pedra Alvarinho Vinho Verde, **121**

CALIFORNIA

★★★Brander 1996 Cuvée Natalie, Santa Ynez Valley, **154**

★★★Geyser Peak 1996 Sauvignon Blanc, Sonoma County, **142**

★★★Martinelli 1996 Gewürztraminer Martinelli Vineyard, Russian River Valley, **154**

★★★Rosenblum Cellars 1995 Zinfandel, Contra Costa County, **149**

★★★ Seghesio 1995 Zinfandel, Sonoma County, **149**

★★Beringer Vineyards 1995 Alluvium Blanc, Knights Valley, **155**

★★Brander Vineyard 1996 Sauvignon Blanc, Santa Ynez Valley, **142**

★★ Edmunds St. John 1995 L'Enfant Terrible Mourvèdre, California, **151**

★★ Estancia Los Altos 1994 Cabernet Sauvignon, California, **144**

★★ Ferrari-Carano 1996 Fumé Blanc, Sonoma Coast, **142**

★★ Fetzer Vineyards 1995 Merlot Eagle Peak, California, **146**

★★ Gallo Sonoma 1995 Chardonnay Stefani Vineyard, Dry Creek, **139**

★★ Handley Cellars 1995 Chardonnay, Anderson Valley, **139**

★★ Handley 1996 Gewürztraminer, Anderson Valley, **154**

★★ J. Rochioli 1996 Sauvignon Blanc, Russian River Valley, **143**

★★ Mondavi 1995 Malvasia Bianca, California, **154**

★★ Quivira Vineyards 1995 Dry Creek Cuvée, **152**

★★ St. Francis 1995 Cabernet Sauvignon, Sonoma County, **144**

★★ Sanford 1996 Sauvignon Blanc, Central Coast, **142**

★★ Seven Oaks 1996 Chardonnay, California, **139**

★★ Terra Rosa 1995 Cabernet Sauvignon, North Coast, **144**

★★ Wild Horse 1996 Malvasia Bianca, Monterey, **155**

OREGON
★★★ Willamette Valley Vineyards 1996 Pinot Gris, Oregon, **160**

★★ Bridgeview Vineyard 1996 Pinot Noir, Oregon, **158**

★★ Cristom 1995 Chardonnay, Willamette Valley, **161**

★★ Duck Pond Cellars 1996 Pinot Gris, Willamette Valley, **160**

★★ Erath Vineyards 1996 Pinot Gris, Willamette Valley, **160**

★★ Firesteed 1996 Pinot Noir, Oregon, **159**

★★ Oak Knoll Winery 1995 Pinot Gris, Willamette Valley, **160**

★★ Willamette Valley Vineyards 1996 Dry Riesling, Willamette Valley, **161**

WASHINGTON STATE
★★ Columbia Crest 1995 Sauvignon Blanc, Columbia Valley, **163**

★★ Columbia Winery 1993 Cabernet Sauvignon, Columbia Valley, **166**

★★ Columbia Winery 1996 Cellarmaster's Reserve Riesling, Columbia Valley, **164**

★★ Covey Run 1995 Chardonnay, Columbia Valley, **164**

★★ Hogue Cellars 1996 Late Harvest White Riesling, Columbia Valley, **165**

★★ Kiona Vineyards 1995 Lemberger, Washington State, **168**

★★ McCrea Cellars 1995 Chardonnay, Columbia Valley, **164**

★★ McCrea Cellars 1994 Tierra del Sol, Columbia Valley, **169**

★★ Washington Hills 1995 W. B. Bridgman Merlot, Columbia Valley, **166**

AUSTRALIA
★★ d'Arenberg 1995 The Olive Grove Chardonnay, McLaren Vale, **173**

★★ d'Arenberg 1994 The Old Vine Shiraz, McLaren Vale, **175**

★★ Geoff Merrill 1994 Owen's Estate Shiraz, South Eastern Australia, **176**

★★ Mitchelton 1996 Preece Chardonnay, Victoria, **173**

★★ Mitchelton 1996 Thomas Mitchell Marsanne, **174**

★★ Mitchelton 1995 Thomas Mitchell Shiraz, **175**

★★ Rosemount Estate 1996 Sémillon, Hunter Valley, **174**

★★ Rothbury Estate 1996 Chardonnay, Hunter Valley, **172**

★★ Rosemount Estate 1996 Shiraz, South Eastern Australia, **176**

★★ Yalumba 1994 Bush Vine Grenache, Barossa, **178**

★★ Yalumba 1995 Chardonnay Reserve, Eden Valley/Yarra Valley, **173**

NEW ZEALAND
★★ Nautilus 1996 Sauvignon Blanc, Marlborough, **182**

★★ De Redcliffe 1996 Sauvignon Blanc, Marlborough, **182**

★★ St. Clair 1996 Chardonnay, Marlborough, **183**

SOUTH AFRICA
★★★ Clos Malverne 1995 Cabernet Sauvignon, Stellenbosch, **188**

★★★ Clos Malverne 1996 Pinotage, Stellenbosch, **188**

★★ Backsburg 1993 Shiraz, Paarl, **189**

★★ Beyerskloof 1996 Pinotage, Stellenbosch, **188**

★★ Groot Constantia 1995 Weisser Riesling, Constantia, **187**

★★ La Motte Estate 1992, Franschhoek Valley, **189**

★★ Mulderbosch 1996 Sauvignon Blanc, Stellenbosch, **187**

★★ Neil Ellis 1996 Chardonnay, Elgin, **187**

CHILE
★★★ Casa Lapostolle 1995 Cuvée Alexandre Merlot, Rapel Valley, **194**

★★ Caliterra 1994 Cabernet Sauvignon Reserva, Maipo Valley, **194**

★★ Caliterra 1996 Merlot, Valle Central, **193**

★★ Casa Lapostolle 1995 Cuvée Alexandre Cabernet Sauvignon, Rapel Valley, **194**

★★ Casa Lapostolle 1995 Cuvée Alexandre Chardonnay, Casablanca Valley, **192**

★★ Concha y Toro 1996 Chardonnay Casillero del Diablo, Casablanca Valley, **192**

★★ Santa Carolina 1992 Cabernet Sauvignon Gran Reserva, Maipo Valley, **194**

★★ Santa Rita 1996 120 Sauvignon Blanc, Lontue Valley, **192**

★★ Santa Rita 1995 120 Cabernet Sauvignon, Rapel Valley, **193**

★★ Undurraga 1995 Cabernet Sauvignon, Colchagua Valley, **193**

ARGENTINA
★★ Alamos Ridge 1995 Chardonnay, Mendoza, **198**

★★ Bodega Norton 1995 Malbec, Mendoza, **197**

Best Values by Variety

ALL RATED TWO STARS OR HIGHER, ALL UNDER $15

CABERNET SAUVIGNON-BASED

★★★ Clos Malverne 1995 Cabernet Sauvignon, Stellenbosch, 188

★★ Caliterra 1994 Cabernet Sauvignon Reserva, Maipo Valley, 194

★★ Casa Lapostolle 1995, Cabernet Sauvignon Cuvée Alexandre, Rapel Valley, 194

★★ Columbia Winery 1993 Cabernet Sauvignon, Columbia Valley, 166

★★ Estancia Los Altos 1994 Cabernet Sauvignon, California, 144

★★ St. Francis 1995 Cabernet Sauvignon, Sonoma County, 144

★★ Santa Carolina 1992 Cabernet Sauvignon Gran Reserva, Maipo Valley, 194

★★ Santa Rita 1995 120 Cabernet Sauvignon, Rapel Valley, 193

★★ Terra Rosa 1995 Cabernet Sauvignon, North Coast, 144

★★ Undurraga 1995 Cabernet Sauvignon, Colchagua Valley, 193

See Bordeaux, 14, for more Cabernet Sauvignon-based wines

CHARDONNAY

★★ Alamos Ridge 1995 Chardonnay, Mendoza, 198

★★ Antinori 1996 Castello della Sala Chardonnay, 97

★★ d'Arenberg 1995 The Olive Grove Chardonnay, McLaren Vale, 173

★★ Bodegas Nekeas 1996 Vega Sindoa Chardonnay Cuvée Allier, Navarra, 112

★★ Casa Lapostolle 1995 Chardonnay Cuvée Alexandre, Casablanca Valley, 192

★★ Concha y Toro 1996 Chardonnay Casillero del Diablo, Casablanca Valley, 192

★★ Covey Run 1995 Chardonnay, Columbia Valley, 164

★★ Cristom 1995 Chardonnay, Willamette Valley, 161

★★ Gallo Sonoma 1995 Chardonnay Stefani Vineyard, Dry Creek, 139

★★ Handley Cellars 1995 Chardonnay, Anderson Valley, 139

★★ McCrea Cellars 1995 Chardonnay, Columbia Valley, 164

★★ Mitchelton 1996 Preece Chardonnay, Victoria, 173

★★ Neil Ellis 1996 Chardonnay, Elgin, 187

★★ P.V.Q 1995 Quinta de Pancas Chardonnay, Estremadura, 121

★★ Rothbury Estate 1996 Chardonnay, Hunter Valley, 172

★★ St. Clair 1996 Chardonnay, Marlborough, 183

★★ Seven Oaks 1996 Chardonnay, California, 139

★★ Yalumba 1995 Chardonnay Reserve, Eden Valley/Yarra Valley, 173

See Burgundy (Chablis, 30; Côte d'Or, 25; Côte Chalonnaise, 31; and Mâconnais, 33) for more sources of Chardonnay

MERLOT

★★★ Casa Lapostolle 1995 Merlot Cuvée Alexandre, Rapel Valley, 194

★★ Bodegas Nekeas 1995 Vega Sindoa Merlot, Navarra, 109

★★ Caliterra 1996 Merlot, Valle Central, 193

★★ Fetzer Vineyards 1995 Merlot Eagle Peak, California, 146

★★ Torres 1995 Las Torres Merlot, Penedès, 110

★★ Washington Hills 1995 W.B. Bridgman Merlot, Columbia Valley, 166

PINOT GRIS/PINOT GRIGIO

★★★ La Cadalora 1996 Pinot Grigio Vallagarina, 86

★★ Duck Pond Cellars 1996 Pinot
Gris, Willamette Valley, **160**

★★ Oak Knoll Winery 1995 Pinot
Gris, Willamette Valley, **160**

★★ Tiefenbrunner 1996 Pinot
Grigio, Alto Adige, **86**

*See Alsace, 37, for more sources of
Pinot Gris*

PINOT NOIR

★★ Bridgeview Vineyard 1996
Pinot Noir, Oregon, **158**

★★ Firesteed 1996 Pinot Noir,
Oregon, **159**

*See Burgundy (Côte d'Or, 25, and
Côte Chalonnaise, 31) for more
sources of Pinot Noir*

RIESLING

★★ Columbia Winery 1996 Riesling
Cellarmaster's Reserve,
Columbia Valley, **164**

★★ Hogue Cellars 1996 Late
Harvest White Riesling,
Columbia Valley, **165**

★★ Groot Constantia 1995 Weisser
Riesling, Constantia, **187**

★★ Willamette Valley Vineyards
1996 Dry Riesling, Willamette
Valley, **161**

*See Germany, 129, and Alsace, 37,
for more sources of Riesling*

SAUVIGNON BLANC

★★★ André Neveu 1995 Sancerre
Le Manoir Vieilles Vignes, **47**

★★★ Célestin Blondeau 1995
Pouilly-Fumé Les
Rabichottes, **47**

★★★ Domaine Déletang 1996
Touraine Cépage
Sauvignon, **46**

★★★ Jean-Claude Dagueneau 1996
Pouilly-Fumé, **47**

★★★ Lucien Thomas 1995 Sancerre
Clos de la Crèle, **47**

★★ Brander Vineyard 1996
Sauvignon Blanc, Santa Ynez
Valley, **142**

★★ Clos Roche Blanche 1996
Touraine Sauvignon, **46**

★★ Columbia Crest 1995 Sauvignon
Blanc Columbia Valley, **163**

★★ De Redcliffe 1996 Sauvignon
Blanc, Marlborough, **182**

★★ Domaine de Coussergues 1996
Sauvignon Blanc, VdP d'Oc, **72**

★★ Ferrari-Carano 1996 Fumé
Blanc, Sonoma Coast, **142**

★★ J. Rochioli 1996 Sauvignon
Blanc, Russian River Valley, **143**

★★ Maurice Barbou 1996 Touraine
Sauvignon, **46**

★★ Mulderbosch 1996 Sauvignon
Blanc, Stellenbosch, **187**

★★ Nautilus 1996 Sauvignon Blanc,
Marlborough, **182**

★★ Sanford 1996 Sauvignon Blanc,
Central Coast, **142**

★★ Santa Rita 1996 120 Sauvignon
Blanc, Lontue Valley, **192**

SYRAH/SHIRAZ

★★ d'Arenberg 1994 The Old Vine
Shiraz, McLaren Vale, **175**

★★ Backsburg 1993 Shiraz, Paarl, **189**

★★ Geoff Merrill 1994 Owen's
Estate Shiraz, South Eastern
Australia, **176**

★★ Mitchelton 1995 Thomas
Mitchell Shiraz, **175**

★★ Rosemount 1996 Shiraz, South
Eastern Australia, **176**

*See Northern Rhône, 52, and
Languedoc-Roussillon, 67, for more
Syrah-based wines*

PAIRING WINE & FOOD

FIRST COURSES

ANTIPASTI OR HORS D'OEUVRES
Champagne, 41; Muscadet, 51;
Orvieto, 96; Prosecco, 86; Sancerre,
46; Soave, 85; Verdicchio, 96

CAVIAR
Aged Champagne, 41; Alsace
Riesling, 38; German Riesling, 129

CHARCUTERIE AND SALAMI
Beaujolais, 35; Côte Chalonnaise
Pinot Noir, 32; Dolcetto, 81;
Provençal Rosé, 65

CRUDITÉS
Dry Sherry, 114; New Zealand
Sauvignon Blanc, 182; Pouilly-Fumé,
46; Provençal Rosé, 65; Vinho
Verde, 120; Young Beaujolais, 35

DIM SUM
Alsace Muscat, 39; Moscato d'Asti,
83; Vinho Verde, 120

FISH TERRINES AND PATÉS
Alsace Pinot Blanc, 39;
Champagne, 41; Orvieto, 96;
Washington Sémillon, 162

FOIE GRAS
German Auslese Riesling, 129;
Pinot Gris, 38; Sauternes, 20;
Vendange Tardive Alsace
Gewürztraminer, 37

GOAT CHEESE
Albariño, 111; California Sauvignon
Blanc, 142; New Zealand Sauvignon
Blanc, 182; Pouilly-Fumé, 46;
Sancerre, 46

HAM OR PROSCIUTTO
Dolcetto, 81; Off-Dry Sherry, 114;
Prosecco, 86; Verdicchio, 96

**MACKEREL, SARDINES OR
OTHER OILY FISH**
Albariño, 111; Alsace Riesling, 38;
French Rosé, 65; Muscadet, 51;
Soave, 85; Vinho Verde, 120

MEAT TERRINES AND PATÉS
Barbera, 81; Beaujolais, 35;
California Zinfandel, 149; Côtes
du Rhône Reds, 62; Southern
French Rosé, 65; Valpolicella, 85

ONION TART
Alsace Riesling or Gewürztraminer,
38; California Sauvignon Blanc, 142

QUICHE LORRAINE
Alsace Pinot Gris, 38; Mature
Champagne, 41

SHRIMP, BOILED
Dry Vouvrey, 49; Mâconnais Whites,
33; Orvieto, 96; Soave, 85; Vinho
Verde, 120

**SHRIMP, SQUID OR OYSTERS,
FRIED**
Albariño, 111; California Sparkling
Wine, 153; Champagne, 41; Dry
Sherry, 114; Dry Vouvray, 49

SMOKED SALMON AND GRAVLAX
Alsace Riesling, 38; Chablis, 30;
Champagne, 41; German Riesling
Kabinett, 131; New Zealand
Chardonnay, 183

**VEGETABLE TERRINES AND
PATÉS**
California Sauvignon Blanc, 142;
Dry White Bordeaux, 14; Pouilly-
Fumé, 46

PASTA

CREAM-BASED SAUCES
Alsace Riesling, 38; Dry Vouvray,
49; Orvieto, 96; Pinot Bianco, 85;
Pouilly-Fumé, 46; Sancerre, 46;
Soave, 85

GARLIC-AND-OIL-BASED SAUCES
Pinot Grigio, 85; Provençal Rosé,
65; Verdicchio, 96

MEAT-BASED SAUCES
Barbaresco, 81; Barbera, 81; Barolo,
78; Chianti, 90; Côtes de Provence
Reds, 64; Rosso di Montalcino, 92

TOMATO-BASED SAUCES
Barbera, 81; Beaujolais, 35; Côtes
du Rhône, 62; Dolcetto, 81

RISOTTO

FISH-BASED
California Chardonnay, 138;
Mâconnais Whites, 33; Orvieto, 96;
Provençal Rosé, 65; Soave, 85

MUSHROOM-AND-TRUFFLE-BASED
Bandol, 64; Barbaresco, 78; Mature
Red Burgundy, 24; Rosso di
Montepulciano, 92

VEGETABLE-BASED
Champagne, 41; Pinot Bianco, 85;
Pinot Grigio, 85; Pouilly-Fume, 46;
Sancerre, 46; Verdicchio, 96

FISH & SHELLFISH

BASS, FRESH WATER
California Sauvignon Blanc, 142;
Mâconnais Whites, 33; Soave, 85

BASS, SEA
Alsace Riesling, 38; Champagne,
41; Oregon Pinot Gris, 158;
Pouilly-Fumé, 46; Sancerre, 46

BOUILLABAISSE
California Sparkling Wine, 153;
Cava, 112; Provençal Rosé, 65;
Spanish Rosé, 110

COD
Alsace Pinot Gris, 38; California
Chardonnay, 138; Mâconnais
Whites, 33; Oregon Pinot Gris, 158

CRAB (BOILED, CAKES OR SALAD)
Champagne, 41; Mâconnais
Whites, 33; Oregon Pinot Gris, 158;
New Zealand Sauvignon Blanc,
182; Washington Sémillon, 162

CRAB, SOFT-SHELL
Alsace Riesling, 38; Champagne,
41; Mâconnais Whites, 33; Soave,
85; White Bordeaux, 14

FISH, FRIED
California Sparkling Wine, 153;
Dry Vouvray, 49; Vinho Verde, 120

FLOUNDER
Alsace Pinot Blanc, 39; Chablis,
30; Pinot Grigio, 85

HALIBUT
California Chardonnay, 138;
Condrieu, 55; Oregon Pinot
Gris, 158

LOBSTER
Condrieu, 55; Finer White
Burgundy, 24

OYSTERS, CLAMS AND MUSSELS
Champagne, 41; Premier Cru
Chablis, 30; Sancerre, 46

RED SNAPPER
Chablis, 30; Oregon Pinot
Gris, 158

SALMON, GRILLED
Bourgueil, 48; California
Chardonnay, 138; Chablis, 30;
Chinon, 48; Provençal Rosé, 65;
Red Burgundy, 24

SALMON, POACHED
Alsace Pinot Gris, 38; Oregon
Pinot Noir, 158; White Bordeaux,
14; White Burgundy, 24

SCALLOPS
Champagne, 41; German Riesling
Spätlese, 129; Pinot Grigio, 85;
Vouvray Demi-Sec, 49; White
Burgundy, 24

SHRIMP
Chablis, 30; Manzanilla, 114;
Muscadet, 51

SKATE
Alsace Pinot Gris, 38; Mâconnais
Whites, 33; Pouilly-Fumé, 46;
Washington Sémillon, 162

SOLE
Alsace Riesling, 38; Pinot Grigio, 85;
Premier Cru Chablis, 30; Soave, 85

SQUID OR OCTOPUS, GRILLED
Oregon Pinot Gris, 158; Pinot
Grigio, 85; Soave, 85

SUSHI AND SASHIMI, LIGHTER FISH
Albariño, 111; California Sparkling
Wine, 153; Champagne, 41; Dry
Vouvray, 49; Sancerre, 46; Unoaked
White Bordeaux, 14

SUSHI AND SASHIMI,
RICHER FISH
Beaujolais, 35; Chinon, 48; Oregon
Pinot Noir, 158; Richer
Champagne, 41

SWORDFISH
Australia Chardonnay, 171;
California Chardonnay, 138;
Oregon Pinot Gris, 158

TROUT, GRILLED
Alsace Pinot Gris, 38; California
Sauvignon Blanc, 142; Pouilly-
Fumé, 46; Provençal Rosé, 65

TROUT, PAN-FRIED
German Riesling Kabinett, 129;
Mâconnais Whites, 33;
Sancerre, 46

TUNA, GRILLED
California Chardonnay, 138; Cru
Beaujolais, 35; Lighter Red
Burgundies, 24; Oregon Pinot
Noir, 158

TUNA, SEARED
Alsace Pinot Gris, 38; Blanc de
Blancs Champagne, 41; Côte d'Or
White Burgundy, 28

CHICKEN & TURKEY

CHICKEN, GRILLED WITH HERBS
AND GARLIC
Beaujolais, 35; California "Rhône
Clones," 151; California Sauvignon
Blanc, 142; Provençal Rosé, 65

CHICKEN, ROAST
Argentine Malbec, 197; Beaujolais,
35; Côtes du Rhône, 62; Dolcetto,
81; Lighter California Zinfandel,
149; Lighter Rioja, 105; Oregon
Pinot Noir, 158

CHICKEN, STIR-FRIED
Alsace Pinot Gris, 38; California
Sauvignon Blanc, 142; California
Sparkling Wine, 153

COQ AU VIN
Cru Beaujolais, 34; Lighter Northern
Rhône Syrah, 62; Red Burgundy, 24;
Ribera del Duero Reds, 107

TURKEY, CLASSIC
THANKSGIVING-STYLE ROAST
Australian Shiraz, 175; Beaujolais,
35; Chianti, 90; Côtes du Rhône,
62; Crozes-Hermitage, 56; Red
Rioja, 105; Zinfandel, 149

GAME BIRDS

DUCK WITH FRUIT GLAZE
OR SAUCE
Australian Chardonnay, 172;
Beaujolais, 35; Côtes du Rhône, 62;
Rioja, 105; St-Joseph, 53;
Valpolicella, 85; Young Chianti, 90;
Zinfandel, 149;

DUCK, ROAST
Barbaresco, 78; California Pinot
Noir, 154; Chinon, 48; Côte Rôtie,
53; High-End Burgundy, 24; Oregon
Pinot Noir, 158; St-Joseph, 53

DUCK CONFIT
Australian Shiraz, 175; Bandol, 64;
Barbera, 81; Chinon, 48; Côtes du
Rhône, 62; Cru Beaujolais, 35;
Languedoc Reds, 68; Provençal
Rosé, 65; Red Bordeaux, 15

GOOSE, ROAST
Alsace Vendange Tardive Riesling,
38; Bourgueil, 48; California Pinot
Noir, 154; Chianti Classico, 90;
Chinon, 48; Oregon Pinot Noir,
158; Red Burgundy, 24

PHEASANT
Bandol, 64; California "Rhône
Clones," 151; Chilean Cabernet
Sauvignon, 193; Côtes du Rhône,
62; Hermitage, 56; Oregon Pinot
Noir, 158; Zinfandel, 149

PIGEON, SQUAB, QUAIL OR
GUINEA FOWL
Bandol, 64; California Pinot Noir,
154; Chianti, 90; Minervois, 70;
Oregon Pinot Noir, 158; Red
Burgundy, 24; Rioja, 105

OTHER GAME

RABBIT, SADDLE OF
Bandol, 64; Chianti Classico, 90;

Côte Rôtie, 53; Côtes du Rhône, 62; Gigondas, 61; Loire Valley Cabernet Franc, 48

VENISON
Bandol, 64; Barolo, 78; Biggest Zinfandel, 149; Cornas, 57; German Riesling Auslese, 129; Languedoc Reds, 68

VENISON DAUBE
Australian Shiraz, 175; Châteauneuf-du-Pape, 59; Côtes du Rhône, 62; Cru Beaujolais, 35; Dolcetto, 81; Zinfandel, 149

WILD BOAR
California "Rhône Clones," 151; Côtes du Rhône, 62; Dolcetto, 81; Rioja, 105; Washington Merlot, 166; Zinfandel, 149

BEEF

BARBECUED RIBS
Australian Shiraz, 175; California Merlot, 146; Châteauneuf-du-Pape, 59; Dolcetto, 81; Languedoc Reds, 68; Minervois, 70; Rioja, 105; Young Zinfandel, 149

FILET MIGNON
California Merlot, 146 ; Chianti Classico, 90; Hermitage, 56; High-end Burgundy, 24; Mature Bordeaux, 15; Mature Rioja, 105;

FLANK STEAK
Bandol, 64; California Pinot Noir, 154; Chianti, 90; Chilean Cabernet Sauvignon, 193; Corbières, 70; Languedoc Reds, 68

HAMBURGERS
Australian Shiraz, 175; Beaujolais, 35; Chilean Cabernet Sauvignon, 193; Dolcetto, 81; Languedoc Reds, 68; Zinfandel, 149

HOT DOGS
Beaujolais, 35; Chianti, 90; Chinon, 48; Provençal Rosé, 65

ROAST
Argentine Malbec, 197; Barbaresco, 78; Bordeaux, 15; Valpolicella, 85

STEAK (NEW YORK STRIP, SHELL PORTERHOUSE OR T-BONE, SEARED OR BROILED)
Australian Cabernet or Shiraz, 175; California Cabernet or Zinfandel, 149; Cornas, 57; Rioja, 105; Washington Merlot, 166

STEAK AU POIVRE
California Syrah, 151; Chianti, 90; Côte Rôtie, 53; Crozes-Hermitage, 56; St-Joseph, 53; Young Rioja, 105

STEAK SHISH KEBABS
Barbera, 81; Beaujolais, 35; Bourgueil, 48; Chinon, 48

STEW
Beaujolais, 35; Corbières, 70; Rioja, 105; Simple Bordeaux, 15; South African Pinotage, 188; Young Zinfandel, 149

LAMB

LEG
Argentine Malbec, 197; Bandol, 64; Bordeaux, 15; California Cabernet Sauvignon, 143; Rioja, 105

RACK OR CHOPS
Aged Rioja, 105; Barolo, 78; Barbaresco, 78; Best Bordeaux, 15; Best California Cabernet Sauvignon, 143; South African Cabernet, 188

STEW
Australia Cabernet Sauvignon, 176; Chianti, 90; Cru Beaujolais, 35; Young Bordeaux, 15; Zinfandel, 149

PORK

BARBECUE
California Sauvignon Blanc, 142; Pouilly-Fumé, 46; Provençal Rosé, 65; Vouvrey Demi-Sec, 49

CHOPS, CLASSIC PAN-FRIED
Argentine Malbec, 197; Beaujolais, 35; Cabernet Franc, 45; Côte Chalonnais Burgundy, 32; Côtes du Rhône, 62; Dolcetto, 81; Loire Valley, 45

TENDERLOIN, GRILLED
Beaujolais, 35; California Merlot, 146; Young Rioja, 105; Zinfandel, 149

VEAL

OSSO BUCCO OR VEAL CHOPS
Bandol, 64; Barbaresco, 78; Barbera, 81; Bordeaux, 15; Chianti Classico, 90; Valpolicella, 85

SCALLOPINE
Chinon, 48; Cru Beaujolais, 35; Dolcetto, 81

ORGAN & VARIETY MEATS

BRAINS
Alsace Riesling, 38; Champagne, 41; Muscadet, 51

FOIE GRAS, PAN-SEARED OR ROASTED
Aged Champagne, 41; Alsace Gewürztraminer, 38; German Riesling Auslese, 129; Vouvray Demi-Sec or Moelleux, 49

LIVER AND ONIONS
Barbera, 81; Chinon, 41; Simple Beaujolais, 35; Zinfandel, 149

SWEETBREADS
Bordeaux, 15; California Chardonnay, 138; Mature Red Burgundy, 24; Richest White Burgundy, 25

TRIPE
Beaujolais, 35; Côtes du Rhône, 62; Young Rioja, 105; Zinfandel, 149

VEAL KIDNEYS IN MUSTARD
Bandol Rosé, 64; Barbaresco, 78; Beaujolais, 35; Côtes de Provence Red, 64; Côtes du Rhône, 62; Valpolicella, 85

GREEN SALADS

CAESAR
California Chardonnay, 138; Côtes du Rhône/Ventoux, 62; Provençal Rosé, 65; Youngest Beaujolais, 35

MIXED (MESCLUN) WITH GOAT CHEESE
California Sauvignon Blanc, 142; New Zealand Sauvignon Blanc, 182; Pouilly-Fumé, 46; Sancerre, 46

NIÇOISE
California Sparkling Wine, 153; New Zealand Sauvignon Blanc, 182; Provençal Rosé, 65; Vinho Verde, 120

SPINACH
California Sauvignon Blanc, 142; California Sparkling Wine, 153; Pouilly-Fumé, 46; Muscadet, 51

OTHER SALADS & VEGETABLES

ARTICHOKE VINAIGRETTE
Alsace Muscat, 39; California Sauvignon Blanc, 142; Loire Valley Sauvignon Blanc, 46

ASPARAGUS VINAIGRETTE
California Sauvignon Blanc, 142; New Zealand Sauvignon Blanc, 182; Orvieto, 96; Sancerre, 46

GREEK SALAD
Albariño, 111; New Zealand Sauvignon Blanc; Pouilly-Fumé, 46, 182; Sancerre, 46; Soave, 85; Vinho Verde, 120

LENTIL SALAD
Beaujolais, 35; Provençal Rosé, 65

PANZANELLA (TOMATO AND BREAD)
Pinot Grigio, 85; Provençal Rosé, 65; Soave, 85

PEPPERS, ROASTED
California Sauvignon Blanc, 142; Provençal Rosé, 65; Soave, 85

TOMATO, MOZZARELLA AND BASIL SALAD
Soave, 85; Verdicchio, 96; Vinho Verde, 120

CHEESE

BLUE, AGED
Bual Madeira, 126; Châteauneuf-

du-Pape, 59; Chianti, 90; Sweet
Sherry, 114; Vintage Port, 122;
Young Bordeaux, 15;

BLUE, YOUNG CREAMY
Australia Chardonnay, 172;
Beaujolais, 35; California
Chardonnay, 138; Dolcetto, 81;
Provence Rosé 65

CHEDDAR-TYPE
Beaujolais, 35; California Pinot
Noir, 154; Oregon Pinot Noir, 158;
Rioja, 105; Young Bordeaux, 15;
Young Red Burgundy, 24

GOAT, AGED
Beaujolais, 35; Bourgueil, 48;
Chinon, 48; California Sauvignon
Blanc, 142; Dolcetto, 81

GOAT, FRESH
Pouilly-Fumé, 46; New Zealand
Sauvignon Blanc, 182; Sancerre, 46

**HARD (CHESHIRE, EMMENTALER,
GOUDA, PARMESAN, ETC.)**
Barbera, 81; Dolcetto, 81; Tuscan
Red Wines, 89

ROQUEFORT
Châteauneuf-du-Pape, 59;
Minervois, 70; Sauternes, 20

**SOFT, MILD (BRIE,
CAMEMBERT, ETC.)**
Champagne, 41; Muscadet, 51;
Soave, 85; White Burgundy, 24

**SOFT, PUNGENT (EDEL DE
CLERON, ETC.)**
California Chardonnay, 138;
California "Rhône Clones," 151;

Côte Chalonnaise Reds, 32; Côtes
du Rhône, 62; Rioja, 105;
Zinfandel, 149

**WASHED-RIND
(ÉPOISSES, TALEGGIO,
LIVAROT, ETC.)**
Big Italian Reds, 75; Bordeaux, 15;
Burgundy, 24

DESSERTS

CHEESECAKE
Loire Valley Late-Harvest
Chenin Blanc, 50

CHOCOLATE-BASED
Australian Liqueur Muscat, 179;
5- and 10-Year-old Madeira, 126;
Ruby or Tawny Port, 122; Sweet
Sherries, 114

**CRÈME BRÛLÉE, CRÈME
CARAMEL AND FLAN**
German Beerenaulese or Sweeter,
129; Sauternes, 20

FRUIT, FRESH OR SALAD
Alsace Riesling or Muscat, 38;
Champagne, 41; German Riesling
Spätlese or Auslese, 129

FRUIT TARTS OR PIES
Alsace Late-Harvest Wines, 38;
German Auslese Riesling, 129;
Sauternes, 20; Vouvray
Moelleux, 49

NUT-BASED
5- and 10-Year-Old Madeira, 126;
Oloroso and Sweeter Sherries, 114;
Tawny Port, 122

FOUR STAR WINES
(NEVER MIND THE PRICE)

The wines listed below generally go beyond the price ranges covered in *Food & Wine Magazine's Official Wine Guide 1998*. These are bottles for times when you're looking to astound a friend or associate with your largesse, elevate a special meal or just hunker down by your own deserving self with a truly exceptional bottle.

RED BORDEAUX

Château l'Angélus 1995, St-Émilion ($75–$100)

Château Cheval-Blanc 1995, St-Émilion ($100–$125)

Château Cos d'Estournel 1995, St-Estèphe ($60–$80)

Château Ducru-Beaucaillou 1995, St-Julien ($60–$80)

Château Haut-Brion 1994, Graves ($80–$100)

Château l'Evangile 1995, Pomerol ($75–$90)

Château Latour 1995, Pauillac ($100–$150)

Château Latour 1994, Pauillac ($90–$120)

Château Margaux 1995, Margaux ($100–$150)

Château Margaux 1994, Margaux ($80–$110)

Château Mouton-Rothschild 1995, Pauillac ($100–$150)

Château Pétrus 1995, Pomerol ($350–$500)

Château Pétrus 1994, Pomerol ($400–$600)

Château Pichon-Lalande 1995, Pauillac ($60–$80)

Château Trotanoy 1995, Pomerol ($90–$120)

SWEET BORDEAUX

Château Climens 1990, Barsac ($60–$80)

Château Rieussec 1990, Sauternes ($60–$80)

Château d'Yquem 1990, Sauternes ($200–$250)

Château d'Yquem 1988, Sauternes ($200–$250)

CHAMPAGNE

Krug 1995 Brut ($120)

Krug 1995 Clos du Mesnil ($210)

Laurent Perrier 1988 Grand Siècle ($110)

Moët & Chandon 1990 Dom Pérignon ($100)

Pol Roger 1986 Cuvée Sir Winston Churchill ($125)

Taittinger 1988 Comtes de Champagne ($120)

Taittinger 1991 Rosé Comtes de Champagne ($150)

Veuve Clicquot 1988 La Grande Dame ($100)

RHÔNE VALLEY

Chapoutier 1995 Hermitage Le Pavillon ($120)
Chave 1995 Hermitage ($60)
Guigal 1996 Condrieu La Doriane ($60)
Château Rayas 1995 Châteauneuf-du-Pape ($65–$80)

ITALY

Aldo Conterno 1993 Barolo Bussia Soprana Vigna Cicala ($90)
Giacomo Conterno 1990 Barolo Monfortino Riserva ($150)
Angelo Gaja 1993 Barolo Sperss ($100)
Angelo Gaja 1993 Barbaresco Sorì San Lorenzo ($159)
Bruno Giacosa 1993 Barbaresco Santo Stefano ($75)
Castello di Ama 1993 Merlot Vigna L'Apparita, Tuscany ($90)
Felsina 1993 Fontalloro VdT, Tuscany ($38)
Montevetrano 1995, Campania ($50)
Dalforno 1990 Amarone ($162)

PORT

Fonseca 30-Year-Old Tawny ($90)
Fonseca 40-Year-Old Tawny ($125)
Taylor 40-Year-Old Tawny ($125)
Dow 1994 Vintage Port ($50–$60)
Fonseca 1994 Vintage Port ($80–$125)
Graham 1994 Vintage Port ($60–$75)
Taylor 1994 Vingage Port ($80–$125)

CALIFORNIA

Araujo Estate 1994 Cabernet Sauvignon Eisele Vineyard,
 Napa Valley ($50)
Dalla Valle 1994 Maya Proprietary Red Wine, Napa Valley ($80)
Dominum Estate 1994 Red Table Wine, Napa Valley ($75)
Dunn Vineyards 1994 Cabernet Sauvignon, Napa Valley
 ($40–$50)
Robert Mondavi 1994 Cabernet Sauvignon Reserve,
 Napa Valley ($50–$60)
Matanzas Creek 1994 Merlot, Sonoma Valley ($43)
Mount Eden Vineyards 1995 Chardonnay Estate, Santa Cruz
 Mountains ($40)
Philip Togni 1995 Cabernet Sauvignon, Napa Valley ($48)
Ridge Vineyards 1994 Monte Bello, California ($80–$100)
Spottswoode 1994 Cabernet Sauvignon, Napa Valley ($45)

INDEX OF TASTING NOTES